THE CASE OF THE JOURNEYING BOY

"Innes enthusiasts will be glad to know that his new book is one of his best, a fine suspense novel with the kind of penetrating and humorous observations on the frailty of human nature that one has come to expect of him." —*The New York Times*

"Skillful and entertaining." —*The New Yorker*

THE CASE OF THE JOURNEYING BOY

BY MICHAEL INNES

PERENNIAL LIBRARY
Harper & Row, Publishers
New York, Cambridge, Philadelphia, San Francisco
London, Mexico City, São Paulo, Sydney

A hardcover edition of this book was published by Dodd, Mead and Company under the title *The Journeying Boy* in 1970. It is here reprinted by arrangement.

THE CASE OF THE JOURNEYING BOY. Copyright 1949 by J. I. M. Stewart. All rights reserved. Printed in the United States of America. No part of this book may be used or reproduced in any manner whatsoever without written permission except in the case of brief quotations embodied in critical articles and reviews. For information address Dodd, Mead and Company, Inc., 79 Madison Avenue, New York, N.Y. 10016. Published simultaneously in Canada by Fitzhenry & Whiteside Limited, Toronto.

First PERENNIAL LIBRARY edition published 1983.

LIBRARY OF CONGRESS CATALOGUE CARD NUMBER: 82-48245

ISBN 0-06-080632-X (previously ISBN: 0-575-00394-4)

83   84   85   86   10   9   8   7   6   5   4   3   2

CHAPTER I

ON THE MORNING OF MONDAY, the 4th of August, 1947, Mr Richard Thewless walked in pleasant sunshine through the West End of London. His object was commonplace enough, being simply that of obtaining temporary employment as a private tutor. Nevertheless, he had the sense of an occasion, and of an interest much transcending that which commonly accompanied his finding a new pupil. For *this* pupil—if indeed he landed the job—was somebody. Or rather —since small boys are necessarily nobodies—he was the son of one very decidedly somebody. Sir Bernard Paxton's reputation was worldwide. He was beyond question the greatest of living physicists.

From his proposed connection with this eminent person, Mr Thewless already extracted considerable satisfaction—to the point, indeed, of being quite unwontedly disposed to a somewhat premature counting of his chickens. It was, to begin with, with the learned and professional classes that, in general, he got on best. He liked people substantially of his own sort, and often continued to like them when they turned out not very readily able to meet his bills. Impecunious barristers, bankrupt country gentlemen or harassed provincial professors with sons who must either win an Eton scholarship or be swept into the hideous maw of national education: these were persons whom Mr Thewless took pleasure in succouring. True, it was his duty sometimes to represent to them that Magdalen or Christ Church, King's or Trinity—those farther goals—might be as readily attained through new and virtually costless establishments as through others still addressing themselves to the world of Alfred the Great or William of Wykeham or the Prince Consort. Nevertheless, Mr Thewless profoundly sympathised with the conservative disposition evinced by this category of his employers. For by instinct he was, as he sometimes told himself, a sober and self-respecting snob, just as by vocation he was a hanger-on of people themselves now no more than desperately hanging-on. And precisely here lay the particular attraction of Sir Bernard Paxton. Already—Mr Thewless reluctantly admitted it—the lower stratum of the intellectual class was being proletarianised, and there was always a limit to what the most conscientious tutor could achieve in households in which there appeared unnaturally and perpetually to preponderate distracting vistas of unwashed dishes and unsegregated babies. In that particular world nowadays only the high-ups had their heads substantially above the soapsuds. Yet here, surely, Sir Bernard Paxton must belong. . . . Mr Thewless, hoping that his services might be retained by this eminent scientist, looked forward to a congenial environment still materially cushioned by a substantial prosperity.

But Mr Thewless was a man of measure. Mounting as he presently did the broad flight of steps to Sir Bernard's front door, and responding with practised certainty to sundry preliminary indications of what lay within, he was visited by sharp misgiving. Often enough before he had been in this sort of house, but never with satisfaction for very long. Positive opulence was something which he found uncomfortably to jar with the spirit of the time; the poet whose social occasions obliged him to spend a day at Timon's villa was not rendered more uneasy by its splendours than was Mr Thewless by anything resembling their latterday counterpart. And why—the question suggested itself even as he raised his hand to the door-bell—yes, why in the world should a really great man take the trouble to surround himself with so emphatic a material magnificence?

A large element of taking trouble there must certainly be. Not even wealth (and what he was confronted with, he saw, was inherited wealth rather than the mere fruits of a substantial earned income)—not even wealth made this sort of thing trouble-free nowadays. Anxiety about where the housemaids were to come from and how the place was to be heated must, under present conditions, tiresomely creep out of housekeeper's room and butler's pantry and assault the owner. Nor—Mr Thewless understood—was there a Lady Paxton. Sir Bernard was a widower, so that female vanity could not be responsible for the maintaining of these splendours. Doubtless there were noblemen and others in high place for whom the utility of such a way of life still outweighed its inconvenience; people, Mr Thewless vaguely thought, who give political parties. But for a man whose labours were on that frontier where the higher physics passes into the inapprehensible it was distinctly odd.

And Mr Thewless shook his head. Whereupon Sir Bernard's butler, taking this as indicating a disinclination on the part of the visitor to remove his overcoat, made a noise at once respectful and peremptory. Mr Thewless took off the overcoat. He handed the man his hat, and suffered the discomfiture of seeing an expert scrutiny passed upon the unimpressive label inside the crown. He had already relinquished his umbrella, which happened to be a good one; he had the impression that he was suspected of having purloined it during some momentary failure of surveillance in just such another resplendent place as this.

Then he was ushered into a library, where he waited for some time.

This interval, had he known it, was heavy with destiny. But Mr Thewless was aware of no more than a growing sense of oppression which he put down partly to the sultry quality of this London morning and partly to the sombre richness of the apartment. The furniture was ancient, carven and massive, upholstered in dark velvets upon which glinted dull silver studs. Horripilant velvet, thought Mr Thewless—and being unable without discomfort even to think of sitting down he discreetly prowled about. It must all be Spanish, he decided, even to the heavy presses sheltering the books. And, of course, both pictures in the room were Spanish; indeed they were almost certainly the original work of Velasquez. Mr Thewless was somewhat humiliated to find that his first impulse before these masterpieces was in the direction of financial calculation. Persons who moved more familiarly among private collections of Old Masters were presumably superior to this vulgarity. Conscientiously then Mr Thewless elevated his mind to æsthetic contemplation. The first painting represented a peculiarly repulsive court dwarf; the second was of a radiant little prince, dark-haired and dark-eyed, who clasped a formidable musket in his right hand and glanced slantwise out from a scene of improbable carnage among wolves and boars. It was a vision of the felicity of childhood, and the whole room —it suddenly occurred to Mr Thewless—was contrived to contrast with it and set it off. And this made Mr Thewless uneasy. His uneasiness in turn made him feel bourgeois and provincial. And by this his uneasiness was increased yet further.

Caught in this unfortunate circle, Mr Thewless found himself distrusting everything around him. He distrusted an eminent physicist who lived like a grandee; he even distrusted his butler. But this was absurd. Why should he nurse dark suspicions of a man simply because he had been impertinently curious about a visitor's hatter? Mr Thewless realised what was happening. He was simply more and more distrusting *himself*—and of the burden of this abasement he was endeavouring to lighten his ego by projecting the occasions of his distrust upon the world around him.

If Mr Thewless was not altogether confident about himself, this was certainly not because he had disappointed any very general expectations. Little had been prophesied of him, either by himself or others, which he had not fulfilled. First as a schoolmaster and later as a private coach he had given satisfaction to his employers, and these in return fed, clothed and housed him, as well as providing small but fairly regular sums of money for recreation and to set against old age. This was the whole history of Mr Thewless as he sat in Sir Bernard Paxton's library waiting to be interviewed. It is true that he sometimes found himself believing that other situations, had they come his way, would have aroused in him responses not altogether inadequate. But such secret persuasions were no doubt commonly harboured by the unsuccessful, and Mr Thewless attached small significance to them. On the other hand the self-distrust that intermittently assailed him worried him a

8

good deal. Was it not baseless, after all, since what he was called upon to do he did reasonably well?

However all this might be, Mr Thewless upon the present occasion found himself growing irrationally cross—cross with himself and cross with the environment and presumed personality of Sir Bernard Paxton. This feeling might well have led him to a resolve to proceed no further, to decline the proposed engagement if it were offered to him. But actually it had a contrary effect. Mr Thewless resolved to get the job, and to get it as the result of displaying an uncompromising professional severity. He had just come to this decision when he was ushered in upon Sir Bernard.

It was rather like a trick played by a fashionable physician. From surroundings of elaborately contrived oppression and gloom he was abruptly transferred amid tones, proportions and objects evocative of confidence, repose and a buoyant, nervous tone. The room had all this even while being markedly exotic, for there was almost nothing in it which was not of the authentic arts and crafts of ancient China. Those strangely lyrical landscapes and those birds perched amid blossoms miraculously disposed were, Mr Thewless conjectured, about a thousand years old. In the British Museum he would have appreciated them very much; now, unfortunately, his first thought was again that a lot of money must have been spent on them. And, more than ever, he instinctively disapproved. A man who kept Spain and China cheek by jowl in this way almost certainly ordered his rooms wholesale. Yes, that would be it. Sir Bernard Paxton would simply decree a room and some professional person would forthwith purvey it. And not a merely commercial person by whom Sir Bernard might be roundly and wholesomely cheated. Rather some great connoiseur would be employed, some unfortunate pitchforked out of a ruined continent. . . . At this rambling and undisciplined moment Mr Thewless saw Paxton.

At once everything faded out except the man himself. He was not even "Sir Bernard"; he was a single great name, belonging with Galileo, Bacon, Newton. He might live amid a menagerie; he might indulge not in mere ostentation and

9

acquisitiveness, but in eccentricities, lunacies, deplorable vices—and there would remain the single overwhelming fact of his being Paxton still.

He stood in a window embrasure, bathed in sunshine. He turned as Mr Thewless advanced and the light caught that prodigious brow, that whole skull so tremendous that it would have been freakish and horrible had the man's whole frame not been cast in a gigantic mould. The capacity for profound speculation was evident at once, and a moment later the habit of it was revealed in the settled lines of the forehead and mouth. Mr Thewless was impressed. But when he saw Paxton's eyes he was overcome. Deeply and darkly blue, they were the eyes of a child who sees his first illuminated Christmas tree, or his first fall of snow. Only whereas the child's emotion is transient Paxton's was enduring. Whatever was the universe that Paxton contemplated it was one evoking the response of perpetual wonder and awe. All other men—Mr Thewless suddenly felt—lived with their noses hard up against a wall and their eyes painfully focused upon some few inches of brick and mortar. But Paxton's stature carried him clear of the barrier and he looked out upon an illimitable prospect which he recognised as his heritage and his home.

The impression of all this was for some moments so overwhelming that Mr Thewless went almost automatically through the preliminary exchanges that followed. When the voice of genius did eventually reach him with any clarity it seemed to come, at first, from a long way off.

"One way and another, my son has been unlucky for a number of years. I am afraid that his teaching has been something worse than indifferent. Wartime conditions, no doubt."

Mr Thewless blinked. These were words extremely familiar to him. They might almost be described as standard at this stage of such an interview. Quite automatically, Mr Thewless looked judicial and nodded as does one man of superior understanding to another. But within him he was immediately aware of the impertinence of this when such a one as Paxton was in question.

"A sensitive and slightly nervous boy. He has been judged unruly at times—and it is certainly true that he is not very amenable to discipline of the ordinary sort."

"Quite so." Mr Thewless's tone conveyed complete understanding of the situation and complete confidence in his own power to deal with it. Mr Thewless was in fact (as an inward voice told him) going through his tricks. "Special arrangements may well be necessary in such a case, Sir Bernard. But they should be made with as little fuss as possible. The danger of too much indulgence should be frankly faced. It is no kindness to cocker and coddle a lad who will be obliged to face the world on his own one day. The advantage of a public school lies in its being, roughly speaking, a microcosm of that world. It reproduces that world's rough-and-tumble, among other things. If a boy can stick it, he should. We must not be too quick to think in terms of guarding of the young nerves from shock. On the other hand, when a sensitive child . . ."

Mr Thewless was eying Sir Bernard Paxton firmly and his voice did not falter. Nevertheless, he was keenly aware of the fatuity of presenting this shallow and platitudinous chatter to a man whose views must necessarily be both extensive and profound. Nor was his uneasiness diminished by the observation that Sir Bernard was responding much as commonplace parents did; that is to say, he was slightly disconcerted, slightly hostile and more than a little impressed. And by the time Mr Thewless had reached the conclusion of his remarks (this conclusion being to the effect that, all things considered, young Paxton might well be delivered over to him for just so much modified cockering as a ripe experience should endorse)—by the time Mr Thewless got so far, Sir Bernard showed every sign of eating out of his hand.

For some moments Mr Thewless was triumphant. He had successfully presented just that air of professional severity upon which he had resolved while in the library, and the consequence was that the job appeared as good as his. With Sir Bernard Paxton he had kept his end up; he had been abased by neither his intellectual eminence nor the splendours of his way of living. And this was very satisfying to the ego.

These feelings on the part of Mr Thewless are so natural as scarcely to be worthy of record. More important is the fact that he had other feelings as well. In all this he saw himself as about one millimetre high. Of course Sir Bernard Paxton could be scored off; genius always can. And perhaps *this* genius was more vulnerable than many—for Mr Thewless had come to discern the weakness in the man before him. His will by no means matched his intellect. The creaking magnificence of this great London house attested it, for here was simply the issue of an irrelevant part of himself—his wealth—which he had been unable to resist. But more striking than this was what was already discernible of the relationship between Sir Bernard and his son. The father doted on the son, the son pushed the father around, and now the father was seeking extraneous aid. To Mr Thewless, who contrived to manage boys simply by taking his ability to do so for granted, this was a familiar situation in which there was always something slightly ridiculous. And the absurdity grew when the father was a towering person like Paxton. What was diminutive in Mr Thewless drew him for a moment into an attitude of pleased superiority.

But this was to take the matter basely. One has the duty of reverencing genius in its frailties as well as in its strength. And certainly it was not for Mr Thewless, confronting the intellectual beacon that was Paxton, to pride himself on the continued independence of his own flickering farthing candle. In any perplexity into which this great man had fallen it was his duty to assist to the maximum of his power. . . . This resolution on the part of Mr Thewless, which was sincere and generous, added considerably to the jolt he was presently to experience. But, as it happened, it was to have consequences far wider than that. Upon it, and in the near future, imponderable things were to hang.

Meanwhile, Mr Thewless discoursed on School Certificate. "Still," he said, "substantially below the standard? I am afraid there must be something very far wrong. Is he a capable boy?"

With parents, this was one of Mr Thewless's strongest words.

12

A small boy who was likely enough to become a Senior Wrangler or a Fellow of Balliol he would by no means describe in terms more extravagant. And this he had found was a capital technique.

"Capable?" Sir Bernard sounded dubious. "Humphrey's intelligence quotient is fair. In fact it is very high so far as the common run of able people go. But he does seem to be retarded in certain respects."

Mr Thewless wondered whether he himself might be ranked among the common run of able people. He doubted it.

"On the other hand"—Sir Bernard spoke with an effort—"there are matters in which he is uncommonly precocious. That is particularly so in—um—the sphere of the emotional life."

This sounded far from promising. Mr Thewless considered. "But he has at least held his place at school?"

Sir Bernard looked extremely gloomy. "They wouldn't be in a hurry to turn out my son, you know. I doubt whether latterly the position has been other than that. Humphrey is somewhat ungovernable, as I said."

"But the holidays have begun, and he is at home? I think I had better see the boy, Sir Bernard, before even the most tentative arrangement is made."

"That is very reasonable. And I believe Humphrey is actually in the house at this moment. Only—it is really rather an awkward thing—he is at present quite resolved not to show himself."

Mr Thewless, receiving this information, was expressively silent.

"But he is quite keen on a certain holiday that has been proposed. Cousins on my late wife's side—folk, actually, whom I seldom meet—have asked him to join them in Ireland for a month. It is there that I would wish you to accompany him, and keep him to his reading as well as you can. If Humphrey is given to understand that he may only go on condition that he has a tutor——"

"I quite understand." And Mr Thewless was indeed perfectly familiar with bargaining and compromising parents. "Do these cousins live permanently in Ireland?"

"I know almost nothing about them. But I imagine they merely have a place there to which they go at this time of year for shooting and diversions of that sort."

"In fact, the proposal would be that I should take Humphrey for purposes of study to what will probably prove to be a large house-party in a hunting-lodge or shooting-box? I hardly think that such conditions would be likely to favour application in a wayward lad."

Sir Bernard looked harassed and depressed. "I quite see the force of what you say. And you do very well to insist on it. Only——"

At this moment there came a low buzzing sound from somewhere on the exquisitely lacquered table behind which Sir Bernard sat. With a word of apology, he picked up a telephone receiver. It was merely an instrument, Mr Thewless conjectured, by which he maintained communication with other parts of this ramifying establishment—and indeed what appeared to issue faintly from the ear-piece was the voice of the objectionable butler. Mr Thewless disapproved of a gentleman thus ordering matters as if his home were a laboratory or an office. But genius, he reflected, makes its own rules. And again he surveyed the noble brow and perpetually wondering eyes of the great scientist. It was really satisfactory—it was really very satisfactory, after all—to find onself drawn into the affairs of one so eminent.

"At once," said Sir Bernard. There was something like surprise and relief in his tone. He replaced the receiver, and in the same moment his hand went down in what might have been the action of pressing an electric bell. He looked at Mr Thewless in an abstraction so extreme as to suggest that some profound speculation on the structure of the physical universe had suddenly come to him from the void. And then he spoke. "I shall give myself the pleasure," he said, "of writing to you by this evening's post. Should it be possible . . ."

And thus in a matter of seconds—although not before achieving a full realisation of what had happened—Mr Thewless found himself being shown out. Some more acceptable candidate for the distinction of tutoring young Humphrey

Paxton had turned up. What manner of man was his successful rival? Mr Thewless had his answer as he stood in the hall waiting to be handed his suspect umbrella and his insufficient hat. For through the open door of the library he glimpsed a young man of athletic figure and confident bearing who was beguiling his brief period of waiting by turning over the pages of *The Times*. Mr Thewless knew the type.

He walked down the broad steps of the Paxton mansion into London sunlight. The letter which Sir Bernard would write that evening already lay open in his mind. He had received it before. That it was a disconcerting letter to receive was a fact lying not at all in the economic sphere. Mr Thewless was never unable to obtain employment, and that on terms as good as it ever occurred to him to bargain for. No, the jolt lay elsewhere. . . . Mr Thewless reached the pavement and took a deep breath of air—an air equally redolent of lime trees and petrol engines. He was, he tried to persuade himself, well out of it. The Paxton establishment had irritated him; Humphrey Paxton sounded a most unpromising boy; the proposed arrangement would have been altogether unsatisfactory from a working point of view.

Nevertheless, Mr Thewless was disappointed. And this, since he was an honest man, he presently admitted to himself. Galileo, Bacon, Newton . . . that morning he had been with the gods. Genius had half turned to him in its frailty and he had been prepared to shoulder whatever responsibility followed. In this heart Mr Thewless believed that he would have done not badly. As he turned away from the Paxton portico and walked through the quiet, almost empty square, he felt the universe contracting about him and building up, not many inches from his nose, its old and familiar horizons. It was as if, while in the great man's presence, he too had for a moment contrived to peer over that brick wall. But now—to put it less graphically—the humdrum was establishing itself once more as his natural environment. For some little time his life would feel the narrower as a result of this episode. And then he would forget all about it.

But in this prognostication Mr Thewless was wrong. As a

consequence of his visit to Sir Bernard Paxton, an altogether fuller life was presently to be his. And in this his fate was to contrast markedly with that of the young man whom he had glimpsed in the library.

CHAPTER II

THE SPANISH LIBRARY HAD a good deal impressed Captain Cox, and now the Chinese study impressed him too. Nevertheless, the marked deference with which he shook hands with Sir Bernard Paxton was only partly a tribute to wealth. Captain Cox, quite as much as Mr Thewless, respected genius. And Sir Bernard certainly had abundance of it. He could, likely enough, show you how to press a button and blow up any gang of rascals who were making a nuisance of themselves on the other side of Europe—and was it not something of a red-letter day to be in the presence of *that*?

The mind of Captain Cox as he made this reflection quite kindled to the idea of science; there floated before him such vague images of its unfolding wonders as the genius of the American people has given to the world through the medium of strip fiction. Sir Bernard had a head like an egg, which was entirely as it should be; and he was probably mad. "Honoured to meet you, sir." said Captain Cox, quite carried away. Then, feeling the shockingly foreign lack of restraint in this, he blushed deeply. "Warm day," he added hastily. "Wonderful season, I'm told, up in the north. Birds strong on the wing."

Sir Bernard Paxton bowed. Having among his other endowments a substantial insight into human nature, he saw at once that the muscular young barbarian before him was not a bad fellow. It was for this fundamental fact of character, no doubt, that he had been so highly recommended by persons enjoying Sir Bernard's confidence. For in intellect, clearly, he represented something like absolute zero. But, of course—thought Sir Bernard confusedly—that might be all to the good.

For in undoubted fact Sir Bernard *was* confused. In that part of his life which concerned itself with family responsibilities his son Humphrey had reduced him to sheer muddle-headedness. He was devoted to the boy, and this although he seldom had more than ten minutes of the day in which to think of him. Yet in Sir Bernard obscure forces had come to ensure that when a decision about Humphrey had to be made that decision would generally be wrong. This was hard on Sir Bernard, and of course a little hard on Humphrey too; certainly it did not contribute to the building up in him of the purposive young scientist whom Sir Bernard desired to achieve. And now Sir Bernard, preparing to swallow Captain Cox whole, was no doubt making an error which could have been pointed out to him by his gardener or his cook.

"There are directions," said Sir Bernard, "in which my son has been over-stimulated for his years. I fear that the society which I tend to draw around myself might be charged with being excessively intellectual, and this has reacted unfavourably on the boy."

Captain Cox nodded. "A bit too much of a book-worm, I suppose? Still, we've caught him young, and it ought to be possible to get back to a healthier state of affairs. I generally recommend horses."

"Horses?" Sir Bernard appeared slightly at sea. "No; it is not that Humphrey has become over-studious. It is rather that he has reacted against the intellectual—or at least the scientific —bias of his home. The stimulus has led him—um—to over-compensate in other directions. I do not know even that his morals are good."

"Ah! Well, I should be inclined to say that the answer was cold baths. And perhaps I would cut out the horses at first. Fishing would be better." And Captain Cox, who, like Mr Thewless, was not without his repertory of tricks, appeared to consult some fount of inner experience. "Yes; the thing to do will be to get him out with a rod and line."

"As a matter of fact, I am thinking of sending him to Ireland now. And there will be plenty of fishing with the relations to whom he is to go. As to horses, I cannot say. My recollection

17

is that people keep donkeys in such places." Sir Bernard paused, aware that this was not a very well directed line of thought—aware too that he was somewhat disingenuously concealing the fact that the Irish visit represented Humphrey's own determination. "I have no doubt that an outdoor life would be most desirable. But, as a matter of fact, there is School Certificate to consider. Humphrey should have got that this summer."

"Don't worry, sir—don't worry over that at all." And Captain Cox shook his head dismissively. "I've found it to be just a matter of mugging up the old papers and seeing how the examining blighters' minds work. We'll wangle him through that in no time. It's not as if it were Higher Cerificate. There it does seem as if you have to know the stuff."

Sir Bernard frowned—this being not at all his conception of the right way to pass an examination. But the spell of Captain Cox—of Captain Cox's remoteness, even weirdness—was upon him. Humphrey plainly needed an altogether new type of approach. And no doubt this was it. Cold baths, fly-fishing, possibly equitation whether on horses or donkeys—assuredly this was what a demoralised—or at least problematical—boy required.

And Captain Cox was consulting a diary. "Well," he said, "the sooner we are off the better. Those relations got a shoot? We must decide about a gun. Nothing more important for the lad than that. And I think I know how just the right thing can be picked up. What's his height, sir? Perhaps we'd better have him in."

"Perhaps that would be best." And Sir Bernard hesitated. It was more difficult, he found, with this young man than it had been with Mr Thewless to confess to the distressing fact that Humphrey was not choosing to show himself.

And the simple Captain Cox, misinterpreting this hesitation, again blushed beneath his healthy tan. "That is to say, sir, if you do by any chance think of taking me on. I'd do my best to pull the little blighter together for you, and all that. But perhaps some other fellow——"

Sir Bernard was in a quandary. He recalled Mr Thewless,

18

an experienced person in whom some traces of what might be called mental life had been discernible, and he felt a lingering doubt. And now the healthy automaton before him had brought the matter to an issue. Being not quite able to decide, Sir Bernard adopted the resource of being carefully explanatory. "Captain Cox," he said, "you misinterpret my hesitation. I was merely reflecting"—and here Sir Bernard's courage fairly failed him—"that Humphrey may not at the moment be available."

The effect of this speech was startling—being nothing less than a whoop of satirical laughter from behind a door on the far side of the room. There was a moment's silence, and now it was Sir Bernard's turn to blush. He rose, strode to the door and threw it open. Only an empty ante-room was visible.

Captain Cox took this shocking interruption very well. "Not quite the thing, eh?" he said. "But boys do get out of hand from time to time. I don't know that I'd be severe. Just try to explain, you know, that there are things one doesn't do. Start by insisting quietly on good manners and other matters will probably dry straight."

"It is possible that you are right." Sir Bernard doubted whether this simple code, admirable in a general way, would, with Humphrey, quite see Captain Cox through. But his opinion of the young man rose; he would at least not be brutally heavy-handed, which was clearly the danger with his type. Yes, those who recommended Captain Cox had no doubt substantial reason for doing so.

"Perhaps," suggested Captain Cox helpfully, "I might chase him up now and explain that it is only in comics that people listen at keyholes? It's not quite a thing one should let pass."

"On the whole, I judge that it would be better not." Sir Bernard disliked having his beautiful rooms turned to the uses of a bear-garden. And Humphrey, he knew, whose mental age was bewilderingly variable, would be quite capable of answering the proposed admonitions by seizing a priceless Han vase and pitching it at Captain Cox's head. "The truth is that I have been obliged to enter into a sort of compact with the boy." Before Captain Cox's respectful but uncomprehending gaze he again hesitated. "If he is to have a tutor for the holidays, it is to be not before he sets out for Ireland—where, I ought to have explained, he much wishes to go."

Captain Cox, being out of his depth in such a family situation, wisely held his tongue. And Sir Bernard led the conversation back to School Certificate and then to the cousins with whom the holiday was proposed. One of them—actually a sort of nephew—had recently called and shown a disposition to improve what had hitherto been only a slender acquaintance, inviting both Sir Bernard and Humphrey to Ireland. That, of course, was impossible, for Sir Bernard had a great deal of work on hand. For years, indeed, holidays had been things unknown to him. But the invitation had suggested a possible solution of the problem of Humphrey's vacation. . . . Sir Bernard talked on, aware that he was not really getting anywhere. And as he talked the clock moved on too. At length he tried to settle the matter. "Captain Cox," he said abruptly, "I would like you to——" And then a last twinge of doubt assailed him. "I would like you to stop to luncheon, if you are not engaged."

And the luncheon—at which Humphrey did not appear— was quite a success. Sir Bernard, who rarely sat down at table in company other than that of fellow members of the Royal Society, did his best to accommodate his conversation to the interests of his guest. He ought, after all, to know more about this prospective tutor than he did. He proceeded therefore to draw him out. This proved not at all easy—and that for reasons which were entirely to the credit of Captain Cox's good sense and modesty. Already Sir Bernard knew that the young man was something of a fire-eater; now he gathered that he had been a good deal about the world upon missions in which courage and steadiness were required. And in the war he had certainly seen his share of fighting. Pursuing this theme first with pertinacity and then with downright authoritativeness, Sir Bernard eventually extracted from Captain Cox the admission that he had been awarded the Victoria Cross. And Sir Bernard, who was as impressed by this circumstance as any normal schoolboy would be, wondered how it would strike Humphrey. It might be a strong card—on the other hand, to this too that unaccountable child's response might be a hoot of satirical mirth. . . . Sir Bernard, still doubtful as to a decision in this matter of tutors, found that the mere progress of the meal had made that decision for him. Over the soup it was an open question, but the serving of the sole virtually committed him—and to this commitment Sir Bernard's butler, moving softly about the room, was a sort of gloomy witness. By the time that Captain Cox plunged his fork into a second pancake it had become apparent that there was no drawing back. Sir Bernard, therefore, went forward.

"It will be best," he said, "that you should leave on Thursday, should that be convenient to you."

"That's A1 by me, sir."

"I am glad to hear it. The Heysham boat-train leaves Euston at four fifty-five, and I will arrange that the necessary bookings shall be made."

Captain Cox produced a pocket diary. "In that case, I had better be along here about half-past three."

Sir Bernard hesitated. "I am afraid," he said, "that it is a matter in which Humphrey must be a little humoured. I shall bring him to Euston myself and introduce you there."

"I see." Captain Cox sounded slightly dubious. "In fact, Humphrey and I will be pretty well pigs in a poke to each other until we are on our way together?"

Sir Bernard nodded a little stiffly. "I trust that you will not find him objectionable. Although difficult, he is really a very attractive lad. Nor do I think that you will find the relations in Ireland altogether uncongenial. They are near a place called Killyboffin. The name is Bolderwood and the family is most respectable."

"Ah," said Captain Cox. "They wouldn't be the Bolderwoods I know."

Sir Bernard, who took this for a pleasantry and found it not quite to his liking, signed to the butler for a final glass of claret. "I was remarking that the Bolderwoods are of considerable antiquity—I believe in the county of Kent. Latterly, however, the main branch of the family has lived much in

South America, where I understand them to have considerable interests. We must not disparage commerce, Captain Cox—provided, of course, that it is on the large scale." And Sir Bernard (in whose eyes, as we have seen, shone the awe of one whose universe is on a very large scale indeed) sipped his claret with some complacency.

Captain Cox, who appeared not given to undercurrents of satirical feeling, concentrated upon writing "Bolderwood" in his diary—a quite new diary, unseasonable to the time of year, which he might have bought for the express purpose of recording the requirements and occasions of his prospective employer. "And the address?" he asked.

But Sir Bernard's mind had strayed elsewhere. "Humphrey——" he began—and paused as he observed Captain Cox's pencil once more travel over the paper. It was perhaps a sleepiness following upon the excellent Paxton claret that thus momentarily reduced the young man to an automatism so accurately recalling the jurors in *Alice in Wonderland*. Becoming conscious of what he was doing, he blushed and hastily thrust the diary into his hip-pocket—this apparently as the most inaccessible place he could at the moment command.

"Humphrey——?" said Captain Cox.

"I was about to remark that Humphrey, not unnaturally, has a good deal interested such schoolmasters as he has had. It is a pity they have not managed to make a little more of him. Understanding, I am sure, is what he needs. But these people have at times written quite voluminous reports, and it occurs to me that you might usefully run through them. If we take our coffee in the study, it will be possible for you to do so."

If Captain Cox reflected that Humphrey himself might be a good deal more illuminating than his reports he had the tact not to say so, and Sir Bernard's plan was accordingly adopted. Many of Humphrey's previous preceptors, it turned out, had expatiated at some length on his abilities and shortcomings in Latin, Maths, Geography, Scripture and similar intellectual pursuits, while others had made remarks on his industry,

22

degree of personal cleanliness, attitude to manly sports, table manners, veracity, loquacity and sundry other character traits commonly coming beneath a schoolmaster's eye. Captain Cox conscientiously perused these memorials for about an hour, and at the end of this period informed Sir Bernard that no very clear picture of the boy emerged. Sir Bernard, approving of this honesty, gloomily concurred. He then wrote out a cheque, requested the new tutor to buy a shot-gun and any other necessary gear, led him out into the hall and bade him farewell.

As Captain Cox walked away from the Paxton mansion and its magnificence, and as the Paxton coffee continued to settle down upon the Paxton claret, he reflected upon a certain unacknowledged mistrust which had lurked in his consciousness for some time. Was young Humphrey Paxton such that any prospective tutor might be expected to retreat in dismay upon a first ripening of acquaintance? Certainly there was ground for suspecting something of the sort. For, as matters at present stood, they were to meet only in the uncompromising atmosphere of Euston railway station, and some ten minutes thereafter they would be travelling together in an express which made its first stop at Crewe. Was this the cunning of Sir Bernard, who was so plainly a terribly brainy old bird? Captain Cox feared that it was. He had, in fact, let himself in for what might prove an uncommonly tiresome job. But this did not, perhaps, greatly disturb him. He would do his conscientious best with Humphrey. And as they were going to stay with people apparently adequately provided with lakes and streams, there ought to be enough salmon, snipe and waterfowl to compensate for his tutorial labours.

No; it was by something else that Captain Cox was obscurely troubled. It had been the occasion of that odd abstraction which had led him into the little misadventure with his diary. . . . Captain Cox, who was now walking through the square next adjoining to Sir Bernard Paxton's, had advanced so far in his meditations when they were interrupted by the sound of rapidly running feet behind him. He glanced back in time to see a slender youth come dashing round the corner he had himself turned a minute before. "Hi!" shouted the youth. "Hold on!"

Captain Cox halted. That this untidy, fair-haired boy was Humphrey Paxton appeared certain, and he found it necessary positively to brace himself for the unexpected encounter. But his first impression was favourable. The lad possessed a turn of speed and ease of breathing that suggested a very fair athletic trim. Moreover, he looked Captain Cox straight in the eye. "Are you my new tutor?" he asked.

"I am. And I think you were at that keyhole quite long enough to know it."

"Keyhole?" The boy appeared momentarily disconcerted. "Oh well, why not?"

"It isn't done. Not by our sort. A housemaid might do it because she isn't a lady." Captain Cox frowned. "I mean, might do it if she hadn't the *feelings* of a lady. You mustn't do everything that you see young louts doing in comics."

"All right. I'll drop it." Humphrey, Captain Cox reflected, appeared suitably abashed. "Are we going to Ireland together?"

"Certainly we are. We leave at four fifty-five on Thursday. And I've suggested to your father that before that I'd better buy you a gun."

"A gun? I say, that was jolly decent of you." The boy, however dark a view he and the public-school system took of each other, appeared to possess the right articulations—which were made the more attractive in his case by a very slight lisp. Not that Captain Cox was wholly reassured as to his charge, for in the lad's eye as it confidently met his there was an impression of remote and rapid calculation which, in one so young, was not altogether inspiring of confidence. But his total bearing was frank enough. "Couldn't we," he asked, "buy it together?"

"Well, perhaps we could. In fact, it mightn't be at all a bad idea."

"What about Thursday afternoon? That's the first time I'm free. Only I want to go to the Metrodrome at two-fifteen and see *Plutonium Blonde*."

"Whatever is that?"

"It's a film with an atom bomb in it. They say it's absolutely smashing."

"It might well be that." And Captain Cox chuckled, pleased with this unwonted flight of wit in himself. "Well, I'm afraid you will have to choose."

The boy considered. "I say, couldn't you come to *Plutonium Blonde*, too? It really is sticking out. We could buy the gun first, and then go to the flicks, and then straight across to the railway station. I'd have sent my things ahead."

"I think your father was intending to bring you to Euston."

"Dad can meet us at the station for the proper sort of farewells. Do come."

Captain Cox considered. This eagerness for his earlier society on the part of the kittle young Humphrey was distinctly gratifying, and his forebodings were beginning to dissipate themselves. "We could have the gun sent straight to Euston and put in the Left Luggage," he said. "And if we met at half-past one——" He made rapid calculations. "We could just do it. But I shall consult your father first."

"Ring him up this evening. Where do we meet?"

"At Bone's in Piccadilly for a quick snack first. And now you'd better cut along." Captain Cox was a great believer in the moral effect of abrupt dismissals of the young. "You won't see many films in Ireland. We shall have other things to do. Goodbye."

And Humphrey Paxton's new tutor strode on his way. The holiday job, he felt, was going to be satisfactory, after all. Snipe drummed and salmon leapt before him as he marched.

CHAPTER III

Sir Bernard Paxton to Mr Thewless

DEAR MR THEWLESS,—Since our meeting this morning it has unfortunately proved necessary to make arrangements other than those of the kind then contemplated. I am greatly obliged to you for your kindness in calling.

Yours v. truly,

BERNARD PAXTON.

Humphrey Paxton to Universal Stores

DEAR SIRS,—Please deliver at once by special mesanger one pair of strong binoculars for bird-watching and a good camera (not box). Please send also these books: *Biggles Flies East, Biggles Flies West, Biggles Flies North, Biggles Fails to Return,* Bertrand Russell's *History of Western Phisolophy,* George Moore's *Daphnis and Chloe, Biggles and the Camel Squadron,* Bleinstein's *More and More Practical Sex,* Blunden's *Life of Shelley,* also *Atalanta in Calydon, Biggles in Borneo, Women in Love* and any *close* translations of *Cæsar's Civil Wars,* Book III and *Phædrus' Fables.* I repeat special mesanger and charge to my account.

Yours truly,

BERNARD PAXTON (*p.p.* H. P.).

Humphrey Paxton to Miss Mary Carruthers

MY DEAR MISS CARRUTHERS,—I am leaving on Thursday for Ireland. As you know about my wanting to go I hope you won't mind my writing to tell you. I shall miss not being able to come and see you while I am away but I hope you will let me come when I get back. It has been so very wonderful

26

really meeting you and then hearing you read your wonderful poems. As you know I have not been happy among the oppressive and deadening influances of this place where there is nothing but

> a world of woes
> The harsh and grating strife of tyrants and of foes

but I hope that in Ireland amid the influances of Nature (about which you write so beautifully in your Ode) I shall

> burst.
> My spirit's sleep.

I have also to read a lot of Latin they say but when I return it will be

> So now my summer task is ended, Mary,
> And I return to thee, mine own heart's home.

I think Latin silly particularly since you said you do not read it very much. But fortunitly I shall be able to take some other books won from Opression by Guile!

> nothing that my tyrants knew or taught
> I cared to learn, but from that secret store
> Wrought linked armour for my soul, before
> It might walk forth to war among mankind.

> Your sincere and admiring friend,
> HUMPHREY PAXTON.

Humphrey Paxton to Master John Potter

DEAR POTTS,—I can't come to look at your stamps on Thursday afternoon because I'm going to Ireland—as I jolly well said I would. Actually I'm not going till late in the afternoon but I have to be at the dentists's all the time before that.
> HUMPHREY PAXTON.

Humphrey Paxton to Miss Beverley Anne Crupp

BUXOM BEVERLEY,—I am going away on Thursday afternoon but first I will take you out. Be at the usual place at half-past twelve. I will give you a meal and take you to the pictures. I will book two seats in the back row. Do not muffle

27

yourself up as for Siberian snows. Among those wanting to sit beside a cloakroom or clothes-horse

Is not Numbered

H. P.

P.S.—Alas, that love should be a blight and snare
To those who seek all sympathies in one!

You need not trouble with this.

TUESDAY MORNING

Universal Stores to Sir Bernard Paxton

DEAR SIR,—We enclose a letter received from your address this morning and await the favour of your further instructions. Assuring you of our best attention at all times,

We remain,
Yours faithfully,
J. MUIRHEAD
(Universal Stores Ltd.).

Telegram to Sir Bernard Paxton

MUCH REGRET SUDDEN DEATH RENDERS IT IMPOSSIBLE ACCEPT POST AS ARRANGED COX.

Sir Bernard Paxton to Universal Stores

DEAR SIRS,—Please deliver the goods ordered on my behalf by my son. You may however omit the treatise *More, and More Practical Sex*, and add a reliable pocket compass.

Yours faithfully,

B. PAXTON.

Sir Bernard Paxton to Mr Thewless

MY DEAR MR THEWLESS,—Since writing to you yesterday afternoon I find the situation again changed. It will be best to say frankly that I had engaged as tutor to Humphrey a young man highly recommended to me, whose chief virtues appeared to be athletic interests and simplicity of mind: these I thought might commend themselves to the boy in the particular circumstances of the holiday proposed. But this gentle-

28

man has been called away—seemingly by a family bereavement—and I am hoping that you may still be free, and inclined, to assist us. If so, would you have the great kindness to ring up, or send a telegram, upon the receipt of this, in order that we may arrange to meet at Euston on Thursday?

It is not within my recollection that we discussed terms. If you are now so good as to undertake the work, would you please let me know whether, for the month or so that it will last, the sum of fifteen guineas weekly would appear to you to be reasonable? I am uninformed in these matters and you must forgive me if this should be to propose an inadequate remuneration.

With kind regards,
Yours sincerely,

BERNARD PAXTON.

P.S.—May I say how much I enjoyed, in the *Journal of Roman Archæology*, your lucid and informative account of the villa which you assisted in excavating at Little Slumber some years ago?

B. P.

TUESDAY EVENING

Mr Thewless to Sir Bernard Paxton

THANK YOU FOR YOUR LETTER STOP WILL TAKE HUMPHREY TO IRELAND SUBJECT RETURN AT DISCRETION SHOULD ENVIRONMENT IN MY OPINION BE PREJUDICIAL MORAL AND OR NERVOUS AND OR INTELLECTUAL PROGRESS OF PUPIL STOP TERMS SATISFACTORY BUT PLEASE REPLY ON ABOVE THEWLESS.

Sir Bernard Paxton to Mr Thewless

MY DEAR MR THEWLESS,—Very many thanks for your telegram to which I reply at once by special messenger. I am glad that you find it possible to take Humphrey on his holiday and need hardly say that I highly approve the reservation you make. However, although I know little of the Bolderwoods I have a substantial hope that they will provide the quiet and stability which are so desirable. They have been apprised of Humphrey's present somewhat unsettled state.

I enclose a cheque for £65, being three weeks' salary as agreed between us and a further sum upon which to draw for such expenses as you may incur. Humphrey will be provided with pocket-money, but you will of course make any further disbursements of this kind that you think judicious.

It was my intention on Thursday afternoon to take Humphrey to visit an aunt and then come straight to Euston. He now tells me, however, that he has made an appointment with his dentist, so I suggest that we all meet at the station at half-past four. Near the main hall you may recall a plan showing the location of the various buildings and platforms, and this would seem to be a convenient place for our rendezvous. Unfortunately there is a possibility that within the next couple of days I may be called urgently away. In this event Humphrey will have the necessary tickets, and a note with anything further that it may occur to me as being convenient for you to know. I need only add now that he is looking forward to the change and already appears to be drawing benefit from its prospect. He has taken occasion to acquire various books and objects—some of them very sensible—which he proposes to take with him. What alone causes me some anxiety is a growing tendency to imagine various conspiracies and enmities as hovering around him. I will later consult Lord Polder (a very old friend) about this, and he may recommend some form of psychiatric treatment. Meanwhile, Humphrey will be in excellent hands.

Yours very sincerely,
BERNARD PAXTON.

Humphrey Paxton to Mr A. B., c/o Bunce, Newsagent, Bolt Road

SIR,—You make a misstake. I am ashamed of nothing I say or do. So you may see me with whom you like, when you like. Wretched man! if I did not think that all law was Tyrrany I would have you put in goal. If you approach me personally I will punch you on the nose.

Farewell and beware
    ＼ HUMPHREY EDWYN HONYEL PAXTON.

30

Miss Margaret Liberty to Miss Agnes Hopper

MY DEAR AGNES,—I am writing to excuse myself, with many apologies, from what I am sure will be a most delightful Mah Jong party on Friday. The fact is—I am going for a holiday—and to the West of Ireland! I leave on Thursday! And this means such a terrible *rush*!

You will wonder how this has come about. Well, when my brother, Sir Charles, came to see me a short time ago it appeared to him that I was (only, I am sure, ever so slightly) *run down*, and he recommended the change and was so very generous as to provide for the financial side. You will appreciate the thoughtfulness of this the more when I tell you that my brother's work is now *extremely important and most confidential* —and so absorbing that it is really charming of him to give such thought to the happiness and health of an elderly spinster sister. Were my dear father, Sir Herbert, alive he would, I am sure, be proud of his *equally distinguished son*. Woollens are the problem, even at this time of year, and particularly when one is going abroad. I am sure to be particularly interested in everything I find in Eire, as my father, a truly liberal man, was a great supporter of the late Mr Gladstone. And on the literary side there will be, I believe, views of Slieve League, Ben Bulben, and other places most romantically associated with Allingham, Mr Yeats and other wonderful Irish writers.

In great haste from one who is about to go out and hunt for *woollen stockings* (!!) and who remains

Your affectionate friend,
MARGARET LIBERTY.

Captain Cox to Miss Joyce Vane

DEAR JOYCE,—I'm terribly sorry I shan't be seeing you for some time, as on Thursday I'm off to Ireland with a kid who sounds a bit of a handful all round. This is a terrible bore! I've been making enquiries since I got the job and it appears that the lad's father is a terrible scientific swell. He has a laboratory in which he cracks atoms much as you and I might crack nuts when lucky enough to be having one of our jolly dinners together. Perhaps this is why the lad is insisting on taking me to see a film with atom bombs in it just before we leave. It's called *Plutonium Blonde*. But there is only one blonde for me and I will see her again as soon as I can.

Love,
PETER.

Ivor Bolderwood to Cyril Bolderwood, Killyboffin Hall, C. Donegal

MY DEAR DAD,—I shall be returning by Stranraer to-morrow night, nearly everything here being satisfactorily cleared up, I am glad to say. Meanwhile this ought to catch this evening's plane and let you have one piece of news. I called on cousin Paxton and expressed the hope that, being now more settled on this side of the world, we might a little better our acquaintance with him. Bernard is very much the great man (as is right and proper) but perhaps a little lacking in the simplicity of life and manner which one likes to think of as attaching to genius. He is—as we rather expected—unable to visit us this summer, having very important re-searches in hand. I was of course sorry about this but at the same time a shade relieved—suspecting that when he does go into the wilds it is to do all the orthodox things during the day, and to express complete rustication of an evening by donning nothing more elaborate than a boiled shirt and a black tie. But he did accept your invitation for his only boy, Humphrey, who will be crossing with a tutor on Thursday. Humphrey is of public-school age and will presumably want to fish and perhaps shoot. Billy will no doubt be able to do something about that. Bernard hinted darkly that Humphrey is something of a handful, and indeed that he has sometimes been afraid of his running away! What do you think of that? But soon he soft-pedalled on this theme, no doubt as not want-ing to scale off relations like ourselves benevolently prepared to "solve the problems of the holidays." As for the tutor, I gathered in a telephone conversation that he was to have been a Captain Peter Cox, V.C., a worthy much too straight out of the romances of "Sapper" to be quite our cup of tea. Do not, however, be alarmed! Now, it seems, the charge has been transferred to a Mr Thewless, whom Bernard described as "a very genteel man and something of a scholar." Bernard had looked him up in some work of reference and found that he is given to writing little articles on Roman remains. So he may be quite a congenial man, and it occurs to me that he might be interested in the conical mound near Ballybags, which appears to me to be almost certainly defensive in type. Humphrey and this excellent bear-leader will be taking the light railway from Dundrane on Friday and you will no doubt send Billy to meet them.

> Your affectionate son,
>
> IVOR.

CHAPTER IV

AS HE DROVE TO Euston, Mr Thewless, having a tidy mind, endeavoured to sort out his misgivings. He did not believe that Sir Bernard Paxton had read his article on the Roman villa excavated at Little Slumber. Being anxious to secure his services after all, Sir Bernard had simply looked him up in the likelier bibliographies and added a postscript designed to please. Every summer, as Mr Thewless very well knew, scores of Thewlesses attach themselves to little archæological enterprises and happily potter away their holidays in insignificant siftings of the rubbish-dumps of the legionaries. . . . But in Ireland—thought Mr Thewless irrelevantly—the armies of Rome had never set foot. There the Imperial Eagles had never been borne along the unending arrow-like roads that were the arteries of Latin culture. And the island was the worse of it to this day. Because the prætors of Augustus had left it to the generals of Elizabeth, to the Earl of Essex and Lord Grey de Wilton. . . .

But these scholastic reveries—thought Mr Thewless, bumped awake as his taxi jerked to a stop in a traffic-block— were off the present point. Sir Bernard was paying too much, too. For a residential holiday post five guineas would have been adequate and eight handsome. Fifteen was merely ominous. And along with the offer of it there had come fresh and disconcerting information. Humphrey Paxton was not merely difficult. There was now the suggestion that the unfortunate lad was a little off his head, and disposed to imagine conspiracies and dangers around him. It was with this that Mr Thewless was to be landed in the depths of Ireland and in a household of which he knew nothing.

Mr Thewless frowned at the humped back of the taxi-driver. These were merely the reactions of a new housemaid who learns that it is two miles to the nearest bus-stop. Rightly regarded, if the job was difficult it thereby carried only the more dignity. This was Paxton's boy—say Newton's, Galileo's boy. The child of genius. . . . And it was up to the new tutor to see him through.

But there was the additional annoyance that Sir Bernard himself might not appear again. There had been the suggestion that the great man might be "urgently called away." The quite childish suspicion came to Mr Thewless that he was really, in the vulgar phrase, being led up the garden path—or left holding the baby. Perhaps Sir Bernard had reason to avoid or dread a parting at a railway station. Perhaps in all innocence, but at the beckoning of the unconscious mind, he had contrived that the urgent calling away should happen. Perhaps here at Euston there would be immediate and embarrassing difficulty. Mr Thewless had a horrid vision of a lusty fifteen-year-old boy indulging in a hysterical fit on the platform. . . . Various ineffective schemes occurred to him. They would see if any of the automatic machines were working. They would walk up and look at the engine. They would buy large numbers of banal illustrated journals. They would look for chocolate-coated ice-creams. Distraction was the proper technique.

The taxi-door was flung open and Mr Thewless, emerging, gave directions for the disposal of his luggage. Unlike many of those who excavate Roman villas, he never found small matters of this sort harassing and he seldom muddled them.

It was already a couple of minutes after half-past four as he made his way to the appointed rendezvous. There was nobody there.

Misgiving returned. If Sir Bernard was indeed not bringing the boy to the station, what reason was there to suppose that the boy would actually come? It was true that his father believed him anxious to go to Ireland—but what more likely than that when it came to the point panic might seize a nervous child? Mr Thewless paced up and down. He bought some tobacco and paced up and down once more. It was after twenty-five to five. Suddenly a fantastic thought—or rather a fantastic mental experience—came to him. Sir Bernard Paxton was one of the most important men in England—and not important in any insulated world of science merely. There no longer existed such an insulated world. He must be important—vastly important—to those who played for power. For *ultimate* power. For the very dominion of the earth. Was it not conceivable that his only child . . .?

Mr Thewless halted, amazed at himself. He never read gangster stories. He never even read that milder sensational fiction, nicely top-dressed with a compost of literature and the arts, which is produced by idle persons living in colleges and rectories. Whence, then, did this sudden vivid fantasy come? He found himself staring unseeingly at some unintelligible piece of machinery displayed in a glass case. He turned and hurried out into the main courtyard of the station.

A taxi was just drawing up. The door burst open and he saw untidy black hair and black eyes glancing slantwise from a pale face—with crowning these the sort of flattened bowler hat which some public schools still consider essential for young travellers. The boy jumped from the taxi, and as he did so hauled from an inner pocket a large watch on a leather strap. Mr Thewless went up to him. "Are you Humphrey Paxton?"

Startled eyes regarded him. "Yes."

"I thought"—and Mr Thewless nodded at the watch—"that I recognised Master Humphrey's Clock."

The boy gave a yelp of laughter, instantly taking and joyously appreciating the unremarkable joke. Then his eyes narrowed and Mr Thewless saw them suddenly flood with anxiety, suspicion, distrust. "Are you Mr Thewless, my tutor?" he asked abruptly.

"I am. And you have arrived just in comfortable time."

"Let me see your passport, please."

Mr Thewless opened his mouth—and checked himself. From an inner pocket he produced the document and handed it over.

And the boy scanned it with extraordinary intensity. Then he handed it back. "Excuse me." He turned away and tumbled some coins into the hands of the taxi-driver—and his own hands, Mr Thewless noticed, were trembling. Another taxi had drawn up behind. The boy spun round upon it. An elderly lady got out. The boy gave an odd gasp; it might have been of either relief or dismay. "Well," he said, "here I am. And I'm most terribly sorry to be late. I've got the tickets and my gear is in the Left Luggage. Daddy couldn't come. It's not *too* late?"

"Not a bit. Did the dentist keep you?"

"The dentist?" The boy looked blank. "Oh, well—it was all horrid. And then I had to go home for something. I just *had* to go. I'm frightfully sorry. It was terrible cheek, keeping you waiting." He paused, and his eyes flashed again at Mr Thewless. "What's the first line of the *Æneid*?"

"*Arma virumque cano, Troiae qui primus ab oris.*" And Mr Thewless smiled. "Perhaps you can tell me the second?"

"The second?"

"Certainly. If you want to be sure it's me, I want to be sure it's you."

"I see." And Humphrey Paxton gave a quick and decisive nod. "*Italiam fato profugus Lavinaque venit.*" He frowned. "Would we have time to make a short telephone call?"

"Only just."

"Is there anyone in London that you know very well?"

"I have a sister who lives in London."

They had been walking through the station, and now Humphrey halted by a telephone box. "Will you ring her up and say just the words I tell you?"

Mr Thewless nodded gravely. "Unless they are quite

unsuitable words, I have no objection at all. Come along."
They entered the telephone box together and he produced
two-pence. "What is it that I am to say?"

Humphrey considered. "What is your sister's name, please?"

"Harriet."

"Then say 'Hullo, Harriet, I hoped I'd find you in'—and
hand the receiver to me."

Mr Thewless did as he was bid. The lad, he thought, *was*
quite unbalanced. Nevertheless, he was capable; he ought
certainly to have got School Certificate long ago. . . . He
heard his sister's voice. "Hullo, Harriet," he said, "I hoped
I'd find you in." And he handed the receiver to Humphrey.

"I'm so sorry." Humphrey's voice was apologetic, but not
exaggeratedly so. "Would you mind telling me who has just
spoken to you?" He listened. "Thank you," he said. "Would
you please hold on?" He handed the receiver back to Mr
Thewless. "You may care to explain," he said seriously. And
he slipped from the telephone box.

Mr Thewless explained—briefly, for his eye was on his
watch. He set down the receiver and emerged briskly. "And
now we run for it, Humphrey. We have ten minutes, but
there's often a queue at the Left Luggage. Porter!" And he
hurried forward. Humphrey Paxton, it was clear, fought with
phantoms, and a sympathetic understanding was necessary.
After all, it was only in point of their intensity that such dire
imaginings as apparently beset the boy were abnormal. Only
a few minutes before his own well-ordered mind had been
invaded by some sensational and alarming notion—fleetingly
indeed, so that he no longer remembered what it had been
about. . . . At the moment he must simply show Humphrey
that the phantoms had no power over the actual world; that
the holiday upon which they were embarked went smoothly
forward on its predetermined way. "What about the tickets?"
he asked briskly.

And Humphrey produced an envelope. "Everything is there,
sir." His voice was meek and suddenly that of a much younger
boy. Mr Thewless glanced at him. He was moving dreamily
forward, sucking his thumb.

They still had seven minutes when Humphrey's suitcases had been added to those of Mr Thewless on a barrow. Their porter was moving off when he was recalled by the man at the counter. "Paxton, was that? There's something else came in later." And he pushed forward a heavy and slender object in a canvas case.

Humphrey's thumb came out of his mouth; he turned and himself seized this new piece of luggage with quick curiosity. "It's a *gun!*" he cried—and so loudly that people turned to stare. His eyes blazed. To be young! thought Mr Thewless. To have so swift and passionate a capacity for pleasure, for exultation! A clatter disturbed this reflection. Humphrey had flung the swathed shot-gun back on the counter. "I don't want the horrible thing," he said. "Take it away. It's not mine."

Mr Thewless looked at the label. "It's addressed to you, Humphrey, and has been delivered here by special messenger. Your father must have meant it for a surprise."

"He wouldn't do such a thing—unless prompted. Did *you* prompt him?" And Humphrey looked at his tutor accusingly. "Do *you* think I want a horrible gun to go shooting living things with?"

"I can see you don't. And I certainly didn't suggest a gun to your father. But there it is."

Humphrey shot out a finger and pointed at the clerk behind the counter. The whole scene was uncomfortably dramatic, and there was now a little crowd to watch it. "Do you think *he* would like it? He could sell it and buy toys for his children."

Mr Thewless smiled. "I don't think he would be allowed to take it, just like that. But if you don't want it we can leave it here and make some arrangement when we get back."

"I don't know that we *shall* get back." Humphrey's glance as he uttered this dark absurdity was travelling rapidly over the people round about. "We'll take it," he said abruptly. "Come on." And he tucked the shot-gun under his arm and strode forward.

Mr Thewless, had there been leisure for the action, might

have paused to mop his brow. As it was, he hurried after the porter, who was trotting in sinister haste far in front of them. Their coach was A3, which meant right at the front of the interminable train. They gained it, however, with a good half-minute to spare. The man piled their luggage on the racks. Mr Thewless handed him a shilling and then, after rapid calculation, a further sixpence. The train was moving.

"We've done it!"

Humphrey's voice had rung out surprisingly. So might the earth's first space-traveller exclaim as his rocket took off for the moon. The two other occupants of the compartment looked up, smiling. One was a bearded man with pebbly glasses. The other was the elderly lady who had been in the taxi behind Humphrey's. On one side a towering brick wall was gliding past them; on the other were lines of sleeping-cars, themselves apparently fast asleep in the afternoon sunshine. Presently the whole sprawl of North London would be hurtling southwards. Then the Midlands. There would be no pause till Crewe.

Mr Thewless, tucking his gloves into a crevice on the rack above his head, heard a sigh behind him, and when he turned to his pupil it was to observe that some quick reaction had seized the boy. Humphrey was curled up in the corner seat opposite, his head just above the level of the window-frame, staring out with unseeing eyes. He had grown to a casual seeming smaller and younger, and yet at the same time he appeared to be supporting some unnatural burden of years. His brow was slightly puckered and for the first time Mr Thewless noticed that there were dark lines under his black eyes.

In fact, Humphrey Paxton had retired into a sort of infantile privacy, like some unhappy small boy being taken to his first private school. And into that privacy it was necessary to intrude. That, Mr Thewless saw with some misgiving, was a condition of getting anywhere. Somehow—and the sooner the better—he had to rap firmly on the door and walk in.

But it would assuredly be useless to force the lock. For the moment at least it might be best to leave Humphrey alone.

Mr Thewless, therefore, got out his book—it was a volume of verse—and opened it. He read a page with reasonable concentration—it would never do to let his professional problem of the moment obsess him—and turned over to the next. And here his mind must a little have wandered, for it was some moments before the oddity of what had occurred came home to him. What he had stumbled on was in the form of a rhetorical question; and it was substantially the question that he now realised to be forming itself with some urgency in his own mind about his new pupil. Acting on impulse, he leant forward and handed Humphrey the book. "Do you know this?" he asked. "The one called 'Midnight on the Great Western.'" And he pointed to the place on the page:

> "*What past can be yours, O journeying boy,*
> *Towards a world unknown,*
> *Who calmly, as if incurious quite*
> *On all at stake, can undertake*
> *This plunge alone?*"

Humphrey read the lines, frowning. He read them again and abruptly sat up. "Is that by Shelley?" he demanded.

"No; it's by Thomas Hardy."

"Was he as good a poet as Shelley?"

"I happen to like some of his poetry better. But he was not nearly so good a poet. He kept on being depressed. And although you can write poetry out of despair, just as you can write it out of joy, it's very hard to write it out of depression."

"I see." Humphrey sounded as if, in fact, he did see, and he was looking at his tutor wide-eyed. "I wasn't told you knew about those things." His voice was, if anything, rather hostile, and he handed Mr Thewless back his book at once. "Have you been told to find out about *my* past?" he demanded abruptly.

Mr Thewless smiled. "I've been told to give you a hand with your future. But if you care to tell me about your past I shall be quite interested."

Humphrey ignored this. "Did you show me that poem

40

because I look as if I'm taking a plunge into a world unknown?"

"You do a little look as if you think you are."

"The poem says 'calmly.' Do I look as if I'm doing it that way?"

Mr Thewless hesitated. "No; you don't. You look as if you found it rather more exciting than is comfortable. But I think you could manage quite a lot of calmness at a pinch."

Faintly but perceptibly, Humphrey Paxton blushed. "About poetry," he said abruptly. "Do you know the verse Mary Carruthers writes?"

"Yes."

"Do you think it good?"

"No."

Humphrey's eyes widened further. He looked almost guiltily round him. "Not good! I—I know her quite well. She has me to tea. She's awfully decent."

"As a person? Perhaps she is. But not her poetry. It's awfully indecent, as a matter of fact."

Humphrey gave a sudden whoop of wild laughter. "Do you mean because it makes you blush inside?"

"Just that. You see, you know it's no good, really."

Humphrey gasped. It was an unambiguous gasp this time— like that of a person who has been lightened of at least one of many confusions. "I say," he said, "do we get tea?"

"Yes. I think I hear the fellow coming now. Let's go along. And we get dinner on the train, too."

"Wizard!" And Humphrey Paxton tumbled himself into the corridor. He looked like any one of the innumerable small fry whom summer releases from English schools. Without any illusions, Mr Thewless followed him.

The first-class restaurant car was empty when they entered it; a minute later the elderly lady from their own compartment came in and sat down in a far corner. Humphrey picked up a printed card from the table and handed it politely to his tutor. Mr Thewless glanced at it. "I don't think it tells one much."

"And not about the dinner either." Humphrey shook his head so that his gleaming black hair tossed on his forehead. "Some man in Whitehall sits and tells the railway just how many slices of bread and scrape it may give us, and just how thick to cut the railway slab. It's tyranny."

"Is it? Suppose that we——" Mr Thewless looked across at Humphrey. "Are you a Cavalier or a Roundhead?"

"I'm a Roundhead." Humphrey spoke decidedly.

"Very well. Suppose we were a group of Roundheads besieged in a castle and that there were only so many tins of biscuits——"

"They didn't have tins. And I don't know that they had biscuits."

"Then say so many kegs of salted beef. Would it be tyranny in the man in charge to insist on a proper share-out?"

"It would depend on how he was elected."

Mr Thewless shook his head. "I don't think it would. As long as he made a good job of it, the particular manner of his election would be irrelevant. Irrelevant, that is to say, to the particular point at issue. And if he worked very hard at his job——"

Humphrey gave his sudden peal of laughter. "You work terribly hard at *yours*," he said.

This was a disconcerting thrust. Mr Thewless was somewhat inclined to the doctrine that education should go on all the time. But now he abandoned the Roundheads and poured himself out a cup of tea. "Can you eat all right?" he asked.

"Eat all right? Why ever not?"

"Because of the dentist. He sometimes leaves one a bit sore."

"Oh, that! Old Partridge is never too bad."

Mr Thewless put down his cup. "Is that Mr Partridge in Devonshire Crescent?"

"Yes. I always go to him." And Humphrey looked his tutor straight in the eye.

Mr Thewless felt a sudden sinking of the heart. For Mr Partridge happened to be his sister's dentist and that very morning Mr Partridge's nurse had rung up to cancel an appointment. When Humphrey claimed to have visited his dentist that dentist had been in bed with influenza.

Prevarication in a pupil is always tiresome. But in this instance, Mr Thewless found, it was also strangely disturbing. Why? He could discover no sufficient answer, and was aware only of the elements of some fantastic suspicion stirring anew in the depth of his mind. He decided on an obstinate return to education. "My point," he said, "was that England is rather like a besieged castle to-day. And that's why we none of us get more than our share."

"I did. I just asked." And Humphrey pointed to his plate.

The boy had certainly managed to get two pieces of cake. "I imagine," said Mr Thewless austerely, "that you were given mine as well."

"No, sir. As a matter of fact you've eaten yours. Only you were thinking so much about the Roundheads—or Mr Partridge—that you didn't notice."

Looking down at his own plate, Mr Thewless saw sufficient crumby evidence to substantiate this. Humphrey Paxton, he realised, could be extremely annoying—and only the more so because he was not in the least impertinent. He had good manners. Or perhaps he had merely a natural and undisciplined charm which passed as these. Whatever he had—Mr Thewless reflected with sudden irritation—he abundantly needed. The world is never for long very patient with its Humphrey Paxtons. To get along at all, they must necessarily exploit whatever powers of pleasing they may possess. For a moment—and all inconsequently—Mr Thewless felt himself invaded by an unwholesome sense of pathos. Just so must Thomas Hardy have felt as he contemplated that journeying boy—docketing him both for a doleful poem and for the most shattering of his novels. But it was not Mr Thewless's business to develop cosmic feelings about young Humphrey. What was required was some provisional analysis of the lad's strength and weakness—and not merely in mathematics and Latin. How serious was this queer sense of surrounding conspiracy and danger amid which he moved?

Mr Thewless glanced across the table. Humphrey, having eaten all there was to eat, was showing a disposition to curl up once more and suck his thumb. This clearly was a species of retreating to the nursery and locking the door. But against what? Mr Thewless looked out at the window. Perched on a fence, two little girls were waving at the train and behind them on a long, dull canal a gaily painted barge was moving southwards; sitting on the deck in the level evening sunshine was a woman peeling potatoes. There could have been no more peaceful scene; all the security of England lay in it. But Humphrey, it was to be presumed, moved during much of his waking life in an invisible world, stubbornly sustaining nerve-racking roles. Humphrey Paxton, Special Agent . . . Humphrey Paxton, the Secret Service Boy. And all this had begun to usurp upon reality, as had been instanced by the absurdities at Euston. Yes—thought Mr Thewless, laboriously reassuring himself against unformulated alarms—that was how the matter stood. It was a state of affairs common enough, and nothing was more foolish than to make a profound psychological pother over it, as the boy's father was perhaps unhappily prone to do. Yet——

And Mr Thewless frowned absently at the bill which had been laid in front of him. For something, he found, prompted him to distrust this simple diagnosis. About Humphrey when he was alert and aware there was a sense of covert calculation which was disturbingly of the waking world. He had been sizing Mr Thewless up. And he had been sizing up too a novel but perfectly actual situation—one which his day-dreams had perhaps helped in building, but which was itself by no means a day-dream. Or so some instinct in Mr Thewless declared. And instinct declared further—obscurely and most disturbingly—that more than one sort of danger would attend any disposition to deny that Humphrey Paxton knew a hawk from a handsaw. He did not simply spar with shadows in quite the way that Sir Bernard supposed. He was imaginative, unruly, ill-adjusted—an uncompromising problem at a dozen points. But to explain his conduct, his bearing, the essential impression he gave, by declaring that he was an incipient little lunatic

44

suffering from delusions of persecution: this was to run counter to some powerful inner persuasion.

It would perhaps have been well had Mr Thewless, getting thus considerably far in his speculations in a novel field, as it were paused to take breath. As it was, his mind took a further leap, and found itself thereby on a perch so hazardous that mere vertigo was for a time the result. The impulse to scramble down again—only made the more overwhelming by a certain nightmarish power of reproduction with variation which the horrid eminence was henceforward to display: this must be held accountable for the deplorable muddle with which he was ever afterwards to associate the successive stages of his journey to the west of Ireland. It was as if the celebrated twilight with which that region is romantically associated were already a little clouding his intellectual processes.

What now at once came to him was a suspicion, a sudden and topsy-turvy suspicion having for the time much more of power than of precision. Something of the sort had come fleetingly into his mind earlier, when he had been perturbed by the tardy appearance of his charge at Euston. But his new speculation elaborated upon that. If the atmosphere of lurking melodrama which this totally unknown boy carried with him belonged somehow not to a fantastic but to an actual world, then what significance must attach to that extraordinary performance at the station whereby Mr Thewless's first encounter with him had been entirely a matter of his, Mr Thewless's, having elaborately to establish *his* identity? And why had the boy told a lie about Mr Partridge the dentist? Why had he not known that Mr Partridge was ill? Why had the shot-gun taken him wholly by surprise? Why, above all, did he involuntarily give the impression of one embarking with full awareness upon a novel and hazardous adventure requiring constant wary calculation?

It is very possible that had Mr Thewless continued this surprising train of thought undisturbed he would have been able to lay out a number of alternative hypotheses in an orderly manner, and so have begun to see some way round the problem by which he was confronted. Unfortunately at this moment he looked up and caught the boy's eye. It was this that gave him his sudden and disabling impression of being perched or poised as it were above some horrid precipice. For the boy's gaze was no longer abstracted. It was directed upon Mr Thewless in naked distrust and fear. But just so—Mr Thewless realised with horror—was he looking at the boy. It was as if a nameless and corrosive suspicion had instantaneously propagated itself between them.

Hence Mr Thewless's hasty hunt, one may say, for a downward path. This would never do. In a moment of indiscipline (he told himself) he had allowed a bizarre and sinisterly-beckoning mistrust to seize him. And Humphrey Paxton, this nervous and unfortunate boy, was instantly aware of it. Almost irreparable damage to their tentative and insecure relationship might be the result. Mr Thewless, partly because he remembered that this was Paxton's boy, and partly for reasons more immediately human, cursed himself heartily. It was essential that he should try to retrieve the situation as quickly as might be. And he must begin by sweeping his own mind clear of the penny-dreadful rubbish which—perhaps through the operation of some suggestive force from the teeming brain of Humphrey—had so unwontedly invaded it. Here—Mr Thewless in headlong downward scramble reluctantly asserted to himself—was a nervous boy who fancied things; who went in fear of all sorts of non-existent threats to his security. His confidence must be restored. These threats must be treated as the shadows they were.

Thus did Mr Thewless march his thoughts to the top of the hill and march them down again—or rather (to put it frankly) did he give them licence, which they were abundantly to take advantage of quite soon, to scurry up and down as they pleased. At the moment, however, he had them more or less quietly stowed—permitting them, indeed, but one more mild foray. In other words, one final flicker of queer distrust he did at this moment allow himself. "Humphrey," he asked, "have you ever met any of these cousins we are going to stay with?"

The boy shook his head. His gaze had gone blank and

uncommunicative. "No," he said; "they've never set eyes on me." There was a long silence. Humphrey's thumb stole towards his mouth. Then he checked himself and looked at his tutor steadily. With a movement as of abrupt decision he leant across the table. "Sir," he asked seriously, "have you ever been blackmailed?"

Mr Thewless, because now determined at all costs to be sedative, smiled indulgently and leisurely filled his pipe. "No," he said; "nothing of that sort has ever happened to me."

"It has to me."

"Has it, Humphrey? You must tell me about it." Mr Thewless paused. "But when I was a boy I used to get a good deal of fun out of telling myself stories in which things like that happened. Only sometimes the stories got a bit out of hand and worried me."

"I see."

And Humphrey Paxton gave an odd sigh. Mr Thewless rose to return to their compartment. Once more something illusive and disturbing had invaded his consciousness. As he swayed down the corridor—following Humphrey and with the elderly lady behind him—he realized that it was the profound isolation of Hardy's journeying boy.

CHAPTER V

WHILE MR THEWLESS AND his charge were moving unsteadily down the corridor of the 4.55 from Euston Detective-Inspector Thomas Cadover was crossing a broad London thoroughfare with the unconcern of a man once accustomed to controlling the traffic in such places with a pair of large white gloves. Nowadays his attire was pervasively sombre and his hair the only thing that was white about him: it had gone that way as the result of thirty years of fighting Metropolitan crime. During this long period he had seen many men come to the same job and not a few of these leave again—promoted, demoted, retired, or resigned. The fanatical

Hudspith was gone and so was the wayward Appleby. But Cadover himself hung on, his hair a little thinner each year as well as whiter, his expression a little grimmer, his eyes sadder, his mouth compressed in an ever firmer line. He had seen tide upon tide of vice and lawlessness rise and lap round the city. Of low life and criminal practice he had seen whole new kinds sprout and flourish; he had seen criminology, answering these, transform itself and transform itself again. Sometimes he thought it about time he was giving over. Still, he was not giving over yet.

He paused on the kerb and bought an evening paper. He turned to the stop press. *West End Cinema Tragedy*, he read. *Scotland Yard Suspects Foul Play.*

Well, *he* was Scotland Yard—and the cinema was still a hundred yards off. Newspapers were wonderfully ahead with the news these days. He walked on and the Metrodrome rose before him. Across its monstrous façade sprawled a vast plywood lady. If erect, she would be perhaps fifty feet high; she was reclining, however, in an attitude of sultry abandon amid equatorial vegetation and in a garment the only prominent feature of which was a disordered shoulder-strap. As a background to the broadly accentuated charms of her person— pleasantly framed, indeed, between her six-foot, skyward-pointing breasts—was what appeared to be a two-ocean navy in process of sinking through tropical waters like a stone. One limp hand held a smoking revolver seemingly responsible for this extensive catastrophe. The other, supporting her head, was concealed in a spouting ectoplasm of flaxen hair. Her expression was languorous, provocative, and irradiated by a sort of sanctified lecherousness highly creditable to both the craft and the ardent soul of the unknown painter who had created her. Poised in air, and in curves boldly made to follow the line of her swelling hips, were the words AMOROUS, ARROGANT, ARMED! Above this, in letters ten feet high, was the title PLUTONIUM BLONDE. And higher still, and in rubric scarcely less gigantic, was the simple announcement: ART'S SUPREME ACHIEVEMENT TO DATE.

There were queues all round the cinema. The crowd could

afford to be patient. Here, as at Eve's first party in the Garden, there was no fear lest supper cool; within this monstrous temple of unreason the celluloid feast perpetually renewed itself. And aloft in her other Paradise that second Eve, a prodigal confusion of tropical flesh and nordic tresses, spread wide the snare of her loosened zone and grotesquely elongated limbs. She was like a vast mechanised idol sucking in to her own uses these slowly moving conveyor-belts of humanity. . . . And the crowds were growing as Cadover watched. People were buying the evening paper, reading the stop press and lining up. For here was sensation within sensation. *Art's supreme achievement to date. Scotland Yard suspects foul play.*

Another squalid crime. . . . Circumstances had made Inspector Cadover a philosopher, and because he was a philosopher he was now depressed. This was the celebrated atom film. This was the manner in which his species chose to take its new command of natural law. Fifty thousand people had died at Hiroshima, and at Bikini ironclads had been tossed in challenge to those other disintegrating nuclei of the sun. The blood-red tide was loosed. And here it was turned to hog's wash at five shillings the trough, and entertainment tax extra. That some wretched Londoner had met a violent death while taking his fill seemed a very unimportant circumstance. To track down the murderer—if murderer there was— appeared a revoltingly useless task. Mere anarchy was loosed upon the world—so what the hell did it matter? Better step into a telephone-box and call the Yard. Then he could send in his resignation in the morning and join some crank movement demanding international sovereignty. . . .

Inspector Cadover's feet carried him automatically forward —as automatically as if he had been on his beat nearly forty years before. He was skirting the long queue for the cheaper seats. There was a woman clutching the hand of a fretful five-year old boy with a chocolate-smeared mouth and sleep-heavy eyes. There were two lovers already beginning to cuddle in the crush. There was an apostate intellectual, furtive and embarrassed, caught by that scanty cincture overhead like a fly on a fly-paper. Cadover went grimly forward and the vast

49

building received him. Underfoot the padded carpet was heavy as desert sand.

Three constables stood in the foyer. They could be no manner of use there; the management had doubtless wangled their presence as a little extra advertisement for its latest, and unforeseen, sensation. Cadover was about to scowl when he remembered that this would dismay them, and that they were only doing what they were told. So he nodded briskly and passed on. A slinky young man had appeared and was proposing to conduct him to the manager. The slinky young man contrived to insinuate that this was a privilege. Cadover, smouldering, marched forward still. Banks of flowers floated past him, gilt and scarlet chairs on which no one had ever sat, little fountains playing beneath changing coloured lights. Hectically tinted photographs as big as tablecloths, each with a disconcering tilt to its picture-plane, presented curly-headed young men with butterfly ties, sleek-haired not-so-young men with smeared moustaches, a Negro in a straw hat, a nude girl knock-kneed and simpering behind a muff, the members of an entire symphony orchestra dressed like circus clowns. . . . A door was opened and Cadover was aware of bare boards and a good rug, of bare walls and Dürer's *Apollo and Diana*. This was the manager's room. Its conscious superiority to the wares peddled outside was very nasty. Cadover's gloom increased.

The manager was sitting at a Chippendale table lightly scattered with objects suggesting administrative cares. On a couch at the far end of the room lay what was evidently a human body, covered with a sheet. By the window stood a glum, uniformed sergeant of police, staring out over London.

The manager rose. His manner appeared to aim at that of somebody very high up in a bank, and he received Cadover as if he came from among the middle reaches of his more substantial clients. "An unpleasant thing, this," he said. "But if we must show a film of which the high-light is a holocaust what can we honestly say of a mere solitary killing in the Grand Circle? 'Irony,' I said to myself at once when they told

50

me about it. 'It's like cheap irony.' And then I had them bring the body straight in here. Now we shall have nothing but standing room for a fortnight. The cinema industry, my dear Inspector, is nothing but a great whore. And you might call this the tart's supreme achievement to date."

The slinky young man giggled deferentially. Cadover, who did not care for this cynical travesty of his own responses, looked round the room. "The tart," he said, "would appear to treat her doorkeepers handsomely enough." There was a brief silence. The slinky young man giggled on another and an abruptly checked note. Cadover walked over to the body and twitched away the sheet. "Unknown?" he asked.

The sergeant had come up beside him. "No identification yet, sir. It's been made deliberately difficult."

"This happened in the auditorium?" Cadover turned to the manager. "And you had the body hauled out on your own responsibility?"

"Certainly. There was nothing else to do. And it wasn't known that the fellow was dead until they had him out in the upper foyer." The manager returned to his desk and consulted a note. "Lights went up at the end of *Plutonium Blonde*, the time being three minutes past four. One of the girls we call usherettes"—and the manager made a fastidious face over this barbarism—"saw the fellow slumped in his seat and went up to have a look at him. He didn't look right, so she called the floor manager. That was the regular procedure. The floor manager gave him a shake, and then saw the blood. By that time there was a bit of a fuss round about, so he sent one of the girls for a couple of commissionaires and to call up a doctor. He supposed, you know, that the fellow had suffered a hæmorrhage, or something like that. By this time the lights were due to go down, and he didn't stop them, since he didn't want more disturbance than need be. But as the body was lifted out he saw that it *was* a body—that the fellow was dead—and he tells me that the notion of foul play did enter his mind. He called two firemen to stand by where the thing had happened—fortunately it was right in the back row—and then he came straight up to me. I gave instructions for the body to be brought in here and for the police to be called up at once. Then I went in to see how it was with the seats where the thing had happened. The row immediately in front was full. But the dead man's seat was, of course, still empty, and so was one seat on his right and three on his left. So I ordered the whole five to be roped off and guarded. Then your men arrived and my responsibility ended. Lights go up again in five minutes. Of course, if you want the theatre cleared and closed, I will have it done. Only you might put me through to your Assistant Commissioner first. I have to consider my directors, you know."

Cadover made no reply. He turned to the sergeant. "Well?"

"We arrived while they were still showing the short that follows *Plutonium Blonde*. There seemed no point in sealing the place. People had been pouring out and in during the previous interval—the one during which the discovery of the body was made. But, of course, there was the question of people nearby when the thing occurred who might still be in the theatre. There was that, and there was what the usherettes might know, and there was clearing a space round the spot where the thing had happened, and searching it in the interval after the short. Inspector Morton is on that now, sir, with half a dozen men from the district. But I understand they've come on nothing yet. The crime appears to have passed unnoticed."

"Unnoticed? But this man was shot. You can't shoot a man in a public place without——"

The remainder of Cadover's sentence was drowned in a sudden crashing explosion which made Dürer's engraving rattle on the wall. The manager sighed resignedly. "Disgraceful," he murmired. "Do you know that between the auditorium and this room there are two supposedly sound-proof walls? We shall have people calling quacks from Harley Street to swear that they've been deafened, and we shall have to pay thousands of pounds. And, of course, it's indecent too. Much more indecent than rows of ghastly little trollops waggling their photogenic haunches. The Lord Chamberlain should intervene. When I was a young man I had idealism, Inspector, I assure you. I saw Film as a great new æsthetic form. Those

52

were the days of the early Claires, and of *Potempkin* and *Storm over Asia*. And to think that it should all come to this . . .! Would you care for a cigar?"

The slinky young man, looking awed, produced a box of Coronas from a drawer. Cadover petrified him with a scowl. "Was that meant to be an exploding bomb?" he asked.

The manager nodded. "An atomic one. The biggest noise in the entire noisesome history of the screen. Sound's greatest triumph. The explosion kills seventy-five thousand supers hired at five dollars a head. It also blows the clothes off a gaggle of girls in a cabaret. It's all very disheartening to people like ourselves. To say nothing of being an invitation to murder. For plainly the shot was fired just as the sound-track triumphantly broke the record. Ingenious, come to think of it. The poor fellow must have been lured in expressly to be shot under cover of that hideous row. And then he was robbed."

"Robbed?" Cadover turned sharply on the sergant.

"I don't think it should be called that, sir. Everything—or nearly everything—was certainly lifted from the body. But there was more to it than that. Bits of the clothing were cut away."

"Bits of the clothing?"

"Yes, sir. You know there are three places where a good tailor usually sews in a tab with a name—an inner jacket pocket, a waistcoast pocket, and the inside of the trouser-tops at the back. Well, all these places have been cut out."

There was a silence while Cadover verified this. "I can understand the shooting," he said. "With a smokeless powder, and when the audience was stunned and distracted by that uproar, the thing would be possible enough. But that anyone should then be able to tumble the body about——"

The slinky young man giggled. "It was in the back row, Inspector, and you must remember how people do behave in a cinema—and particularly there. Lovers embrace and fondle each other in the darkness——"

"That's deplorably true." The manager had assumed an expression of refined repugnance. "With a little care, this bold rifling of the body could be made to bear the appearance of mere amorous dalliance. What a splendid point for the Sunday papers that will be."

Cadover frowned. "Initials? Laundry marks?"

"Yes, sir." The sergeant nodded. "Several of the undergarments have the initials P. C."

Once more the slinky young man giggled. "I don't suppose that they could stand for Police Constable, could they?"

The manager looked offended. "Really, Louis, this is no occasion for unfeeling jokes. A hard-boiled attitude is quite out of place." The manager lit a cigarette, strolled across the room and glanced indifferently down at the body. "About thirty, would you say? And a military type. Nothing like the Army for wiping off any individuality a face may once have been blessed with. You could pick half a dozen almost identical young officers out of any line regiment."

This was true. For that sort of identification which is sometimes achieved with the aid of smudgy photographs exhibited outside police-stations or in the Press there could scarcely, Cadover reflected, be a less promising subject. Not that it ought to come to that. Perhaps, within a few hours, and almost certainly within a few days, there would be a link-up with one of the endless enquiries after missing persons that flow in upon the Metropolitan Police. A body not ultimately thus identified would be a rarity indeed. . . . He turned to the sergeant. "Everything been done here?"

"Yes, sir. And Inspector Morton is in a room just opposite."

"I'll see him now. Have the body removed." Cadover nodded curtly to the manager and walked out. The foyer was crowded. *Plutonium Blonde* was over. The evening's final showing of the programme was about to begin.

Inspector Morton was interviewing a succession of girls dressed in bell-bottomed white trousers and enormous scarlet bows. Two constables were making shorthand notes and another was recording the proceedings on a dictaphone. The room was a humbler version of that occupied by the manager, and there was another Dürer engraving on the wall. Perhaps it belonged to the slinky young man called Louis.

54

"All we found." Inspector Morton had interrupted himself to jerk a thumb at a table behind him. Cadover crossed to it and saw a bunch of keys, a pile of loose change, and pocket diary.

"Finger-prints?"

"Been attended to. The diary was in the hip-pocket and must have been missed when the body was rifled. It has a few interesting scribbles." Morton turned back to the girl before him.

Cadover picked up the diary. It was new and at a first glance appeared entirely unused. He turned to the page for that day. Scrawled in pencil he read:

gun for boy 1.15.

He turned to the preceeding page and found:

N.I. police re guns etc.
Light railway from Dundrane

Two days earlier he found:

Bolderwood
  Hump

He continued to search. Throughout the diary there was only one other entry. It occurred six days before and read:

Smith's 7.30

Cadover put down the diary, picked up the bunch of keys and examined them carefully one by one. Then he did the same with the little pile of silver and copper coins. One florin he inspected for some time. Then he turned round. A pair of sailor's trousers—very tight above and baggy below—was swaying from the room, and Inspector Morton was staring at this departure in unflattering absence of mind. "Cadover," he said, "do you think it might be terrorists?"

"No."

Morton sighed. "It was easy to do, and the setting will give it sensational value. But no doubt you're right. Some of these girls are far from being fools. A lot behind, but something on top as well." Morton paused and, getting no response to this, sighed again. "To begin with, something emerges from the box-office. They have been showing to full houses, but when the lights went up and the body was noticed there was one empty seat on its left and three on its right. Four people had left before the end of *Plutonium Blonde*—before the end, that is to say, of its first showing of the day. So there was no question of those people leaving when the film reached the point at which they had come in. Moreover, for that showing those seats could be booked—and they *had* been booked. So I thought at once of quite a little gang on the job. They had their victim nicely isolated, and after killing him they all cleared out. But there is a point that is pretty conclusively against that."

"The booking?"

"Exactly. When you book, the girl in the box-office hands you the numbered tickets and makes a blue cross on the correspondingly numbered seats on a plan. And here we come upon the blessings of industrial psychology. How to make blue-pencil crosses on a plan with most speed and least fatigue. Pushing up production per man-hour—or girl-hour, in this case."

"Ah." Cadover's expression indicated no appreciation of this embroidery.

"Two seats is *zig-zag, zig-zag*. Three seats is *zig-zag-zig, zig-zag-zig*. In other words, you can study the line of crosses and distinguish the number of seats booked at a time. Of the five seats in question, three were booked at one go, and two at another. There can have been no concerted booking of all five."

"Does that follow? The bookings may have been successive. One fellow comes immediately behind the other and simply says he'll have the next three."

Morton shook his head. "In this case, I think not. The block of three has been crossed off with a much more recently sharpened pencil than the block of two. And if one wanted to make sure of all five seats one would scarcely——"

"Quite. But does the girl in the box-office remember anything about the people concerned?"

"Definitely not. It couldn't be expected. The job is purely mechanical and she must have lost all interest in the faces peering in on her long ago. But it's a different matter when we come upstairs to the usherettes. We get far more than we might hope for from them. . . . Look here, I'll draw a plan. It will explain the situation until you can see for yourself." And Morton reached for a pencil. "The seats in question we'll call *ABCDE*, and you can see that *A* comes next to a gangway. It's the back row, remember, so there's nobody behind. From the people in front and to the right we may get something, though I doubt it now. The body was in *B*. And it was *ABC* that were booked together in a block of three, and *DE* that were booked together in a block of two. . . . I think we may say that something of a picture begins to emerge." And Morton tapped his pencil with some complacency on the table before him.

Cadover grunted. "What about those usherettes?"

"Ah! Well, there's a girl who remembers showing the dead man to his seat. But he didn't bring three tickets; he brought two. And there was already someone—a woman—in *A*. Nobody remembers the woman arriving. She may just have had her counterfoil taken at the entrance and found her way to her seat herself. You can see it was an easy one to find. But her ticket, mind you, had been bought along with *B* and *C*."

Cadover committed himself to his first judgment. "Good," he said.

"And this girl remembers who came with the dead man. It was a boy. He might have been about fifteen. Now, of course, that's pretty queer. It suggests that the crime was perpetrated by a woman and a lad. Not but what the woman's function isn't clear."

"It is at least conjecturable."

Morton nodded. "Put it that way, if you like. The dead man believed that on his left there was a stranger having no interest in him. Actually, the woman may have been his murderer.

57

And certainly she had her part to play as soon as he was dead. Everything that might serve to identify the body——"

"Quite so. The manager here has tumbled to that. The job was done under the appearance of hugging and being hugged." Cadover stared sombrely at Morton's plan. "And then this woman, and the boy who had lured the victim to his fate, slipped out. Did anyone remark that?"

"No. We have nothing but the arrival of the man and boy. By the way, though, it was something about the boy that had struck the usherette's attention. He wore a bowler hat."

"Is there anything so remarkable in that? You and I both wear bowler hats."

Morton chuckled. "That's because we are both a particular sort of policeman. Mere lads don't often wear them nowadays. Possibly some conservatively inclined office-boys in the city still do, but on the whole it's a habit confined to a few public schools which like their boys to dress like that when in Town. That's what attracted the notice of this usherette—the glamour attaching to our fading institutions of privilege." Morton lingered over this phrase with evident pride. "And she says that he didn't look quite right. She *says* that *that's* why she noticed him. Bowler hat and all, he didn't look quite right. . . . But one would expect her to say that now."

"Of course one would—but then might she not be correct?" Cadover smiled a rare smile. "Public schoolboys with lethal intentions are quite wrong." His expression grew dark again. "Commonly they have to wait till they grow up and we turn them into airmen and soldiers."

"No doubt." Morton was slightly shocked. "Anyway, that's all we have about *ABC*. But we also have something about *DE*. Another usherette is sure she noticed two people who must have come from *DE*. She noticed them because they came out in a bit of a hurry and almost caused a disturbance. They came out *to the right*—that is to say, not past *ABC*, but past a much longer line of seats, all occupied, on the other side. People sometimes come blundering out because they are feeling ill, and this usherette came forward in case it was anything like that. She shone a torch for them and then caught a glimpse of them in the light of an opening door. It was a boy and a girl."

"Children, does she mean?"

"Not exactly. As a matter of fact, there's something odd there. She is quite clear that the girl was about seventeen. But when I asked the age of the boy, she first said that he looked no more than twelve, but later corrected that and declared he might have been sixteen."

Cadover considered. "Well, it was only a momentary glimpse, and a conflicting impression of the sort might be quite possible. Did she notice anything about them in particular?"

"It was the lad who was really in a hurry, she says. He was bustling out the girl, who was just bewildered and a little cross. Well, of course there was one attractive explanation of that. This lad, sitting perhaps in D, became aware that something horrid had happened on his left, and he decided to get his girl and himself clear of it. An adult, as we very well know, is apt to behave in just that way, and it would be very understandable in a boy. But, as it happens, there's a big difficulty in taking that view. For the usherette is quite confident that those two young people pushed out *before* the big bang. They were clear of the auditorium *before* the girl in the picture is represented as letting off the bomb."

"The girl lets it off?" Cadover frowned at his own irrelevance. "Of course, the lad may simply have tumbled to the fact that, although nothing nasty had actually happened on his left, something of the kind was working up. Not that that's a likely explanation. The essence of the killing must have lain in sudden and unsuspected assault. Perhaps the film makes another big noise a bit earlier?"

"Apparently it doesn't. Even for a revolver with a silencer—which is a clumsy thing—there would be just the one chance. We must take it that the couple in DE left before either murder or hint of murder. In fact, it looks as if they are out of the picture. Whatever their reason for leaving early, it just doesn't concern our affair." Morton hesitated. "Only the usherette noticed one other odd thing. I wonder if you could guess what it was?"

Cadover shook his head, his expression indicating the conviction that the case stood in no need of conundrums arbitrarily added.

"The lad she saw leaving had a bowler hat."

"Um." Cadover's was a quintessentially noncommittal grunt.

"So it almost looks as if the lad who appeared to leave *DE* was the same who arrived in company of the dead man to occupy *BC*."

"It is far from a safe assumption. And if the booking of *ABC* and *DE* respectively were indeed entirely independent it is also a difficult one."

Morton nodded glumly. "I suppose that's so. But this usherette's response—the one who showed the boy and girl out—corresponds oddly to that of the other—the one who showed a man and boy to *BC*."

"You mean that she felt there was something wrong about the boy?"

"No, not that—although there is the odd fact of her being in doubt about his age. I mean that a bit of class-consciousness again came in. She was aware of the bowler hat as a manifesto —as saying, 'My education costs papa at least two hundred a year.' "

"Your manner of questioning usherettes must be extraordinarily skilful." Cadover spoke quite without irony. "But does this lead out anywhere?"

"Only to this—that the usherette then went on to distinguish the girl as not coming out of at all the same drawer. Whatever the feminine equivalent of the bowler hat may be, the girl didn't possess it. 'A cheap little thing'—that's what the usherette called her." And Morton shook his head. "It's extraordinary how snobbish people are. But it's a little stroke added to the picture—though whether to *our* picture one can't say. We do know one thing we have to look for. If the two lads were *not* the same, and if the usherette's nice social sense was not astray, we have to find and question a prosperous youth of problematical age who was giving some little shop-girl an afternoon at the pictures."

Cadover nodded. "I'm afraid," he said seriously, "that it opens what might be called a wide field of reference. One of the uses of prosperity is to entertain little shop-girls in that way. . . . There is nothing else on the cinema side of the affair?"

"Nothing at all, so far. And I doubt whether more will emerge. It's already more than we might hope for."

"I agree with you. Now, what about this diary which was in a hip pocket and therefore missed? Can we make much of it?"

"It's most tiresomely new." Morton stood up and walked to a window. "One might guess that the dead man lost his diary something like a fortnight ago, that he then bought this new one, and that, anyway, he didn't use such a thing very much. The first entry occurs a week last Tuesday and says, '*Smith's* *7.30.*' Is that right?"

"Just that. It sounds like a dinner engagement."

"And with a pal who couldn't have a less helpful name." Morton was drumming moodily on a window-pane. "'Robinson' wouldn't be so hopeless by half."

"I don't at all know about it's being hopeless." Cadover had looked up sharply. "It might be the restaurant, might it not?"

"Good lord—you've got something there! It's the first real light we've struck, likely enough. Can you work the same trick with the other entries? The next is on Monday, isn't it? Just the name '*Bolderwood*' followed by something odd that I've forgotten."

"It's followed by '*Hump*'—just that. The way it's arranged looks rather like the beginning of an address. We might do worse than look for somebody of the name of Bolderwood living at——" Cadover shook his head. "Some English villages have precious queer names, but I doubt whether we'd find one called Hump."

"What about a house?" Morton's face brightened. "People give the most idiotic names to houses. Dash Bolderwood, Esqre., The Hump. . . . What do you think of that?"

"At the moment I think we'll pass on. The next entry occurs

yesterday. '*N.I. police re guns etc.*'—and immediately below '*Light railway from Dundrane.*'

"Well, *Dundrane* explains *N.I.*, because it's a town in Northern Ireland. And seeing police about guns may not be as sinister as it sounds. If you travel to Eire by way of Northern Ireland and want to take dutiable objects in with you and out again you have to collect some sort of certificate from the Northern Ireland Police on the way." Morton sat down, well pleased with his own grasp here. "Again, it is the remoter parts of Ireland which are served by light railways, and it's a reasonable inference that the dead man was proposing a trip there and had been making some enquiries about how to proceed. And, of course, there seems to be a tie-up with the final entry—that under to-day's date. '*Gun for boy 1.15*' it reads, doesn't it? The figures can scarcely represent a bore, or anything technical like that. They must be a time of day—and presumably not in the middle of the night. At a quarter-past one this afternoon something was to be done about a gun for a boy. And if guns and the dead man were going to Ireland so presumably was the boy. And a boy was with the dead man in this cinema within an hour of that time. Now, you don't *hunt out* a gun for a boy at one-fifteen, or *forward* one, or *pack* one. That note of a precise time means an appointment—and, ten to one, an appointment to *buy* a gun. They bought a gun together—a shot-gun of some sort, one must presume—and then they came on here, and then the boy was a party to the man's murder and to the concealment of his identity. It's a most extraordinary picture."

Cadover as he listened to this efficient analysis was gloomily pacing the room. He paused before the Dürer. This one was a fantastic representation of the Assumption of the Magdalen. She was poised nude in air and appeared to be sprouting cherubs all over her like a Surinam toad. Down below a clerkly person raised a hand as if to study this phenomenon against the glare of the sun. Probably the clerkly person was blankly incredulous. But the world really is full of tall stories. . . . "Yes," said Cadover; "it's a most extraordinary picture."

"But gives us several lines."

62

"Quite so. They will have photographs of the dead man by now. I can try Smith's. In the morning I can try the likely gunsmiths. Then there are possible bookings to Ireland by anyone with the initials P. C. Then what about it being by a light railway from Dundrane that one reaches Mr Bolderwood of the Hump? As you say, there are several lines."

"To be sure there are." And Morton looked at his watch and stood up—a man not dissatisfied. "The problem's a tough one, but it can be worn down in time."

Cadover had risen too, and now he reached for his hat—his bowler hat. "Has it occurred to you," he asked abruptly, "that this crime may have no meaning in itself?"

"In itself?"

"Just that. It may be a mere clearing the ground for some other devilish thing—perhaps in a few hours' time, perhaps to-morrow or the next day. I'll make what speed I can. Good night."

CHAPTER VI

DINNER WAS OVER AND the train still ran through sunshine. Double Summer Time—England's last and most detestable contribution to civilisation, Mr Thewless irritably thought —made the evening uneasy and unreal. The engine, a creature whose ancient pride had been to enter stations unblown and on the dot, now pursued with depressed but dogged wheezings a timetable hopelessly beyond its senescent powers. On either side the forlorn and dismal backs of terrace houses stretched like a tedious and inescapable discouraging argument; through their windows peered hideous vases, iron bedsteads, the plywood backs of showy dressing-tables being bought at eighteenpence a week. As a refined person, Mr Thewless felt guilty and glum as he ran this gauntlet. Those miles of brick concealed squalors at which he could only guess; they also concealed heroisms which he was unlikely to touch. Mr Thewless sat back and meditated the building of a better England. For the achieving of that, after all, how many people more talented and powerful than he must passionately care! And yet how slow, how painful every step that was being won! For his own part, he felt very helpless, very irrelevant. An usher, a comparatively expensive leader of privileged little bears. . . . He looked at Humphrey Paxton, curled up on the seat opposite. And a new thought came to him. Perhaps that sense of his own irrelevance was no more than a discouragement whispered by the Devil—say, by way of protecting those dark satanic mills of his which here smoked on the horizon. Perhaps to set Humphrey straight was to set England straighter forty years on. For how much might a single able and imaginative man achieve!

Mr Thewless frowned at himself, distrusting inflated notions, distrusting these wafts of emotion. He picked up *The Times*. It was true that he had read most of it already. But he would convince himself that he was mildly diverted by the fourth leader. . . .

At this moment the elderly lady put down her book and glanced rather nervously about her. Hitherto she had not spoken. But now she looked at Humphrey. "Have *you* got an exciting story?" she asked.

"Thank you; it is quite exciting here and there."

Mr Thewless stirred uneasily. Humphrey, he had noticed, was provided with a number of books of a suitable if slightly juvenile sort; these dealt with the heroic and surprising exploits of aeronauts in various quarters of the globe. But in addition to these the boy had others, and of these the only one that Mr Thewless had been able to survey was the book he was reading now. It was the late George Moore's version of the erotic romance of Daphnis and Chloe. That Humphrey should inform himself from this volume—and even find it quite exciting here and there—Mr Thewless as an enlightened pedagogue judged not reprehensible. Nevertheless, he was not quite pleased. And now this amiable lady would perhaps peer at the book and be a little shocked.

Sure enough, the lady peered. "*The Pastoral Loves of Daphnis and Chloe*," she read aloud. "Ah, yes—I remember quite liking that. There are pirates, are there not? But I don't remember if they are important in the story."

Humphrey, startled, mumbled some inaudible reply. The bearded man with pebble glasses appeared to consider joining in the conversation and to think better of it. The elderly lady tapped the volume on her lap. "Now, this really makes me quite nervous. In your book there is nothing that could actually happen to one. Is there?"

At this Humphrey blushed a bright scarlet beneath his dark hair and mumbled more hopelessly than before.

"For example, pirates are quite out of date. But this"—and again the elderly lady tapped her book—"is a Secret Service novel. And quite a lot of it takes place in a *train*."

"I should have thought the Secret Service a bit out of date too." The bearded man spoke in an appropriately rumbling voice. "The sort of thing that is exciting in time of war."

"But I assure you that it is always going on!" And the elderly lady nodded with surprising emphasis. "I have been told so by persons who are *most* well-informed. Only this April I met an extremely interesting woman at Bournemouth who had good reason to believe that an intimate friend of her brother's was nothing less than a special agent of the Government! I confess that it is since that meeting that I have been inclined to read novels of this sort."

Humphrey had tucked *Daphnis and Chloe* unobtrusively away and was looking at the elderly lady intently. "My name is Humphrey Paxton," he said abruptly.

"And mine is Margaret Liberty." The elderly lady gave a brisk nod by way of completing the introduction. There was a smile of pleasure on her face.

Mr Thewless's uneasy feeling grew. He was aware of a mounting tension in his pupil. He was aware too of the stirring, once more, of just those alarming doubts and fantasies which he had promised himself to banish from his own mind.

"Do you think," asked Humphrey, "that in things of that sort—spies and so on—truth is really stranger than fiction?"

Miss Liberty shook her head. "I wouldn't say that. I only say that things of that sort do happen, and that sometimes quite ordinary people—people like ourselves in this compartment—become mixed up in them. And that, of course, is why this book makes me a little nervous; one can never be quite sure—and particularly in *trains*."

From behind the shelter of *The Times* Mr. Thewless cursed the woman heartily. For if Humphrey irrationally believed himself to be surrounded by blackmail and conspiracy what sort of talk could be more injurious than this? And Mr Thewless put down his newspaper. "I myself," he said firmly, "am quite sure—even during a railway journey. I have no inclination to believe that melodrama will leap out at me from between the pages of a novel. And, even if I were myself nervous, I would hesitate before doing anything to propagate the feeling."

Some little time before he got to the end of this speech, Mr Thewless became aware that it was not a success. For one thing—and even if the elderly lady called Miss Liberty had prattled foolishly—it was definitely uncivil. But also—and this was more important—it was untrue. Mr Thewless was himself substantially jittery. By what stages the feeling had grown again he could now scarcely say. But it was as if a sinister and improbable world really *had* escaped from Miss Liberty's book. If the man with the beard and the pebble glasses had whipped off both these appearances and incontinently revealed himself as a beautiful adventuress toying with an automatic pistol, Mr Thewless would have been alarmed, certainly, but scarcely surprised.

Miss Liberty smiled brightly. She had every appearance of one who is not easily snubbed. "What the writers of these books know so well how to contrive," she said, "is *distrust*. Who knows anything, really, about anybody else? How often in our casual relationships with others we take their very identity for granted! I am taking it for granted now that this young man's name is truly Humphrey Paxton—just as he is perhaps taking it for granted that mine is Margaret Liberty."

From across the compartment Mr Thewless heard Humphrey give his characteristic gasp. There was now a glitter—a positively frightening glitter—in the concentrated glance he was directing upon this cursed busybody. And suddenly he burst into speech. "That's true," he said. "I mayn't be Humphrey Paxton at all." He laughed queerly. "I may just be having somebody on."

The bearded man rumbled. "You're not having me on, my boy. Do you know you have your pullover on inside-out? And there's a tab that shows when you bend forward. It says 'Humphrey Paxton' in neat red letters." And the bearded man chuckled, his eyes twinkling behind their massive lenses. "*I'm* quite satisfied as to who you are."

"But that is altogether primitive!" With a kindled eye, Miss Liberty was protesting warmly. "If he is pretending to be Humphrey Paxton—other, I mean, than as a mere passing joke—*of course* his things will be appropriately labelled. And he will know a great deal about the real Humphrey Paxton, too. It would probably be quite difficult for anyone not knowing the Paxtons well to catch him out."

"That's right—I'm thoroughly well up in my part." Humphrey was now leaning forward in mounting excitement. He swung round upon Mr Thewless. "Can you catch me out?"

For a moment Mr Thewless was bereft of speech. For it was not the boy whom this detestable woman had unnerved; it was himself. This grotesque conversation, starting up out of nothing, had brought him face to face with that fantastic suspicion which—he realised it now—had been haunting the fringes of his mind for hours. *Was this Humphrey Paxton?*

What had the jabbering woman said? How often in our casual relationships with others we take their very identity for granted! That had been it. . . . Well, the boy had certainly not so taken *his* identity for granted; he had authenticated it by scrutinising a passport, by reference to the *Æneid*, and by an ingenious use of the telephone. But why? Was it really because the boy, being the veritable Humphrey Paxton, had doubted the *bona fides* of his new tutor? Might it not rather have been a sort of bluff, an adroitly distracting turning of the tables designed to drive any answering doubts from Mr Thewless's own mind? What of the boy's scarcely controlled agitation and

67

his recurrent air of rapid and furtive calculation? These might well be the signs of a clever youth playing a dangerous and difficult game. And the dentist! Had the youth an uneasy sense that over the dentist he had somehow given himself away, and was he now attempting to discover how the land lay when he jestingly challenged his tutor to catch him out? Was his queer and spasmodic behaviour an overplaying of the part of a nervous boy which he had been instructed to take up?

Mr Thewless, even as he sat silent and amazed at himself, let this jumble of speculations pour into consciousness. His suspicions were better out in the light of day, he realised, than lurking disturbingly in the depths of his mind. But what had planted them there in the first case? Not the foolish talk of Miss Liberty; that had merely precipitated a crisis. He had, he now saw, been worried from the first. The prospect of taking charge of the difficult son of the great Bernard Paxton had been more formidable than he had allowed himself to think. And the actual circumstances in which the responsibility was transferred to him had been disturbing too. Sir Bernard's failure to appear; the boy's belated arrival and odd behaviour; the queer business of the gun: all these things had contributed to the downright uneasiness he now felt.

And then in a flash Mr Thewless saw the full possibilities of the situation in which he had involved himself. He was conducting a boy who called himself Humphrey Paxton to a remote part of Ireland and upon a visit to relations *who would not know whether he was Humphrey Paxton or not*. If the boy was a fraud and played his part well, and if the ticklish matter of letters home were successfully coped with, there was not the least reason why the deception might not continue successfully for several weeks. And—supposing all this to be true—what end would it serve? The answer was starkly obvious. Humphrey Paxton—the real Humphrey Paxton—was the son of a very rich man from whom large sums of money might be extorted under threats. But he was also—and this leapt to Mr Thewless's mind again at once—the son of one of the world's most eminent scientists, so that it was conceivably something quite other than money that the criminals required. Yes! Criminals had kidnapped the real Humphrey Paxton and now had weeks in hand to get him safely away—out of the country, doubtless —while Mr Thewless with this abominable young villain went goose-chasing off to the wilds of western Ireland!

Quite suddenly Mr. Thewless felt himself to be trembling in every limb. He had an irrational impulse to spring up and pull the communication cord, or to thrust out an arm and take the boy sitting opposite him by the collar. Had the bearded man and the fatal Miss Liberty not been in the compartment, he might actually have adopted this latter course out-of-hand. But for some seconds a mere sense of social decorum kept him immobile in his seat. And in those seconds his mind again began to work—began to work in the deplorable seesaw fashion to which it now seemed committed.

Certainly the boy had joined him in circumstances which would have made a kidnapping and substitution perfectly feasible. Humphrey, since he was under sixteen and travelling with an adult, required no passport to visit Ireland; there was therefore no photograph with which to check his identity. And the matter of the dentist was very striking indeed. But was it conclusive? This wayward boy might have given out that he was going to the dentist when he had some quite different plan for spending his last afternoon in Town. What, then, if Mr Thewless was wrong? What if here were the real Humphrey after all?

Two things seemed to follow. First, it must be admitted that he, Mr Thewless, was of a mind considerably more impressionable and erratic than it had ever occurred to him to own to before. For to have arrived so fast and so far in the spreading of a net of baseless suspicion was an achievement altogether surprising in him; indeed, he found himself obstinately reluctant to believe that nothing but fancy was responsible. Secondly, he had been on the verge of some act of almost criminal irresponsibility. For, supposing that this was in fact the genuine Humphrey, consider the lad's case. He was a highly excitable creature who had surrounded himself with alarming, perhaps with terrifying, figments of conspiracy and persecution. These figments had by some obscure telepathic

69

process communicated themselves to his new tutor; had perhaps served, too, to activate a similarly melodramatic strain in the mind of the fortuitously encountered Miss Liberty. Now these two grown-ups were playing up to Humphrey and building an atmosphere which was bound to intensify his fears. And Mr Thewless himself, although he had attempted a few minutes before to indicate this to the lady firmly enough, was now on the verge of seizing the unlucky lad by the collar and doing, maybe, irreparable nervous harm.

"The technique of such yarns," Miss Liberty was saying brightly, "differs both from the detective story on the one hand and the simple thriller on the other. As I said, it is not primarily a matter of mystery, and not primarily a matter of violent action. What is aimed at is distrust . . . sometimes sudden and apparently fantastic distrust."

The boy leant forward further still. "What about the other thing?" he demanded. "Sudden confidence? Taking a chance?"

"That is very true. It is also an excellent thing to bring in. We have always supposed X to be X—a thoroughly reliable man. But all at once there springs up the spine-chilling question: what if X is really Y . . . Y whom we know only to be our deadliest enemy? That is one of the possibilities. But the other is as you say. Z is wholly problematical. We have every reason to suspect him. But something obscurely prompts us and we take a chance." Miss Liberty laughed. "And of course, it turns out well. He is revealed in the end as nothing less than the ace operator in our own Secret Service."

Humphrey laughed too—his wild and sudden laugh. His eyes were still shining. It was hard to believe that he was the same boy who curled up brooding in a corner and sucked his thumb like a three-year-old. He turned to Mr Thewless. "You look glum," he said. "But I expect we'll have a perfectly calm crossing."

The harmless impudence of this juvenile sally ought to have cheered Mr Thewless up. But he was, he found, too extensively disturbed to be much encouraged by a momentary mood of confidence in his mercurial charge. He heartily wished the two

70

strangers away. If they had the compartment to themselves he could surely have it out with the lad and come to a definite conclusion one way or another—and this without doing any great damage supposing him to be indeed the true Humphrey Paxton. But now there was no chance of that. Preston was behind them. Their two fellow passengers were seemingly bound for Ireland. Not till they were on the steamer would he have a chance of getting the boy to himself. And by the time he could come to any determination on his problem they would be at sea. Mr Thewless frowned. Then, recollecting himself, he smiled benevolently both on his pupil and on the calamitous Miss Liberty. For good measure, he even smiled on the bearded man, who was fiddling with a fishing-rod, and who received this gratuitous emotional display with some signs of confusion. Whereupon Mr Thewless looked out through the window, surveyed a landscape which was now just beginning to admit the shades of evening, and fell to a more mature consideration of his predicament.

Suppose, once more, that this was indeed Humphrey Paxton. The boy had been living in a world of oppressive fantasies, until he had reached a state of hallucinating himself with terrifying day-dreams. But now he was making a break; a change of environment lay before him; in his new tutor he had one who would at least handle the situation as intelligently and conscientiously as he could. Moreover, Miss Liberty had not perhaps, been an unmitigated pest. Her cheerful talk about thrillers and spy stories had produced in Humphrey—if Humphrey it was!—what seemed a healthy response; it was as if he had succeeded for the time in reducing his fantasies to their original status of exciting make-believe. Perhaps, indeed, the lady had unconsciously provided something like a key for dealing with him. But now suppose that Mr Thewless broke through this make-believe with an actual and sober challenge to the lad's identity—such a challenge as the lad on his part had uttered when at his most disturbed at Euston. Could he really do this without the risk of inflicting serious nervous shock? On second thoughts, and without the advantage of professional knowledge on such matters, Mr

71

Thewless doubted it. It would be a step of the utmost gravity. And prompting it there might be nothing more solid than a vagary of his own mind—one induced by those very vagaries in his pupil which in accepting his present employment he had given an implied assurance of his ability to cope with!

But now consider again the other side of the picture. What if, in London, the first stages of an audacious and atrocious crime had indeed accomplished themselves? Humphrey Paxton was to be taken by a tutor who had never set eyes on him to visit relations who were in precisely the same case. His father had been prevented from accompanying him to the railway station; presumably, therefore, Humphrey had set out for it alone. *Had he ever got there?* Could more favourable circumstances for a ruthless kidnapping be conceived? For the criminals had only to be provided with a colourable pseudo-Humphrey and they had a chance of achieving something altogether out of the way—nothing less than a kidnapping unsuspected until they chose to reveal it at their own convenience; an abduction unsucceeded by the slightest hue-and-cry! And in this scheme Mr Thewless, the unsuspecting tutor pottering through Cæsar or Virgil with the pseudo-Humphrey in the depths of Ireland, would be the prime if unconscious instrument.

It was an intolerable thought. Moreover, if he really believed his suspicions to have any substance he had a clear duty to act. Not to do so would be to concur weakly in a train of events leading to none could tell what degree of horror. But what could he do? Insist upon returning to London at once? Communicate his fantastic suspicion to Sir Bernard Paxton and request that somebody be sent to identify the boy? But Sir Bernard had been called away, and it might not be easy to get at once into touch with him. Should he hurry on to the Bolderwood cousins and explain the situation to them? Should he call in the police? Harassed thus by one disagreeable project and another, Mr Thewless heartily wished his problematical pupil to Jericho.

As he did so, he turned from the window to view the compartment, and found that the boy had disappeared.

CHAPTER VII

VERY LITTLE REFLECTION would have suggested to Mr Thewless that here was a circumstance in no way remarkable. On long-distance trains people do leave their compartments and potter down corridors. And as yet the boy who might, or might not, be Humphrey Paxton could not have been more than a couple of minutes gone—for certainly Mr Thewless's troubled abstraction had lasted no longer. Moreover, on neither supposition was there strictly anything to be alarmed about. If this was the real Humphrey Paxton, then the whole fevered supposition which his tutor had been building up was a figment and there was no reason to suppose any sort of plot whatever. And correspondingly if this was a bogus Humphrey, then anything untoward—such as the lad's losing his nerve for the imposture and bolting—could represent no more than a welcome clearing of the air.

But at this juncture Mr Thewless was in the grip not of rational calculation, but of instinct. The boy—very possibly the young criminal—was only two minutes gone, and on the mere score of this even the slightest uneasiness was absurd. Yet Mr Thewless was swept not so much by misgiving as by panic.

The man with the beard and the pebble glasses was gone too. On his seat, like the cast skin of some dingy reptile, lay the canvas case of his fishing-rod. Sections of the rod itself were propped in the corner, and beside them lay a gleaming brass-and-ivory reel. On the rack above was that sort of basket with an oblong hole through which one is supposed to drop fish like letters into a pillar-box. At all these things Mr Thewless absently stared—and as he did so his irrational alarm grew. Quite suddenly the bearded man had become in his heated imagination a figure wholly sinister. *For he had never fished in his life.* All these properties were entirely new—and what genuine fisherman ever renewed his entire outfit simultaneously? Moreover, there had been something in the way in which the fellow had fiddled with his rod——

Having got so far in fantastic speculation, Mr Thewless felt his head begin to swim. It was just as the woman in the corner had said; distrust was spreading itself like a miasma around him; he had a nightmarish feeling that he could be certain of nobody; were he to summon the guard, even that official would presently suggest himself as an emissary of darkness. But Miss Liberty herself, although annoying, was at least genuine; there could be no doubt about *her*. And Mr Thewless glanced across at the elderly lady's corner. As he did so he felt a queer stirring in his scalp, and this was immediately succeeded by an even more unpleasant pricking in the spine. The woman in the corner was *not* Miss Liberty. . . .

Long ago Mr Thewless had been deeply impressed by a certain scientific romance. It told how (just as in H. G. Wells's novel) the Martians wished to possess the earth. But they could do so only by projecting their own intelligences into human bodies—and this they had begun to do. No earthly being was safe. A man might turn to his wife—and in that instant the being who looked out through his eyes might be that of a malign invader from a distant planet. . . . And now, as he looked at Miss Liberty, it was something of the same sort that Mr Thewless experienced. For a second—a mere fraction of time—the person answering his gaze *was someone else*. But this was madness! And even as he held the woman's gaze the hallucination passed. More, it even explained itself. Miss Liberty had been at her exciting book again; its illusion had her in its grip; that absurd impression he had received of a cold mind grappling with a crisis was no more than a reflection of whatever absurdities were transacting themselves within its pages.

Nevertheless, Mr Thewless's perturbation grew. He got to his feet, shoved at the sliding-door giving on the corridor and scrambled out of the compartment. Doing this somewhat blindly, he collided with the bearded man, who was now returning to his seat. The impact would in any event have been not inconsiderable. But at this moment it happened that the train, now spurting like a seasoned runner down the final stretch of track to Morecambe and Heysham, swayed over some system of points—with the result that Mr Thewless found himself precipitated upon the bearded man with all the violence of a deliberate assault. And as a result, the bearded man's glasses were knocked off. For a moment the two men looked at each other—and Mr Thewless realised with a fresh stab of apprehension that the eyes fixed upon his own were perfectly focused. Assuredly they were *not* the eyes of a man who has just been deprived of unusually strong lenses of a genuine sort. Moreover—and this completed Mr. Thewless's dismay—the glance which they fleetingly held had a fresh familiarity which it took only a fraction of time to place. It was that same glance of cold appraisal of some invisible situation that Mr Thewless had fantastically imagined himself to discern in the innocent Miss Liberty. . . .

The bearded man picked up his glasses and rumbled an an apology. Mr Thewless, who had been much more in fault, found himself without the power of reply; he edged past the bearded man in a mere impulse to get away, and found himself stumbling up the corridor. Outside, dusk had now fallen and was deepening rapidly. It was like an impalpable tunnel closing in upon the hurtling train, and already the flying wheels and pounding pistons were taking on the deeper note they seem to sound at night.

The boy was missing. . . . Mr Thewless made his way up the corridor, peering into the succession of first-class compartments on his right. Business men, Army officers, dogs, expensive children: each held its appropriate quota of these. But of the boy there was, of course, no sign. Why should there be? Mr Thewless got to the end of the corridor and tried the lavatory. It was empty. He passed into the next coach. Here there were two lavatories and one was occupied. But even as Mr Thewless paused doubtfully the door opened and something cannoned unaccountably against his knees. Looking down, he had the shock of feeling that open madness had seized him at last. For what he saw was an elderly and rather

75

intelligent looking man—but put together on a scale of something like four inches to the foot. With a word of apology, this apparition scurried down the corridor, occasionally pausing to stand on tip-toe and peer into a compartment. And at almost the same moment a door opened halfway down the coach and there advanced upon Mr Thewless what appeared to be a schoolboy of about Humphrey Paxton's age. Only this schoolboy was some eight feet high and correspondingly broad, and he came down the corridor only by a series of muscular exertions which made him pant as he moved. . . . Mr Thewless glanced in a kind of despair into the first compartment upon which he came—and met the impassive gaze of a Chinese lady who was holding a white monkey on a chain. At the farther end of the compartment two Indians were playing cards, and in the middle an enormous Negro smoked a cigar. And the compartment held a fifth occupant—an inert figure entirely swathed in bandages. . . .

The train swayed. The engine could not be far away, for its roar was very loud. Nevertheless, other sounds predominated. There was a buzz of excited chatter in half a dozen outlandish tongues; there was a further baffling babel of growls and hisses, snarls and chirps; there was an intermittent and wholly mysterious deep reverberation, as if some valve were being periodically opened in a vast and grating machine.

Upon all these appearances and sensations Mr Thewless did not pause to reflect. He was surrounded by a congeries of foreigners and prodigies; he saw in them only the massive menace which anything of the sort may occasion in a mind swayed by primitive impulse; here was the enemy, and that was that! Nor was Mr Thewless any longer very clear on the first promptings of his confusion. The boy was gone. He had vanished in a sinister way. And his genuineness or otherwise—which was really the crux of the matter—had for the moment passed out of focus.

Mr Thewless glanced again at the Negro, who was dressed with great ostentation as an Edwardian dandy. Had he been in possession of his customary lucidity of mind, it is doubtful whether this circumstance would have appeared to him as particularly suggestive of covert conspiracy. But now he had no hesitation. He pushed back the door and entered the compartment.

In the reading of Mr Thewless the romance about the Martians had been an early vagary representing something altogether out of the way. Moreover, with the possible exception of the episcopate and of His Majesty's judges, he frequented the cinema as sparingly as any man in England. What now came to him, therefore, must be regarded as no matter of easy reminiscence, but rather as an exhibition of native intellectual vigour. Mr Thewless pointed sternly at the almost obliterated figure hunched opposite the Negro and pronounced the words, "Remove those bandages!"

For there could surely be no doubt of it. This swathed and limp figure was something below adult size. The boy had been drugged, and was now being thus ingeniously smuggled away. "Remove those bandages!" repeated Mr Thewless, and glanced commandingly round the compartment.

The Indians desisted from their card-playing. "Please?" they said simultaneously. Their eyes were moist; their linen was finical; they had shoes with very pointed toes.

The Chinese lady leant sideways and dived swiftly into a silk bag. Mr Thewless nerved himself for the emergence of a fire-arm. But what actually appeared was a nut, and this the Chinese lady handed to the white monkey. Then she looked at Mr Thewless. "Iss," she said—not very intelligibly but with perfect agreeableness. "Iss."

The Negro, who had been more particularly addressed, took the cigar from his mouth, balanced it carefully on a newspaper beside him, and with the hand thus disengaged gravely took his hat off to Mr Thewless. It was a grey bowler and must, Mr Thewless thought, have been specially manufactured to encompass that enormous skull. And now, having completed this salute, the Negro spoke in a voice the depth of which would have made the bearded man's rumblings sound like a thin falsetto. "Sir," he said, "I am this gentleman's medical adviser. And I cannot agree to your proposal."

Anger welled in Mr Thewless. "Remove those bandages!" he thundered.

The Chinese lady reached for another nut. The Indians looked at each other wonderingly, and then at Mr Thewless. "Please?" they said.

And the Negro considered. He appeared altogether unperturbed. "The fee," he said, "will be half a guinea."

"I beg your pardon?"

"In the common way of business, and at regular hours, the sum required is sixpence, payable at the door. But here I cannot sanction anything of the sort under half a guinea—or, if it is more convenient to you, say a ten-shilling note."

"Release the boy!" said Mr Thewless.

This time the negro looked genuinely surprised. "My patient," he said, "is Mr. Wambus. Professionally, he is known as the Great Elasto, the Indiarubber Man. I insist upon his travelling in this way because of the constant danger of lesion and infection. Technically, of course, his is a morbid condition of the skin. Allow me." Rapidly the Negro untied a bandage on the arm of the listless creature opposite. "Be so good as to pinch," he said; "pinch and pull."

Mr Thewless pinched and pulled. The skin responded with a horrid spongy resilience. As a nasty sensation it would be uncommonly cheap at sixpence; Mr Thewless produced ten shilling, thrust them hastily upon the Edwardian Negro, and stumbled from the compartment, feeling sick. The white monkey gibbered at him as he passed. "Iss," said the Chinese lady. He was again in the corridor.

Humphrey, the pseudo-Humphrey, the Great Elasto . . . in considerable confusion of mind Mr. Thewless continued to plod towards the engine This whole coach must have been reserved for the circus troupe—or whatever the abominable creatures might be—and in the remaining compartments there was nobody upon whom he was prompted to pause. It was now dark outside and he moved down his narrow shaft of swaying space—on one side of him a night grown indefinably ominous; on the other this nightmarish collection of freaks, the unaccomplished works of Nature's hand, abortive, monstrous or unkindly mixed. . . . To the human and sub-human gibbering there was now increasingly added a mere brute bellowing, with above this that deep periodic reverbera-tion which one could almost feel it was beyond the power of the labouring engine itself to produce.

At the end of the coach was a single lavatory. Mr Thewless peered in and found it empty; he passed on and discovered himself to be in a guard's van, dimly lit and full of tumultuous sound. For here in baskets and hutches and cages, or slumber-ing or straining at the ends of chains, were lemurs and Alsa-tians, goats and cockatoos, cobras and Shetland ponies, raccoons and rabbits. Of the animal part of the circus there was missing only the horses, the elephants and the larger carnivora. But even without the roar of lions the place was a pande-monium. For the rest, it was filled with the usual assortment of luggage: trunks, suitcases, baskets, a pair of drums, a cased and swathed double-bass looking unnaturally large in the dim light, a weighing-machine with some heavy weights, a couple of motor-mowers tied up in canvas. But it was neither the animals nor any of these objects that immediately caught and held Mr Thewless's attention; it was the single human occupant of the van. Sitting plumb in the middle on a large steel and leather chair was a woman of gargantuan propor-tions, fast asleep and snoring. It was this snoring, indeed, that had been so mysteriously echoing down the train.

Here, in fact, was the Fat Lady. And there could be no doubt as to *why* she was here. Into no ordinary railway com-partment could her bulk possibly be introduced; only the double doors of a luggage van would admit this mountain of humanity. . . . Mr Thewless stared, fascinated. Despite him-self, he had a sudden and acute vision of this creature stripped of the gaudy clothes in which she was swaddled—a vision of flesh piled upon flesh in continental vistas.

> "*Licence my roving hands, and let them go,*
>   *Before, behind, between, above, below* . . ."

Mr Thewless felt his brain reel. Not often did his well-ordered mind behave in this way. *O my America! my new-found-land!* . . .

79

At this moment the engine hooted and the Fat Lady woke up.

She opened one eye—an operation involving the systematic redisposition of fold upon fold of puffy and proliferating tissue. She gave a single vast respiration under the influence of which her bosom heaved like a monstrous and straining dirigible (*the Sestos and Abydos of her breasts*, thought Mr Thewless wildly) and then she opened her other eye with the same laboriousness as the first. "'Ullo," she said suspiciously. "Wot are you after?" And, much as if she divined the extreme impropriety of Mr Thewless's disordered imaginings, she drew several yards of outer garment with a careful modesty more closely around herself. "If you come to water them dorgs," she said, "stop making passes and get on with it. 'Ere, where's my tablets?"

"I am looking for a schoolboy." Mr Thewless raised his voice to a shout in order to be heard above the animal noises around him. "A *schoolboy*, ma'am! You haven't seen him pass through here?"

"I ain't seen no schoolboy. 'Aving my forty winks, I been. But likely enough 'e taken my tablets." The Fat Lady began systematically to shake and wobble the several parts of her person, apparently with the idea of dislodging and so discovering the missing articles. Mr Thewless followed the resulting undulations with horrid and unabated fascination; they were seismic or oceanic in character, or they suggested the sort of deep rubbery shudder which a passing bus may communicate to an adjacent building. Strangely, before this spectacle, the erotic imaginings of the poet Donne continued to possess him:

> "*Succeeds a boundless sea, but yet thine eye*
> *Some Island moles may scattered there descry;*
> *And sailing towards her India, in that way*
> *Shall at her fair Atlantick . . .*"

"'Ere they are!" cried the Fat Lady, and held up a bottle triumphantly. "I don't care to be without them—not between one forty winks and the next, I don't. You 'ave to remember the night starvation orl right when you 'ave a domestic economy like mine." The Fat Lady tapped herself on what the poet would have described as the Hellespont of her bosom.

"And 'ave you reckoned the turning over? The doctors cal-
culate as 'ow we turn over thirty-five times in the night. Now,
just consider what that means with me!" And the Fat Lady
shook her head darkly, so that her cheeks quivered like pallid
jellies. "Burning up sugar all the time—that's me!"

"You cannot tell whether a boy has passed through here?"

"Of course I can. You can't get no further than this van.
Try and see."

Mr Thewless did so and found that the Fat Lady was right.
Perhaps the engine was immediately ahead. Certainly the
door at the end of the van was locked. "But you have been
asleep?"

"Of course I been asleep. It's lonesome sitting in here among
all them brutes. Makes you feel 'ardly 'uman." The Fat Lady
was suddenly tearful. "I can tell you, I sometimes feel I'd
rather be a dwarf or a monster. Yes, a monster"—reiterated
the Fat Lady emphatically—"or a freak. I'd as soon be a freak,
I often say, if in all this dratted travelling I could enjoy the
society of my own kind. Two 'eads, I wouldn't mind 'aving—
or no arms and able to play the piano with my toes. Do you
know what they 'ave to do with me to-night on the steamer?
Do you know 'ow they 'as to stow my sort? Why——" At this
moment one of the Fat Lady's eyes closed. "Why——" she
repeated—and her other eye closed too. "As if I were one of
them Indian's heffalumps," she murmured. . . . The Fat
Lady vastly respired, and was asleep.

For a moment Mr Thewless paused, irresolute. A cream-
coloured donkey, diminutive as if in a toyshop, began to bray
in a corner. The sound, mingled with the Fat Lady's snoring,
the pounding of the engine, and the miscellaneous animal
hullabaloo all around, seemed for the moment to represent to
him a final overthrow of all sanity; he hastily quitted the
guard's van and made his way down the train. The Chinese
lady, he noticed, was still giving nuts to the white monkey,
the Indians were still at their cards, the Great Elasto—Mr
Wambus, in private life—lay back inert as before, the
Edwardian Negro was puffing at his cigar again and perusing
a copy of the *British Medical Journal*. Mr Thewless moved on,

81

somewhat somnambulistically continuing to try the lavatories as he went. Near his own compartment he met Miss Liberty, who squeezed past him with every appearance of faint maidenly embarrassment. Perhaps he would find the boy back in his place, and this whole episode to have been mere eggs in moonshine.

Eggs in moonshine, Mr Thewless repeated to himself—and dimly wondered from what odd corner of his reading the phrase had started up. Eggs . . . but the boy was not in the compartment. Nor was the bearded man. The compartment showed nothing but luggage and a litter of books and papers. In Mr Thewless's excited imagination this void and upholstered space was hurtling through the night in an uncommonly sinister way.

Moreover, it was no time since the bearded man had returned from a prowl in one direction; why should he now be off in another? And at once Mr Thewless felt that he knew the answer. He and the pseudo-Humphrey were accomplices; they had planned to confer in privacy; but by some misunderstanding the boy had gone the wrong way. At the moment of that odd collision in the doorway the bearded man had been returning from a false cast. He was off again now in the other direction—and it was in that direction too that the boy must have vanished.

Once more Mr Thewless set out on his wanderings. But this time, he knew, a virtually endless succession of coaches lay before him, and most of them would be very crowded. In order to confer together, moreover, the pseudo-Humphrey and the bearded man could easily lock themselves in a lavatory —and unless he told his sensational story to a guard and invoked assistance it would be impossible to check up on this possibility.

Nevertheless, Mr Thewless plunged down the train, for a sort of automatism now possessed him. Firsts and thirds were alike for the most part overflowing, and he marvelled at the number of people who had the ambition to sail for Belfast that night. Many were soldiers, sailors and girls in uniform; it was deplorable, thought Mr Thewless vaguely, to see how England had become like any Continental country before the war, its railway stations and public places a perpetual filter of drifting and shabby conscripts. A small professional Army, decently clad in scarlet and black——

The reflection, for what it was worth, remained unfinished. For at this moment, and at the farther end of the coach down which he was plunging, Mr Thewless descried the bearded man hurrying before him. But although evidently in haste, he was making an exact scrutiny of each compartment as he passed it—and even in the moment in which he was thus descried he turned round and his pebble glasses glinted as he cast a wary look behind him. Mr Thewless, with remarkable quickness for one not accustomed to this sort of thing, doubled up as if to tie a shoe-lace. The number of people lounging or squatting in the corridor was such that he had a confident belief that this manœuvre had saved him from detection. But now he proceeded more cautiously. That the bearded man was making his way to an assignation he took to be established. If it was indeed with the boy, and if the two could be glimpsed together, the main point of doubt in this dreadful adventure would be resolved.

The train was here increasingly crowded, each coach seemingly more crammed with travel-weary humanity than the last. It was that stage of a long journey that is consecrated to a haze of tobacco-smoke, the smell of orange-peel and a litter and silt of abandoned periodicals and newspapers. Astonishing, thought Mr Thewless, how many people contrive to sleep amid these mild miseries; everywhere around him was the sprawl, the pathos and the strange vulnerability of human bodies sagged and slumped into slumber. Did a large part of the adult population spend too little time in bed? Mr Thewless stepped carefully over a straying infant, negotiated a woman who was rummaging in a suitcase, and became aware that the bearded man had disappeared. Perhaps he had simply put on an extra turn of speed and gained the next coach. But Mr Thewless believed that he had at last dived into a lavatory. He therefore hurried forward to reconnoitre. Fortunately, the corridor was so crowded that one could squeeze oneself into virtually any position without exciting remark. He succeeded in getting himself close up to the suspected lavatory door—so close indeed that he could unobtrusively put his ear to it.

That such a drab proceeding caused Mr. Thewless some discomfort is a point requiring no emphasis. It was to this that the somewhat ineffective termination of the incident was due. That voices were to be heard behind the door was unquestionable, and that the second voice had a boy's higher pitch Mr Thewless almost persuaded himself to believe, and his plain policy appeared to be to stand his ground and achieve a decisive *exposé* there and then. But, even as he decided upon this, there was a general stir and bustle in the corridor. Mr Thewless conjectured—inaccurately, as it happened—that the train was about to reach its destination. And he was alarmed.

It may be that in this whole succession of episodes there was more of alarm than was altogether creditable to Mr Thewless's nervous tone. It must be recalled, however, that he had most abruptly become involved in events—or in the suspicion of events—altogether remote from his common way of life, and that he was enduring a period of intensive acclimatisation. Be this as it may, his alarm now was not discreditable, for it proceeded from a renewal of his power of judgment. Coolly regarded, it was surely overwhelmingly probable that he had merely in all this involved himself in fantasy after all, and that in twelve hours' time he would be looking back on it with mingled amusement and embarrassment. But if this was so he was at present being most remiss in relation to his charge. Wherever Humphrey had strayed to on the train, he would presumably return to his own compartment—and his tutor should certainly not be absent from it as they ran into Heysham. If he were not at hand during what would probably be something of a rush for the steamer, the boy might be considerably upset.

These were rational reflections—but the answering behaviour of Mr Thewless was not wholly so. There is something in a whole train load of people beginning to stir that can communicate a mysterious inner sense of insecurity and the need for hurried action. It was this that had gripped him. And he

84

turned now and began to hurry back towards his base. But as he reached the farther end of the corridor he turned, as it were, one longing, lingering look behind upon his late suspicions—and with a mildly catastrophic result. The bearded man had reappeared and was following him down the train. In this there was nothing sensational. The privy conference which had been held in the lavatory was over, and the bearded man was returning to his compartment. What was startling was the appearance of somebody whom Mr Thewless just glimpsed disappearing in the other direction. This was the back of just such a schoolboy as the lad calling himself Humphrey Paxton, and clad precisely as he.

Once more, perhaps, cool reason would have been able to render Mr Thewless a somewhat different estimate of this incident to that which his agitated imagination formed. A psychologist would have spoken to him on the theme of eidetic imagery, and of the power of the mind to see the image of what painfully absorbs it, not within the brain but projected upon the world without. A critic not thus learnedly equipped but endowed with moderate common sense would have represented that schoolboys are frequent enough, that their formal attire varies little between individual and individual, and that the particular specimen thus glimpsed (not even as having been in any certain communication with the bearded man, but merely in a relation of simple contiguity) might well have been any one under the sun. But whatever promptings of this sort his own mind was capable of Mr Thewless was at the present moment deaf to. And to the marked facility of his suspicion now must be ascribed the fatal absoluteness of his revulsion later. In this mechanism of emotional recoil (the final lurch, as it were, of that seesaw upon which we have already seen him rather helplessly ride) lay the occasion of much disaster to follow.

Clambering over kit-bags and babies, Mr Thewless hurried back to his compartment—physically as mentally a shuttlecock in the swaying corridors of this interminable train. That the bearded man did stand to him in some profoundly malign relationship he was convinced; there was nothing shadowy or intermittent about this; he could feel as he stumbled and squeezed his way forward that the fellow's eyes behind their bogus lenses were boring uncomfortably into his back. But around this there was only wild surmise. The boy was a fraud; with rather shaky logic, Mr Thewless felt him to be a traitor; the real Humphrey Paxton was in the hands of these same people who were plotting thus mysteriously around him and leading him this harassing and humiliating dance; action must be taken at once if he was not to be a mere cat's-paw in the commission of an atrocious crime. . . .

The compartment was still empty. Mr Thewless entered it and sat down heavily in his seat. He had now been in a state of more or less continuous agitation for more than five hours—and to this the last half-hour had stood as a sort of mounting climax. Such excitement told upon an elderly man. Not that Mr Thewless felt himself beaten. Nothing indeed was to be more remarkable about the whole history of these days than that he never felt himself to be precisely that. He was slow; he was bewildered; he was even irresolute at times. But Nature did appear to have given him the obstinate feeling that it was always possible to fight back.

He took breath. And as he did so the bearded man entered the compartment. His expression was not easy to discern, but his manner had become amicable. "That's done with, praise heaven!" he rumbled, and fell to packing up his suspect fishing-rod.

What was done with, presumably, was the journey, and Mr Thewless felt called upon to make some reply. "We are coming into Heysham?" he asked. It went against the grain thus casually to converse with the enemy, but it might be as well to give no appearance of suspicion.

"No, sir—that's some way off yet." The bearded man dumped his pillar-box basket on the seat beside him. "The train stops at Morecambe first, and I myself go no further." The bearded man paused. "Having no occasion to," he added. Mr Thewless seemed definitely to discern an inflexion of sinister triumph in this. "Capital place for fishing, More-cambe. You can make an uncommonly big catch there."

Mr Thewless had no means of telling whether these words were literally true, but as pronounced by the bearded man he felt that they bore some sardonic secondary sense. And for a moment he found himself surprisingly near to random violence. Already, and by mere accident, he had knocked the bearded man's glasses off. In this perhaps he had tasted blood. For he certainly felt now that it would be pleasing to set about this questionable fisherman and give him a bashing. It was a long time since he had cherished such an impulse towards a fellow man. Mr Thewless grabbed *The Times* and took shelter behind it once more. And in a matter of seconds the train had stopped and the bearded man had left the compartment.

Mr Thewless dropped his paper, lowered the window and looked anxiously out. If his charge had been the real Humphrey Paxton, and he had gone into hiding on the train, what more likely than that he should now be proposing to make a bolt for it? And, correspondingly, if his charge had been an imposter, was it not possible that the same thing was taking place? There might have been no plan to maintain a long-continued deception in Ireland; the criminals might feel that they had already been given sufficient grace. And Mr Thewless peered up and down the platform for signs of an absconding boy. But all he saw was the bearded man once more. The fellow had been joined by what appeared to be a private chauffeur, and this retainer was assisting a porter to unload something from the van. The light was poor at just that point, and Mr Thewless had for a moment the absurd impression that what the two men were grappling with was a coffin. . . . But the reality, when he succeeded in distinguishing it, surprised him scarcely less. The bearded man, it appeared, was the owner of that swathed double bass which had kept the Fat Lady and the various circus creatures company in the guard's van. The instrument was being extricated with considerable difficulty—almost as if it were heavy as well as bulky—and the bearded man (whose piscatorial paraphernalia looked doubly absurd in one now revealed as a devotee not of the naiads, but the muses) was superintending the operation with some anxiety. Even as Mr Thewless watched, however, the thing was accomplished, and the bearded man and his retinue made their way to a waiting car. To do so they had to pass close by once more, and upon seeing his late travelling companion the bearded man gave a cordial wave. "I hope you'll have a good crossing!" he called cheerfully, and was about to pass on. But an afterthought appeared to strike him, and he turned. "You and the boy, that is to say. Good night!" He was gone. And at the same moment Miss Liberty re-entered the compartment.

Mr Thewless had forgotten about her. But now he turned his eyes on her suspiciously—and noticed that hers were upon the retreating form of the bearded man. At once his suspicions grew. Between these people—and between these people and the boy—he felt some occult connection. Perhaps this harmless-seeming female was being left as a sort of rearguard to keep an eye on him. . . .

But this was insanity. A more harmless type than Miss Liberty, with her trepidations over an exciting novel, it would be impossible to conceive. And to break the ridiculous spell which he felt growing upon him Mr Thewless spoke out. "May I ask," he said, "if you have seen my young companion? He has been missing for some time, and I am getting quite worried about him."

Miss Liberty withdrew her gaze into the compartment and directed it upon her interrogator. Since she wore no pebble glasses, it was possible to assess something of its quality. What Mr Thewless read in it was distrust. But it was not, he felt, a muzzy and generalised distrust, such as a mind seeped in sensational fiction might evince. It was rather the suspended judgment of one before whom he had by no means as yet passed some crucial examination. "Humphrey?" said Miss Liberty. "I am sure he must be quite all right. Ah, we are moving again! A delightful boy, if I may say so, only perhaps a little highly-strung. He will be back any minute, I expect." She glanced towards the corridor. "Indeed, here he is."

It was certainly Humphrey—whether the true or the feigned. Without a glance at either of his companions, he pushed the door to and tumbled into his seat. He was deathly
88

pale, breathing hard, and—it seemed to Mr Thewless—oddly crumpled. His eyes between their dark eyebrows and dark shadows held a brighter glitter than they had yet shown—a piercing gleam which might have been of fear or excitement or even anger. He curled himself up and his thumb stole towards his mouth; suddenly he straightened himself with a jerk, sat up and thrust his hands into his trouser pockets. "Is the next stop Heysham?" he asked.

Mr Thewless, who had been about to make some reference to his unaccountable disappearance during the past half-hour, was startled by the voice, which was at once unnecessarily loud and trembling beneath some uncontrollable agitation. "Yes," he said. "We shall be there in a few minutes now."

"And go straight on board the steamer?" The boy laughed —and his laugh was more disturbing still. "Do you believe in tests?"

"Tests?" Mr Thewless looked at him blankly.

"*I* believe in tests." It was Miss Liberty who spoke.

And the boy turned to her eagerly. "You don't turn back?"

"Not so long as something inside says to go forward."

"Not even if it's all plainly going to be more than you bargained for?"

"Not even then. To go on, you see, may make you. And to turn back may—well, may mar you quite."

"Is that from a poem?"

Miss Liberty smiled. "I believe it is."

"From Shelley?"

"No. But it is something that Shelley thoroughly believed in, I should say."

The boy peered out into the dark. As he did so the engine whistled, and the sound was eerie. He spoke without looking round, and in a strangely adult voice. "One may not be what one dreams," he said. "I think I *shall* turn back." He wheeled upon Mr Thewless. "You may as well know——" He hesitated and his glance wandered to Miss Liberty. "Is that right?" he asked her.

"It entirely depends on your inner mind."

"I see." The boy was silent. The engine hooted again and

89

the train began to slow down. "One should have a sword upstairs," he said.

Miss Liberty looked puzzled. "A sword upstairs?"

"Yes. Even if one was going to be a poet one should have that." He sprang to his feet. "But at least I've got a gun!" He climbed on the seat and brought down from the rack the mysterious parcel that had caused such perturbation at Euston. "The bump at the end must be some cartridges to be going on with. I say! We've stopped."

"This is Heysham."

"Then here goes." The boy's face was lit up strangely. "Do you remember Protesilaus? He was first ashore at Troy, even though he'd had a warning. I think I'll be first ashore at Heysham."

And the boy thrust open the carriage door and leapt out. Mr Thewless, who had sat through this odd talk in a sort of misdoubting daze, reached for luggage. Had his mind been more actively working, the queer experience of the next few seconds might not have come to him—or if it had come at all must have done so with modified effect. But the fact is that by this time Mr Thewless's thinking had set into a groove of deepening suspicion. And in this mood the boy's dark conversation with this foolish old woman appeared to him as no more than the impudent mystery-mongering of a young rascal conscious of playing the central part in a successful conspiracy —one which had led him, only a little time before, into horrid confabulation with the sinister bearded man in a lavatory.

And so Mr Thewless's mind was made up—so definitely so that he now opened his mouth and stretched out his arm with intent to denounce and apprehend the imposter. As he did so the boy, already on the platform, turned his head——

Sound died upon Mr Thewless's lips; his gesture froze. For this—just *this*—he had seen before. The bare-headed boy set in a sort of deep chiaroscuro by the harsh station light; the bare-headed boy glancing slantwise at him from beneath raven hair; the boy, thus lit and thus standing, grasping a gun . . . all this he had seen, fixed for ever by Velazquez, in Sir Bernard Paxton's Spanish library. And that was why Sir

Bernard *had* such a library—as setting for a picture acquired because of its overpowering likeness to his cherished son. Humphrey had produced a passport after all, and one authenticated far more certainly than by any photograph.

A sadder and a wiser man, Mr Thewless descended quietly to the platform. During these nightmarish five hours he had allowed the strange power of suggestion to carry him into a land of shadows, of figments as insubstantial as those in Miss Liberty's romance. He had believed wonders. And now—and after a fashion strange enough—the simple truth had been restored to him. This was Sir Bernard Paxton's son—a boy hopelessly submerged in highly-coloured fantasies, indeed, but in point of identity none other than he claimed to be. That the future held substantial difficulties was likely enough—but they were only those with which a competent leader of young bears might confidently look to cope.

Mr Thewless took his hat off to Miss Liberty, made an authoritative gesture which secured him one of the few porters in evidence, and with Humphrey Paxton proceeded to board the night steamer for Belfast.

CHAPTER VIII

THE QUEUES HAD GROWN longer outside the Metrodrome. Emerging from the cinema, Inspector Cadover scowled at them as he strode away. Here were people unaware that at their back hurried Time's wingéd chariot . . . people giving half an evening to nuzzling nearer to the armed, the arrogant, the amorous lady. And beyond that less than paper-thin illusion what awaited them? Deserts of vast eternity, Cadover told himself. Assuredly they would miss the Blonde. But they would get the Plutonium, likely enough, in its nastiest fissile form. . . .

At this point Inspector Cadover, an experienced Londoner, was nearly killed by a bus. In which case the laugh would have been distinctly with the folk in the queues, he thought. And it would have been awkward. For nobody else seemed to feel that in the death of this unknown man in a cinema there lay a challenge that was urgent.

> "*But at my back I always hear*
> *Time's wingéd chariot hurrying near.*"

The rhythm of the lines distorted itself as Cadover walked. *I* always hear, *I* always hear, *I* always hear . . . the words thumped themselves out in his brain like a phrase which one has fitted to the inescapable jolt of rails or pounding of pistons as one hurtles through the night in a train. But why think of a train. . . ? Cadover's eye fell upon that rare and blessed visitant of London streets, a cruising taxi. He hailed it. "Smith's," he said.

With the stump of the cigarette between his lips the driver gave a signal of comprehension. Cadover was pleased. He had been by no means certain that Smith's possessed the sort of status that made possible the directing oneself to it in this monosyllabic way; that it was so appeared to lend slightly more colour to the possibility that this small restaurant was indeed what was pointed to in the dead man's diary. How wretchedly meagre the entries that little book had contained! Cadover ran over them once more in his mind.

> *Smith's 7.30*

That had been a week last Tuesday. All the other entries belonged to the present week. On Monday there had been

> *Bolderwood*
> *Hump*

and on Wednesday

> *N.I. police re guns etc*
> *Light railway from Dundrane*

while the final entry was on Thursday—this very day, that was to say, on which the fellow had met his death. And it read:

> *gun for boy 1.15*

For boy. . . . It was conceivable that in a brief jotting a man might so indicate his son. "I must get the boy a gun." Yes, one could hear a father saying that. But the phrase as written down had another flavour. Was it a flavour suggesting a professional relationship? "That lad So-and-So had better have a gun." Was that it? A man whose initials were *P. C.* proposing to take a pupil or ward to Ireland, and as a first step proposing to get the boy a gun. . . . A good deal in the way of inference might proceed from this. For example, a boy is not commonly given a shot-gun, surely, until he is about fifteen. And again, if he is so provided before a trip from London to Ireland there are economic, social and even geographical implications; he is not going to take the thing to Dublin, for instance, for use on Stephen's Green. But likely enough he will be taking a light railway from Dundrane—and travelling first-class should such distinctions carry so far into the wilds of Ireland.

Again, there was a point there. The west of Ireland was not like the highlands of Scotland, a rich man's playground into which there poured at this time of year the residue of England's plutocracy. It was country really remote still; and of such large houses as it had once possessed many were now ruins or burnt-out shells. One might, of course, go off with guns to stay at an hotel, but if P. C. had been taking the boy to stay with landed folk approached by a light railway from Dundrane the hunt from that direction might not be altogether hopeless. But assuredly it would take time. . . . And here was Smith's. Cadover jumped from the taxi.

It was a small restaurant which he had not entered for years. From the outside it looked shabby enough and he eyed it gloomily. The probability was that like many of its kind it had tumbled hopelessly downhill and that its only pronounced feature would be in a tacit, dogged denial—hanging heavy in the air as the smell of synthetic gravy—that the human palate exists. But this—Cadover told himself conscientiously—was neither here nor there, except as it might affect the probability of the dead man's frequenting the place. He pushed open the door and entered.

Smith's, he saw, had gone in for being discreet. Partitions,

93

alcoves and the sort of lighting that is described as subdued
appeared to be its chief selling-point. Behind decaying palms
elderly and besotted men argued with elderly and anxious
women; younger women were paired tensely in corners;
here and there youths given over to ignoble calculation
pressed chianti or what was doubtless execrable brandy upon
predatory girls. Over these futilities presided a frock-coated
proprietor and half a dozen waiters so softly and sinisterly
confidential as to suggest that they kept unnamable horrors
conveniently disposed in an annex at the back. Actually,
thought Cadover, all one would find there would be black-
market butter and a quantity of illicit horseflesh in process of
being transmogrified into venison. He sat down and ordered
something out of a tin. Nobody was near him except two
undergraduates in *demodé* polo-jumpers, endeavouring before
two revolting-looking troughs of *minestrône* to preserve that
sacramental attitude to exotic foods publicised in the writings
of Mr Evelyn Waugh. Cadover beckoned the proprietor.

"I am from Scotland Yard and engaged upon an enquiry
in which it is possible that you can help me. Have you a
regular customer—a young man with the appearance of an
Army officer—whose initials are P. C.?"

The proprietor looked blank. "We don't often know their
names," he said.

"Oh, come. In a restaurant like this you must have a great
many habitués—people who dine here quite regularly."

The proprietor looked as if he would like to have the hardi-
hood to declare that this was indeed so. But he was a man
whom discouragement was beginning to render indifferent
and therefore almost honest. "Well, we don't have so many
of that sort as we once had. People have become very floating
—very floating, indeed. Of course there are people who ring
up and book tables fairly often." The proprietor paused, as if
he suddenly saw that there was something rather odd in this.
"Yes, people do book tables and give names. Browns, mostly.
You'd be surprised at the number of Browns who dine at
Smith's. But I can't place your P. C. Sounds like a postcard,
don't it?"

Cadover received this inane pleasantry coldly. "There are about twenty people in here now," he said. "Just look round, will you, and tell me how many you recognize."

The proprietor made a slow survey of the room. Then he shook his head. "Really, it's difficult to say. Quite a lot of them do *seem* familiar." His gaze was upon the two undergratuates. These, having some dim knowledge of the ways of their kind before the deluge, had ordered a carafe of red wine and were now contemplating it in a gloom which might be either gustatory or financial. "But, do you know, I think it's just their *expressions*?" The proprietor looked puzzled. "Yes—I think it is only that."

"Here is the man I am talking about." And Cadover produced a photograph which had arrived just as he left the Metrodrome. "Do you recognize him?"

"I think I do." The proprietor hesitated. "Or is it just the expression again? I'm afraid it's only that. People who have been dining here . . . there's some odd likeness. . . ."

"This man is *dead*. It's the photograph of a corpse."

The proprietor nodded—as if the matter now explained itself. "Ah," he said. "Well, life is a banquet, after all. And here we have the expression of one who is finished with it. . . . Will you have some venison? It is the *spécialité de la maison.*"

"I'll have tinned pears, please—without custard. And I congratulate you on your baked beans."

The proprietor received this compliment with a deep bow, dredged up from the nineteen-twenties. "To receive the praise of our patrons," he said, "is our only happiness. Our *chef*——"
He was interrupted by one of the undergratuates, who had risen from table with a complexion gone suddenly pea-green and was now making his way to some inner chamber with both hands clutched to his stomach. "But about this *P. C.* it is to be feared that I cannot help you. The features are not distinguished and he would not dwell in the memory."

This, Cadover had already realised, was deplorably true. He put the photograph down on the worn tablecloth before him and produced a bunch of keys. "You don't happen to have noticed anybody with these?"

"I am afraid not."

"Nor with this?" And Cadover produced the dead man's pocket diary.

"No. These are really very insignificant objects. Even if a customer were to produce them over and over again——"

"Quite so. And here is my last exhibit." Cadover brought out a little pile of silver and copper and spread it on the table. "What about that?"

The proprietor looked bewildered. "But of course not! How can one hope to identify a man from a heap of coins?"

"I'm afraid that's very true. How could one identify your restaurant from a plate of tinned pears? Now, if it were the *spécialité de la maison* . . ." Cadover was spreading out the coins on the table. "But have a look at them, all the same. You see, we've nothing else to go on."

Markedly without enthusiasm, the proprietor poked among the coins. Suddenly he picked up a florin. "But this is most remarkable," he said.

"Ah." Cadover's comment had the carefully restrained quality of a man who plays out of a deep bunker and incredibly sees his ball make the green and trickle straight towards the hole.

"It is a counterfeit, and rather an odd one. The waiter brought it to me and I explained to the gentleman."

"And how did the gentleman respond?"

"He was most correct and took it back with an apology. There were reciprocal expressions of esteem and he remarked on the excellent quality of the venison. Just as you have done on the—um—baked beans. Just occasionally it is quite like old times. . . . Good heavens, what is that—an ambulance?"

The pea-green undergraduate was indeed being carried out on a stretcher; his agonised voice could be heard incoherently repeating from *Brideshead Revisited* the majestic passage on *caviar aux blinis* and the hot, thin, bitter, frothy *oseille*. . . . But Cadover paid no attention to this unsurprising incident. He had produced his photograph again. "And was this," he asked, "the man?"

The proprietor studied it anew and then shook his head. "I really cannot say. It is so much less characteristic than the florin, is it not? And the gentleman himself was assuredly of the kind who is like so many gentlemen. *That* I do remember. It is unfortunate that I am so little able to assist you."

"But at least you can remember approximately when this took place?"

"It would be about ten days ago."

"And did the fellow have a companion or companions?"

"There was a lady. But I cannot say that I recall her to mind. She was of the kind who is like so many ladies." The proprietor shook his head mournfully. "You have noticed how it is nowadays? Nothing of individuality any longer attached to the idea of style. And it is to be feared that the same influence attaches to modern cuisine. Times are hard and distinction difficult to attain. Even when one is so fortunate as to receive ample supplies of venison from Sutherland—or is it Ross and Cromarty?—one is sometimes at a loss——"

"You do not recollect that you had ever seen either the man or the woman before? Neither came here regularly?"

"I begin to recollect. Yes, I believe they have come together from time to time." The proprietor brightened. "Perhaps they may come again."

"The man is dead, remember. As a matter of fact, he has been murdered. So *he* won't come again—unless he decides to haunt your kitchens. But the woman is another matter. If she——"

"But she is here now!" Even as he spoke the proprietor visibly blenched. "They are *both* here now—over at the table in the corner." He looked wistfully at Cadover. "Do you think a ghost might be good for trade?"

"I think he might—if he were of the affable and familiar sort. Of course, if he went from table to table clutching his bowels and crying '*Revenge!*' it might be another matter." Having delivered himself of this unkind nonsense, Cadover felt that he might allow himself to glance cautiously over his shoulder. The man whom the proprietor had discerned was certainly not unlike the man who had died in the Metrodrome that afternoon. Nevertheless, nothing supernatural was involved; this was no more than another person of markedly similar type. "And the woman?" he asked the proprietor. "You are sure of her?"

"Quite sure. I clearly recall that emerald ring. Yes, the lady is assuredly the same. But the gentleman"—and the proprietor gave a sigh of relief—"is not."

"He is similar—that is all? In fact you might say he is the sort of man the lady dines with?"

The proprietor nodded. "You may put it that way. And she, of course, is the sort of lady who dines with that sort of man. In such moments as I can snatch from supervising the service and the cuisine the study of human nature is my main preoccupation. And here we have an interesting type."

Cadover stirred his coffee and pushed his chair sideways so that he could command the couple in the corner by a sideways glance. "Would you say," he asked heavily, "that she is an improper woman?"

The proprietor sighed nostalgically. "My dear sir, you recall, if I may say so, memories of happier days. An improper woman—how many years is it since I have heard that exquisitely *fin-de-siécle* expression! I should judge that the lady is employed in some secretarial capacity in the City, and that she has a small circle of male friends."

"Also from the City?"

"Possibly so. They will certainly not belong to the intellectual or artistic classes. The lady, although no doubt in one sense as improper as you aver, is extremely respectable. My experience, my dear sir, assures me of that at once. She is attractive to young men who, certain sharply defined necessities apart, require a healthy moral tone, such as every headmaster of a public school would approve."

"I see." Cadover felt old, and that the world and its types were passing beyond him. "Are the relationships to which you refer of a mercenary nature?"

"The lady will undoubtedly receive presents—quite substantial ones. But she will herself give presents of lesser value. It is all quite simple. And I judge that she will have no special lover or protector behind the scenes. It is life, is it not?" And the proprietor, although his eye was uneasily on a customer who looked as if he might be about to give trouble over the fricassee of chicken, contrived to look nebulously philosophic.

Cadover, having clearly formed notions of the nature of vice, scowled unappreciatively. But he was studying the young man in the corner. "Would you say that the young man has been in the Army?"

The proprietor considered. "The Air Force, I should venture to judge."

"And that he is sociable, with an extensive but vague acquaintance, and that he hasn't much in the way of brains?"

"That would be very much my impression." The proprietor was gratified by these reiterated appeals to his judgment. "Distinctly what they used to call an operational type."

Cadover rose. "I am going out to ring you up from the nearest call-box. You will then fetch that young man to the telephone."

"But we do not even know his name! Such a summons would be quite without plausibility."

"Possibly so. But when called to the telephone many people don't pause to think."

"Very well. I shall endeavour to summon him *avec instance*, and we must hope for the best. I take it that your object is to get rid of him?"

"Precisely. And—unlike that unfortunate youth—without the aid of an ambulance. But it would be as well if you had a taxi at the door, so that he can be whirled away without stopping to think. *À bientôt!*" And with this tactful concession to the cosmopolitan character of Smith's, Cadover slipped from the restaurant.

He found an empty call-box almost immediately, and the proprietor's voice answered his call. He pressed Button A. "Go ahead," he said.

There was silence for something over a minute. Then a slightly surprised but cheerful voice spoke. "Hullo," it said.

"Hullo?" Cadover spoke as one of massively sunny disposition who is momentarily vexed. "Hullo . . . hullo? I can't hear you."

"Hullo," said the voice.

"Hullo . . . am I through? Who's that speaking?"

"Jake Syme speaking," said the voice innocently.

"Good old Jake! Larry here."

"Larry?" The voice was blank.

"Not Larry—Harry."

"Good old Harry!" The voice was instantly expansive. "How goes, Harry, you old whorehound?"

Cadover was disconcerted by this. Appropriate speech failed him. "Very well," he said.

"Like hell? Well, that's grand. Good old Larry."

"Harry," said Cadover.

"Good old Harry. And how's Larry?"

"Like hell," said Cadover.

"Well, that's grand. Come round and have a drink."

"*You* come round and have a drink," said Cadover. "Know the Square Peg? Top-hole little party here. Hop into a taxi and come round now."

"Got a girl here." Jake Syme's voice was suddenly confidential. "Bring her along too?"

"What sort of girl?"

"Girl."

"Better not." Cadover strained his invention. "The mater's here," he said. "Top-hole party, but we've got the mater."

"I see." Jake's voice was properly respectful. "Wouldn't do, of course. I'll leave her here for a bit."

"That's right. Fill the old nose-bag and let her browse."

"What's that?"

"Nothing, old boy." Cadover realised that he had over-reached himself with this outmoded trope. "Come right round now. So long."

"So long."

Cadover left the call-box and walked with modest satisfaction back to Smith's. He grew old, but his dexterity did not altogether fail him. A taxi was drawing out from the kerb as he approached, and he had the satisfaction of catching a glimpse of Jake Syme, his expression alive with innocent anticipations of pleasure. No vice in him, Cadover reflected—

and then shook his head, remembering the lady within. A small circle of male friends. . . . Well, there was a vacancy. And he had better announce the fact straight away.

The girl was eating an ice. Her expression of displeasure might have proceeded either from this or from the fact of Jake Syme's having left her so cavalierly. Cadover sat down opposite her without ceremony. "Good evening," he said. "I want to speak to you."

"I don't think we've met." The girl looked at him coldly. "I am with a friend. He has had to go out to meet somebody's mother, but he will be back in a few minutes. I advise you to go away."

"I am Detective-Inspector Cadover of the Metropolitan Police. What I have to say will not take long, but it may distress you. Would you like to withdraw to the manager's room?"

With a hand that trembled suddenly, the girl pushed away her ice and dived into a bag for her cigarette-case. "I don't think you can have any business with me," she said. "You have no right to interfere with my private affairs."

"I don't intend to." Cadover looked at her austerely and saw with discomfort that she was debating whether to try a little allure. But even as he looked she decided against this. Perhaps, he thought fleetingly, he had not the appearance of one who requires a healthy moral tone, such as every head-master would approve, from the shady ladies of his acquaintance. . . . "I merely want information about a man whom I have reason to believe to be known to you."

The lady raised her eyebrows, and contrived to look at once spontaneously relieved and elaborately puzzled. "A man?" she said—much as if Cadover had mentioned an iguanodon or a tapir. "I don't think I know many men."

"I believe you know a sufficient number for my purpose." Cadover was suddenly grim. "And this is a photograph of the body."

"The *body* . . .?" The girl stared at the square of pasteboard. "Is Peter dead?"

"I am sorry to have to tell you that he died of a bullet-wound in a West-End cinema this afternoon. He appears to have been accompanied by a woman and a boy."

With a nervous and automatic movement the girl smoothed her hair. "I'm terribly sorry," she said. "He was awfully nice . . . a really good sort." Her voice broke. "He was the soul of honour and fair play. I liked him more . . . more than anybody I know. We both liked music." She looked at Cadover with eyes suddenly perfectly ingenuous and swimming in tears. "We usually went to a concert first."

"I am sorry to have such bad news." Cadover's discomfort in this strange world was not abated. "At least I have little more with which to trouble you. What was your friend's name?"

"His name?" The girl was puzzled. "His name was Peter."

"But his surname—and his address?"

"I—I'm afraid I don't know. He—he was rather a casual acquaintance, in a way. We met at a party about a year ago. He used just to drop me a line—not one with any address on it—and we would meet for a show or something."

"I see." Cadover had not reckoned upon this extreme discretion in young men disposed to combine dalliance and moral tone. "But he must have spoken about himself and his circumstances?"

"Hardly at all. I think he had done pretty well at dangerous jobs in the war. I know he had been about the world a bit. And I rather think he was looking for something to settle down to. But he never spoke of his people, or anything like that. He was rather shy."

"That is no doubt one way of expressing it. But about those notes that he sent you—when did you receive the last?"

"Only a few days ago. And it was jolly decent of him to write." The young woman looked at Cadover with suddenly startled eyes. "But there was something in it about a cinema! And about a boy, too. He was going away with a boy. It was nice of him to let me know. . . ." She was now fumbling in a bag. "Yes, I thought so. Here it is." And she handed Cadover a letter.

He looked at the envelope and saw that it was directed to Miss Joyce Vane at an address in Maida Vale; he opened it and read.

DEAR JOYCE,—I'm terribly sorry I shan't be seeing you for some time, as on Thursday I'm off to Ircland with a kid who sounds a bit of a handful all round. This is a terrible bore! I've been making enquiries since I got the job and it appears that the lad's father is a terrible scientific swell. He has a laboratory in which he cracks atoms much as you and I might crack nuts when lucky enough to be having one of our jolly dinners together. Perhaps this is why the lad is insisting on taking me to see a film with atom bombs in it just before we leave. It's called *Plutonium Blonde*. But there is only one blonde for me and I will see her again as soon as I can.

Love,
PETER.

The letter bore no address and it had been posted in the West End; nevertheless, Cadover scanned it with something like exultation. Smith's and the counterfeit florin had been mere wisps of hope—but they had led to what, compared with the situation an hour before, were inestimable riches. He took a slip of paper from his pocket and scribbled. "Miss Vane," he said, handing it to her, "here is your receipt for this document. This is your address in Maida Vale? And you have no other information that you can give?" Cadover's eye as he spoke was on the door; it would be as well to beat a retreat before the return of the indignant Jake Syme. He rose. "By the way," he added, "I think I'd have a drink ready for your friend when he gets back. He may be a little cross. And I'm sorry if my news has been a shock to you. Good evening."

And Cadover hurried into the street, glancing at his watch as he did so. It was eight o'clock. Still compelled by an obscure sense of urgency, he set himself a time-limit. By midnight he would have found a terrible scientific swell who possessed, first, a laboratory in which atoms were cracked like nuts, and, second, a son who was a bit of a handful all round.

But more haste, less speed. He stood on the kerb, waiting patiently. And presently an obvious calculation fulfilled itself. A taxi drew up and there emerged from it an angry and bewildered young man. Cadover took his place and was driven to Scotland Yard.

CHAPTER IX

THE CLOCK STOOD AT eight-twenty when Cadover's call came through. "Information about physicists in London?" said the voice at the other end. "Oh, certainly—no objection at all."

"Nuclear physics," said Cadover. "At least, I think that's the term. Atoms, and so on. The matter is highly confidential."

"It always is." The voice was politely exasperated. "Let people of your sort begin talking about atoms and we are sure to be told how confidential it is. That's all nonsense, you know. Only you can't see it."

"Ah," said Cadover. For to this voice it would be discreet to listen with deference.

"Science has grown up talkative and is bound to remain so. Stop the talkativeness and you stop the science. Whether that would be good or bad is quite speculative. But the fact is undoubted. You see?" The voice rose with the hopeful inflection of one discoursing to a small group of advanced students. "Or don't you see?"

"I see."

"But, of course, if it pleases the police to hold what they consider confidential conversations over a telephone line I am quite willing to join in. Please go ahead."

Cadover scowled at his scribbling-pad. "Time is an important factor, sir, or I would have called. And the enquiry is this. I am looking for a physicist, probably resident in London, who has at least one son somewhere round about the age of fifteen."

"I see. Well, sixteen years ago numerous scientists were

continuing to beget children. In fact, they do it still So it would appear that they are no wiser than other folk. And indeed there are other grounds for supposing the same thing."

"Quite so, sir." This time Cadover spoke with conviction.

"So unless you can tell me something more about this physicist——"

"I have a letter in which he is described as a terrible scientific swell." And Cadover glanced at the note he had obtained from Miss Joyce Vane. "He has a laboratory in which he cracks atoms much as you and I might crack nuts when lucky enough to be having one of our jolly dinners together."

"My dear sir, I don't recall that I ever had the pleasure——"

"I'm only quoting the letter." Cadover made vicious jabs at the scribbling-pad with his pencil. "And it says no more than that. My problem is to identify the scientist quickly."

"Very well." The voice became brisk. "You know, of course, that the writer of your letter is either remarkably ignorant or speaking with conscious extravagance. Scientific swells, however terrible, do not own laboratories in which atoms are cracked like nuts. Unfortunately, the laboratories own *them*. You see?" The voice was not very hopeful this time. "Or don't you see?"

"I see."

"Well, now, your problem is really this. First, how many scientists live in London who are what would propularly be termed 'high up' in atomic research. Second, how many of these have a son or sons round about fifteen years old. I can give you a list of the likeliest men. And for their progeny you can turn to *Who's Who*. It generally tells about people's children—though I can't think why."

"Thank you very much."

"First, of course, comes Sir Bernard Paxton. *You* will have heard of him."

The emphasis in this last sentence was not very flattering. But Cadover scribbled impassively. "Sir Bernard Paxton," he repeated. "Yes?"

"And as a matter of fact, I happen to know that he *has* a son. I recall going to luncheon with Paxton, and this boy

105

being present. A very well-mannered boy. I never quite understood why he threw the cream-jug."

"Why he *what*?"

"Threw the cream-jug at Lord Buffery. An unusual experience for a President of the Royal Society. Buffery had been talking about poetry—surely not a subject to rouse strong emotions in anyone."

Cadover glanced again at his letter. "Do you know," he said, "that that sounds very hopeful? The boy I'm looking for is described as a bit of a handful all round. But, of course, I'd better have your other names as well."

"Lord Buffery himself," said the voice. "Sir Adrian Ramm. Professor Musket, Dr Marriage. Sir Ferdinand Gotlop. . . ."

Cadover sighed as he noted down the long list of names. It looked like being a full night's work. And how would these eminent persons react when hauled out of bed to testify to their having, or not having, a son who was a bit of a handful all round? But at least *Who's Who* might eliminate some. He put down the receiver and reached for the volume. Fifteen minutes later he returned it to the shelf and gloomily picked up his bowler hat. Between atomic physics and schoolboy sons there appeared to exist what his recent informant might have called a high positive correlation. Still, he must tackle it —and tackle it himself. To set a little squad of men seeking information from these eminent persons might have the appearance of saving time. But in general Cadover believed that the solution of a crime ought to be a one-man job. One man trudging from point to point was slow and laborious, but he carried round with him a single probing, pouncing, arguing brain. Set *A*, *B* and *C* to work and, as likely as not, some vital fact would slip through the mesh of the resulting reports. *A*, the man in charge, would fail amid all the material unloaded on him to relate *B*'s *x* to *C*'s *y*. But if both *x* and *y* formed part of *A*'s direct and unmediated experience, then his chance of hitting upon their significant relationship was considerably higher. . . .

In arguing with himself thus, Cadover was no doubt only rationalising an instinct to go about things in an old-fashioned way. Being not without a sort of dogged ingenuity, he could probably have found colourable reasons for continuing to wear the 1912 species of bowler which he was now lodging firmly on the tips of his ears. Thus habited, he strode from the building, climbed into a waiting car and gave the driver Sir Bernard Paxton's address.

It was a quarter to nine and London was still incongruously bathed in the neutral light of early evening. The armed, arrogant and amorous lady of *Plutonium Blonde* was everywhere in evidence upon the hoardings. It struck Cadover that her expression had subtly changed; in addition to animal provocation, it now held a hint of mockery. He felt the stirrings of a sort of personal relationship to this sprawling figure—a sort of confused antagonism which was doubtless, he gloomily reflected, disreputably erotic in origin. Was it desirable, he wondered, that he should see the film? Apart from the fact that the loud noise of the exploding bomb had made the murder in the cinema easy, could there be any relationship between the film and what had actually occurred? The speculation, he saw, was singularly barren; he had no conceivable means of proceeding with it.

The car came smoothly to a halt and Cadover peered out. "Are you sure this is right?" he asked. For the mansion before him was exceedingly imposing and did not at all answer to his notion of a scientists's abode.

"This is it, all right." The plain-clothes constable at the wheel peered out in his turn. "Crime's becoming quite the thing among the upper classes, isn't it? Currency case, I suppose—nobs making the dibs fly on the dear old Riviera?"

Cadover made no reply to these over-familiar observations, but jumped from the car and made his way up a broad flight of steps to Sir Bernard Paxton's front door. He rang the bell and then glanced back over his shoulder at the august square in which the house stood. It was all extremely solid; unlike most of post-war London it was all very adequately painted, glazed and polished. Money still commanded services and materials here. But whereas the folk who had built this square

107

lived comfortably on their income, those who now inhabited it were living—almost equally comfortably—on their capital. Towards the end of the century it would give out, and the reality of social revolution would then become apparent. . . . Cadover became aware that the door had opened and that he was being studied by an unprepossessing but wholly correct manservant. "Is Sir Bernard Paxton at home?" he enquired.

The man was eyeing his bowler hat—and even noting, it might be felt, its propinquity to Cadover's ears. Then his glance travelled down to Cadover's boots, and from thence to the car waiting in the square below. "Sir Bernard," he said impassively, "is not at home."

"Can you tell me when he will be in?"

"Sir Bernard will not be at home to-night."

"You mean he's not sleeping here?"

The man slightly raised his eyebrows, as if to indicate his surprise that even one so uncouth as this caller should be ignorant of the conventions of admittance and exclusion. "Sir Bernard," he said, "is not at present in the house. And he will be unable to receive callers later to-night."

Cadover produced a card. "I am a detective-inspector from Scotland Yard," he said.

"Indeed, sir." Ever so faintly, the tone contrived to imply that some such melancholy fact had already been only too apparent. "I shall not fail to inform Sir Bernard of your call."

"I am afraid the matter is more urgent than that. Is he dining out—or at his club?"

"I'm afraid I don't know, sir."

"Well, what are his clubs? I think I'll try them."

"Yes, sir." For the first time the man hesitated. "As a matter of fact, I am fairly confident that Sir Bernard will be home in about an hour's time. Perhaps you would care to wait?"

"I'll come back."

"Thank you, sir. I would not leave it much later than the hour. It is conceivable that Sir Bernard may be going out again."

"Very well." Cadover nodded and returned to his car—an

inexplicable shadow of misgiving at the back of his mind. "Next address," he snapped.

"That's Lord Buffery's." The car slid from the kerb and the driver spoke over his shoulder. "Blackmail, is it? I rather thought as much."

Cadover frowned. "You appear," he said acidly, "to be a young man remarkably well furnished with hypotheses. But the fact that this is a wealthy part of London is scarcely a sufficient ground upon which to base such an inference. So far as I know, it is *not* blackmail."

"You've got me wrong, sir." The driver was aggrieved. "I wasn't just judging by the fact that we're among the nobs. I was judging by Soapy Clodd. He was lounging at the corner there as we drove up."

"The devil he was!"

"Nasty bit of work, isn't he? Now, if we were getting him a stretch we could go to bed feeling we had done something useful. Think of all them kids he makes miserable! And naturally I thought it was something to do with him."

Cadover shook his head. "Nothing of the sort. And I only know him by name. Never been my line."

"Specialises in blackmailing adolescents, Clodd does. Wealthy people's kids who can raise five pounds now and then to keep his mouth shut. Plays on the queer sense of sin kids have. Have you been petting a girl in the park? Were you coaxed into paying five bob to see something you've always been a bit curious about? I'll tell your mother and she'll be heartbroken for life. That sort of thing. If Soapy had been a bit nearer the kerb I'd have felt like a little hit and run."

"That is a most improper thing to say, even as a joke." Cadover relented. "I rather agree with you, all the same. But Clodd's affairs have nothing to do with us at the moment."

Cadover sank into a reverie which lasted until he was shown into the presence of Lord Buffery. The eminent scientist was playing with an electric train arranged round the circumference of a billiard-room, and he showed no disposition to abrupt this activity when Cadover was announced. "Police?" he said, raising his voice above the rattle of a goods train which was clattering across a viaduct. "Well, what d'you want? . . . Son? Of course I've got a son." He flicked a lever and an express emerged precipitately from a tunnel. "Going away with a tutor? Naturally he is. What else should I do with him in these absurd summer holidays? . . . Peter? Certainly not. Going with a Frenchman to somewhere near Grenoble. . . . Interested in model railways?"

A second goods train had now come into operation and was avoiding the first at sundry crossings in a hair's-breadth way reminiscent of an antique comic film. The refrigerated vans appeared to be particularly noisy. Lord Buffery pressed a button on a switchboard beside him and the express engine instantly emitted a series of realistic and penetrating whistles. And now a great deal of shunting appeared to be taking place in the obscure and extensive area beneath the billiard-table. The uproar grew. Cadover took a pace forward by way of indicating polite attention to these phenomena, and was at once made aware that the floor was an ordered litter of porters, passengers, cars, taxis, Bren-gun carriers, ambulances, motor-cyclists, hay-wagons and other miscellaneous paraphernalia of locomotion all of an appropriate scale. Lord Buffery looked with some apprehensiveness at the size of Cadover's boots, and then at a collection of navvies complete with tools, brazier and nightwatchman's hut which was dangerously in their proximity. "Deuced hard to replace, these," he said apprehensively. "Just mind the steam-roller."

Cadover, minding the steam-roller, resolutely returned to business. "Your son," he asked, "doesn't happen to be a bit of a handful all round?"

Lord Buffery deftly brought another express into action and simultaneously indicated that he had not quite caught the question. Cadover bellowed it anew. Lord Buffery's features assumed an expression of sudden exasperation; he stretched out his hand and the whole various uproar died away on the tracks; he stood up and moved gingerly towards the door. "This way," he said. His voice had sunk into a sudden gloom.

Cadover followed him through a long corridor and saw a door thrown open before him. Inside was a great stillness and clear white light—this and the faint smell which electricity seems to generate when being used in oblique and ingenious ways. The place was some sort of advanced laboratory. And its sole occupant was a small, weedy boy with a bumpy fore-head, large glasses and prominent teeth. For a moment he looked up from the complicated system of retorts and test-tubes over which he was bending, contemplating Cadover without curiosity and Lord Buffery with disapproval tempered with tolerance. And then he returned to his affairs.

Lord Buffery murmured an apology and closed the door. "Harold," he said resignedly, "is entirely given over to study. I call it a damned dull life. Now, if you want to see a boy who *is* a bit of a handful, I advise you to go round to Paxton. Not long ago his lad threw a cream-jug at me." Lord Buffery paused admiringly. "Deuced expensive one too, I should think. Great connoisseur is Paxton—ceramics, pictures—all that sort of thing. . . . But it would be a long time before Harold would throw so much as a calorimeter at you. Would you care to come upstairs and see my workshop? I'm just finishing rather a good model of the Forth Bridge. . . . No? Well, good evening to you."

At least, Cadover thought as he made his way to the car, Lord Buffery appeared untroubled by the larger issues in-volved in the exploitation of atomic power. "Sir Adrian Ramm," he said to the driver, and once more sank back into reverie.

But Sir Adrian Ramm's only son was in a nursing home with appendicitis; he was a reasonably well-conducted child; and there was no proposal that he should go anywhere with a tutor. Sir Adrian could not afford a tutor and would not employ one if he could. As a class of men, he regarded their morals as bad.

But now it was time to return to the Paxton mansion. Cadover realised that his hopes were substantially set in this quarter. For this he had perhaps small logical justification. Indeed, he found that he was attaching obscure significance to the lurking presence of Soapy Clodd, although this petty scoundrel was almost certainly no more than an accidental intrusion upon the picture. All he really had to go upon was this: that the dead man's pupil had been unruly, and that young Paxton had thrown a cream-jug at the President of the Royal Society. Nevertheless, he knew that he would be disconcerted were the Paxton trail to prove a dead end.

The same manservant admitted him—and in what he felt was a sinister quiet. Had some horrid revelation burst upon the household and prostrated it with gloom? Cadover hoped so—and followed the soft-footed butler into a sombre library. A tall, pale man with a high forehead sat writing at a dark, heavily-carved table which served as a desk. He rose as Cadover was announced and advanced across the dimly lit room. "I understand that you are a police officer?" The voice was low and precisely-cultivated. "What is your business with me?"

"I apologise for intruding upon you, Sir Bernard. But the matter is of some urgency." Paxton, Cadover knew, was a person of much consequence in the world—of much more consequence than Lord Buffery. And he found himself treating the great man with a more than usually wary respect—and explaining the reason of his call without at all resenting the fact that he was not invited to sit down.

The tall figure listened in silence. Then he shook his head. "I can be of no help to you. There is no proposal that my son should go away with a tutor."

"The boy is at home now?"

"He is on a short visit to an aunt in another part of London. As it happens, I called upon her and saw them both less than an hour ago."

"Has your son been in any way out of hand recently?"

The tall man could just be discerned in the subdued light as raising his eyebrows. "As my son can demonstrably have no connection with the person who has died in the cinema," he said stiffly, "the question does not arise." Then he suddenly smiled faintly, as if charitably willing to relieve his obscure caller's embarrassment under this rebuke. "As a matter of fact, the boy is sometimes the very devil. Not very long ago he threw a cream jug at Lord Buffery."

At this Cadover, doing what was plainly expected of him, gave evidence of mild mirth. Then, moved by a sudden impulse, he spoke again. "I have another question, which I hope you will not find vexatious, sir. Have you any suspicion that there may recently have been an attempt to blackmail your son?"

"To blackmail him!" The words came with a curious quality —almost as if from one suspecting a trap and momentarily out of his depth. "Certainly not. It is a most improbable circumstance." The tone was confident again now. "Had I reason to suppose anything of the sort I would at once call in the police."

"It is merely that a criminal who specialises in that sort of thing—in preying upon the common misdemeanours and concealments of adolescents—has been observed lurking near your house. It is more than probable that your son is not involved. But I should advise you, Sir Bernard, to bear the circumstance in mind. A sensitive boy so preyed upon may be enduring a very dangerous strain. On our side, we shall see that the man's present activities are investigated. And now I must not take up more of your time."

The tall figure had already touched a bell and was steering Cadover dismissively towards the door. As he did so he appeared to notice Cadover's eye upon a painting at the end of the room. "Ah, yes," he said, "I have that hanging there because it is so uncommonly like my son."

Cadover, thus prompted, looked at the painting more carefully; it was of an aristocratic little boy, dark-haired and dark-eyed, dressed in hunting costume. Cadover wished that the light was better; he was fond of painting—and here surely was an original Velazquez! He remembered Lord Buffery's remarking that Sir Bernard Paxton was a connoisseur. "Surely——" he said.

"Yes—to be sure." The tall figure was now waiting impatiently for the door to open. "It's an old picture—very old indeed. . . . If I can be of further help to you, please let me know. But, as you see, you are on a false scent here. Good evening."

The silent manservant conducted Cadover across the hall and handed him his bowler hat, not without taking a glance inside it first. Cadover set it firmly on his head, and fleetingly inspected himself as he did so in a large mirror before him. This mirror revealed the door through which he had just come; it opened as he looked and the figure of the eminent scientist whom he had disturbed came rapidly out and disappeared into the gloom of a corridor.

The manservant had opened the front door and Cadover saw his car waiting at the bottom of the flight of steps and beyond the broad pavement. And at the same time he heard a voice speaking sharply and authoritatively from what might have been the direction of the main staircase of the house. "Jollard . . ." said the voice. The manservant closed the door softly upon Cadover and he heard no more.

So that was that. The boy who had thrown the cream jug was out of it. Cadover, with an irrational feeling that he had just failed to make a lively acquaintance, climbed wearily but doggedly into the car. "Professor Musket at Dulwich," he said. "Then round to Sir Ferdinand Gotlop at Bromley and on to Dr. Marriage at Greenwich. After that we go right across to Highgate and Wood Green and New Barnet. . . ."

How very queer the association of these familiar and unassuming names with the recesses of atomic physics! How infinitely alarming, when one came to think of it, the spectacle of Lord Buffery and his electric trains! Cadover sat back in the gathering London night and enfolded himself in gloom like a blanket. The car ran over Waterloo Bridge; he peered westward and shook his head at the blank and innocent face of Big Ben, as if doubtful whether those within the shadow of St Stephen's Tower had quite as sharp an eye as was desirable upon that sinister billiard-room. . . . The car, sequacious of Professor Musket, purred through the emptying streets.

Cadover got to bed in the small hours—irritated by defeat; more obscurely irritated by he knew not what. Of those few of London's millions who were on familar terms with proton and electron the male progeny were all comfortably—or in some cases uncomfortably—accounted for. Eminent scientists, it appeared, had no special skill in maintaining amicable relationships with their young. Sir Ferdinand Gotlop's son had run away to sea; another boy made mysterious disappearances for a week at a time, but was at present safely at home studying existentialism; a third was believed to be living in a cellar with a group of juvenile anarchists learned in the manufacture of explosives. But of any youth about to set out for Ireland with a tutor there was no sign whatever.

Restlessly Cadover searched for an explanation. And the likeliest surely was this: that the dead man's letter to Miss Joyce Vane was wholly misleading. The father of the lad referred to might indeed be a terribly scientific swell, while his connection with atomic physics was illusory. The young man might have thrown in this touch just to be impressive—or perhaps he had a vague notion that smashing atoms was the invariable business of all scientists sufficiently eminent. And if something of this sort was the case, the clue provided by this letter was altogether slighter than it had seemed. It was a pointer still, but a pointer into the haystack of London's scientific folk in general. Long before one could get at the matter this way the identity of the dead man would have emerged by some other route. What Cadover had looked for was a short cut. After numerous exhausting windings it had turned out to be only a dead end. And he still had the uneasy persuasion that time was all important in the case.

Dawn was breaking before Cadover fell asleep. He dreamed of interminable journeys through the night, of the deep vibration of steamers and the rattle and sway of trains. Sometimes Lord Buffery would appear gigantic in a fitful moonlight, a portentous presence brooding over interminable sidings, here stooping to pick up a steam-roller and there straddling across a valley like the cantilevers of a bridge. And up and down the corridors of the labouring trains, round the decks and hatches of the plunging steamers strode a great blonde woman in a wisp of shift—amorous, arrogant and armed. Now she was stalking Cadover himself—and now a dark-haired, dark-eyed boy dressed in the rich and sombre garments of imperial Spain.

The rhythm of the train, of the steamer, formed itself into a single word, pounded out a single insistent trisyllabic word. . . .

Cadover woke up, aware of a mind at once dream-sodden and on the verge of discovery. In all that maze of talk which he had threaded through London and its environs the night before—in all that maze of talk there had been a single significant word. Or had there been the *lack* of that word; instead of it had there been an awkward, an unexpected periphrasis? Cadover sat up and shook his head, aware now that he was pursuing only some phantom of thought. He planned the day's work, the new attack that he would make upon the problem of the unknown body in the cinema.

CHAPTER X

THE SEA WAS PERFECTLY SMOOTH; the deep vibration of the steamer was scarcely perceptible; of the myriad stars overhead each was precisely in its appropriate place for that particular hour, century, æon. All these facts were reassuring to Mr Thewless. He stood on deck watching the diminishing lights of Heysham Harbour. Beside him stood a perfectly ordinary boy called—undoubtedly called—Humphrey Paxton. In front of him stretched six weeks or so of considerable but by no means overwhelming difficulty. For these weeks Mr Thewless was already making various competent plans. They would read the fourth book of the *Æneid* and thereby bring sex and the emotional difficulties of adolescence a little into the open. They would give a good deal of time—much more time than would normally be justifiable—to English poetry, and they would incidentally consider fancy, imagination, day-dreaming, and the possible confusions of fiction and fact into which certain types of minds—particularly growing minds—may fall. English composition might take the form of writing, on the one hand, an adventure story in which the narrator was the hero, and, on the other hand, a sober but not uninteresting diary of actual observations made upon people and things.

Such common-sense measures might clear matters up quite as effectively as the probings of child psychologists.

For, of course, that there *were* matters to be cleared up was undeniable. Humphrey, although a perfectly ordinary boy when broadly regarded, had admittedly his uncomfortable side. He imagined things. More than that, he imagined things with such intensity that he set other people imagining too. During the fatigues of the recent railway journey had not Mr Thewless himself been persuaded into imagining quite a lot? He was resolved that with this sort of thing he would have no more to do. Let it be admitted that the boy had an almost hypnotic power of edging one into a world of fantasy. Let this be recognised and firmly guarded against. . . .

"I'm terribly afraid there's something I ought to have told you earlier."

Pitched conspiratorially low, Humphrey's voice came out of the semi-darkness beside him. Mr Thewless smiled as one who now possesses an assured wisdom. For here was the boy off again; his tone betrayed it; he must be briefly humoured and then packed off to bed. It was already unconscionably late and they would be berthed in Belfast long before any normal breakfast-time.

"Something you ought to have told me, Humphrey? Well, out with it. But—by Jove!—what about getting a final ginger-beer? I noticed that the bar is still open." Mr Thewless was uneasily aware that the epithet "sporty" might be applied to his manner of making this proposition. With a movement towards gravity, he therefore continued, "And then we must certainly turn in."

"I suppose so." Humphrey had immediately begun to move towards the bar and the proposed refreshment, but his tone sounded slightly dejected. "Yes, I suppose we must try to sleep."

"Try to sleep!" What Mr Thewless now heard in himself was an unnecessary jollity. "I'm certain you will sleep without rocking to-night. And to-morrow should be a good day. The light railway sounds most amusing."

"Yes." Humphrey sat down and placed his shot-gun (which

117

he now rather absurdly persisted in carrying round) carefully beside him. "Do you know why I brought this? It wasn't to go out shooting helpless birds."

"Perhaps it was in case the sheep look unhappy."

"The sheep?" Humphrey was startled.

"Didn't Shelley somewhere go round with a gun benevolently putting sheep out of what he conceived to be their misery? It made the farmers very cross." Mr Thewless paused and sipped with a dishonest appearance of relish at his ginger-beer. "The story may not be true. But it does represent fairly enough Shelley on his freakish side. It was his marked weakness."

"I see." Humphrey stirred uneasily in his chair. "But what I wanted to——"

"The powerful imagination of a poet," pursued Mr Thewless, "requires ceaseless discipline. Only by being confined within its own proper bounds does it maintain sufficient force and impetus for creative work. For a young artist any involving of his own day-to-day affairs in mere fanciful reverie is bad. It is likely to cripple his final achievement. By a strong effort of the will, therefore, he should abstain." Mr Thewless frowned, momentarily aware of the echo of some magistral voice long ago lecturing his own perplexed innocence on a somewhat different theme. "And this was what was meant by a poet in some ways superior even to Shelley—I refer, Humphrey, to John Keats, whom I am sure you have eagerly read—when he declared that the poet and the mere daydreamer are sheer opposites. And what is the practical lesson of this? We should not allow ourselves to confuse——"

"I didn't bring the gun to shoot sheep. I brought it to shoot plotters and blackmailers and spies." Humphrey Paxton banged down his glass on the table before him and raised his voice to something like a shout. Fortunately, there was still a good deal of noise in the smoke-room and only one or two people looked round. "And I ought never to have left that compartment without it this evening."

"It sounds," said Mr Thewless, "as if what you really need is a revolver."

118

"Exactly." And Humphrey nodded soberly. "Have *you* got a revolver?"

"Dear me, no. You see, plotters and spies don't much come my way."

"I'm terribly afraid they are bound to . . . now." Into Humphrey's voice had come something like compunction and apology. "Perhaps I should have considered that. It wasn't really quite fair to drag you in. I hope Daddy pays you a decent screw?"

Mr Thewless smiled. "As a matter of fact, Humphrey, he is proposing to pay me a good deal more than is customary."

"That's odd." And Humphrey Paxton looked sharply thoughtful. "Would it be dirt money, do you think?"

"That sounds like something rather disagreeable."

"So it is. It's the extra pay dockers and people get when doing something thoroughly nasty. Perhaps Daddy thinks that being my tutor is that." An expression of rather complacent pathos spread itself for a moment over Humphrey's features. "Do you think I might have another ginger-beer?"

Mr Thewless fetched the ginger-beer. "No," he said; "definitely not dirt money. I believe your father finds you a little trying in spots. But he was confident that we should find considerable pleasure in working together. Which reminds me that we can make out a scheme of things when on the train to-morrow."

"Of course *dangerous* work gets extra pay too. Perhaps it was that. Perhaps he really did have an inkling."

"Perhaps he had an inkling that you would pitch me some pretty tall stories." Mr Thewless determined to be good-humoured. "I wonder if I could do it too? To-morrow we might have a competition and see which of us can imagine the biggest adventure."

Humphrey took a gulp at his ginger-beer. "This is going to be difficult," he said. "Of course I didn't mean to tell you at all. I meant you just to find out—as you're pretty sure to do. I meant it to be pretty well my own adventure right through. But now I don't think I can do that. Not after what happened on the train."

Mr Thewless looked at his watch. By one means or another this disjointed nonsense of Humphrey's must be stopped. "I think——" he began.

"I suppose I'm frightened . . . rather." Humphrey looked gloomily at his gun. "Have you noticed how sometimes I get just like a kid?"

"Yes, I have." Mr Thewless responded soberly to this odd appeal. "Our age is not always just what our birthday says. It's the same with grown people sometimes. They can't decide what age it's sensible for them to be. Often people manage to be suddenly much older. Sometimes they manage to stay the same age for years and years. Sometimes they become younger and stay younger for quite a bit. It depends on the sort of things that happen to them. And sometimes people decide that it's time to be no age at all—and then they die. So there's nothing very odd or special in occasionally feeling rather a kid. I've known big chaps do it quite regularly at bed-time. Had to hug a teddy-bear—that sort of thing."

Humphrey, who had listened carefully to this, slightly blushed. Perhaps he had some private reason for finding the reference to teddy-bears embarrassing. "You are a very sensible person," he said seriously. "It's a pity you're going to be such an ass over this." His blush deepened. "Sorry. I oughtn't to have said 'ass.' Not when I wasn't in a temper."

"I certainly don't want to be an ass. But had we not better have this talk in the morning?"

"Very well." And Humphrey got to his feet, submissive but plainly discouraged. "You see," he said, "it was the black-mailing that misled me. I—I handled that. And so I thought—— But this turns out to be different."

Mr Thewless allowed himself an inward sigh. Whatever fantasy was urgently waiting to tumble from Humphrey Paxton's mind had better tumble now. For assuredly he would not sleep if sent to his cabin in his present nervous state. And Mr Thewless produced from his pocket a bar of milk chocolate which he proceeded to divide. "Well, now," he said, "we're pretty private in this corner. So let me hear the trouble, Humphrey. And I'll try not to be an ass."

But Humphrey now seemed to find some difficulty in communication. He munched his chocolate, put up a thumb to lick—and was plainly disposed to let it remain performing the function of an infant's comforter. Mr Thewless tried prompting. "You said something about blackmail before. What was it about?"

"It was about a girl."

"A girl?" Humphrey at this moment seemed so absurdly young that the words now jerked from him came to Mr Thewless without implication. "What do you mean, my dear boy?"

"I know several girls." Humphrey was momentarily circuitous. "There's Mary Carruthers, the poetess—although, of course, she's really a grown woman. But this was Beverley Crupp. She works in a shop. Not that that's any disgrace."

"Certainly not," said Mr Thewless, automatically but forebodingly.

"You *have* to learn about things and do them for the first time."

Mr Thewless judged that a general acquiescence in this sentiment might be inexpedient. So he ate his last piece of chocolate and said nothing.

"I used to fool around with Beverley in parks, and that sort of thing. The way you see people doing all over the place. It used to puzzle me a lot, even although I'd read books about it. But I wasn't puzzled after knowing Beverley. It's quite extraordinary, isn't it? So unlike anything else. So frightfully *exciting*."

By the perfect innocence of this last word Mr Thewless felt considerably relieved. "Well," he said briskly, "what about this Beverley?"

"One day there was a man taking photographs—the sort of man who snaps passers-by with a little camera and then hands them a card. I didn't think anything of it. But it turned out to be blackmail."

"I see." Humphrey's tutor looked at him thoughtfully. "Were you very much worried?"

"At first I was—quite frightfully. It made me feel an

121

absolute kid. But then I managed to use my brains. I could see that the thing was something that this photographer-man did regularly. It was more or less his trade. Well, if I refused to give him money and he sent the photograph to Daddy, or anything like that, it would probably be even more awkward for him than for me. For Daddy, of course, would tell the police, and the fellow would be hunted down and sent to prison. And, anyway, the risk wasn't great. It wasn't as if I had a mother to be upset. Daddy would be cross, but that isn't so—so formidable. And he would quickly come to take a man's view. He would even tell his more particular friends out of a sort of obscure vanity. For a man likes it to be—be borne in upon him that he has a son capable of having sons. A very queer and deep approval of just keeping the human race going is a factor in such cases."

Mr Thewless felt within himself a moment's mild panic. That Humphrey had managed to use his brains was undeniable. Attaining to the mere practical common sense of the matter had been in itself a considerable achievement of intelligence. But his appreciation of what might be called the underlying psychology of the situation was positively intimidating. "I take it, then, Humphrey, that you ignored this criminal's demands?"

"I handled the situation." Humphrey seemed to take particular satisfaction in this phrase. "Actually I don't know that the fellow is quite choked off yet. But he has just ceased to worry me. And that has made me rather uppish. And that's why I'm landed in *this*." Humphrey's glance went warily round the now almost empty smoke-room. "It's a pretty tight place. But I've asked for it."

"There is no doubt that you have had an unpleasant experience." Mr Thewless was genuinely sympathetic—and the more so because he now comfortably felt that full light on Humphrey had come to him. The narrative to which he had listened was sober truth, and at the same time it explained the genesis of a great deal of fiction. Early sexual experience, even of the comparatively innocent kind in which the boy had involved himself with his friend Beverley, may entail considerable nervous strain. Massive feelings of guilt (reflected Mr Thewless, who was a conscientiously well-read man) have to be contended with in the unconscious mind. And upon Humphrey, a sensitive boy so circumstanced, there had broken this horrid business of a petty blackmailer who preyed systematically upon adolescents. Humphrey's brain, it was true—as also, what was not quite the same thing, an ability to use it in an awkward situation—had proved too much for the fellow. But the shock must have been there, all the same. And it had precipitated the deplorable world of fantasy into which the boy now so readily sank.

Mr Thewless felt relieved. There is always great satisfaction in the complete intellectual clarification of a problem. And now surely he had the key—the weapon, indeed, with which he could combat the lad's insubstantial fears. He looked at Humphrey, still clutching his gun, with an increase of benevolence. "I am extremely glad," he said, "that you have told me all this. You don't think, do you, that there was anything deeply shameful in your—your acquaintance with the girl Beverley?"

Humphrey frowned, as if he now had to recover this topic from a considerable distance. "Of course not," he said.

"But the trouble is that there is a part of the mind—particularly of the *young* mind—which does think that. It is very deeply disturbed, and imagines all sorts of punishments which are bound to follow. The person finds himself imagining that he is ill——"

Humphrey looked startled. "I know about that," he said. "Just after I found out about babies I began to think I was going to die of appendicitis. It cleared up when I worked it out that somehow the two things were connected."

"Or the person imagines that he is being plotted against and has all sorts of cunning enemies. In the case of a boy, his father often figures in such fantasies. But we needn't go into the reasons for that."

Mr Thewless had abstracted his gaze in the endeavour to deal discreetly and lucidly with this unwanted territory. Otherwise Humphrey's expression might have given him pause, for it was certainly not that of one who begins to feel lightened of a load of imaginary fears.

"Again, he may feel that he is being dogged or shadowed by spies or avengers, that he will be imprisoned—or even that he has been imprisoned—in dark confined spaces. He may even see his imaginings just as if they were actually happening in the outside world. Shelley did that. He may see himself, or one like himself, apparently involved in similar obscure adventures. And all this just because he believes himself to have come into possession of some dangerous secret."

The hour was late; the ship, although sailing in calm waters, had a gentle motion which Mr Thewless was too poor a sailor to like; the day had produced a succession of obscure and exhausting alarms for which this boy's fevered mind had been assuredly responsible. Moreover, the boy himself, although sometimes extremely young, had a certain intellectual precosity, receptive to mature ideas. Had it not been for all these facts Mr Thewless would scarcely have plunged in this reckless way into what he now supposed to be the well-head of Humphrey's troubles. Naturally, he expected his pupil to be startled; and he was not without an uneasy suspicion that there is much hazard in abruptly exposing or contraverting delusions that have painfully built themselves up in a distressed mind. What he hoped was that by this outspokenness there might rather be achieved some salutary shock. He looked at Humphrey warily and was far from reassured. The boy was now sitting very still. His breathing was short and the pupils of his eyes appeared dilated. But at least he was thinking. Indeed it was evident that some battle was going on between an emotional and an intellectual response to what his tutor had been saying.

And at length he spoke. "You don't think that I could *really* be in possession of some dangerous secret?"

"I think it quite likely that you believe yourself to have gained some guilty knowledge that you ought not to have. You see, Humphrey, having—um—made friends rather early with this girl——"

"Oh, *that*!" There was a disconcerting shade of intellectual impatience in Humphrey's voice. "I'm not talking about that at all."

"It's what sets you imagining things, nevertheless." Mr Thewless was tired, dogmatic. "And you must face the fact."

"I'm facing quite a lot of facts. For instance, the fact that you are right in quite a lot of the things you say. I *do* think that I am being plotted against by cunning enemies. And I *do* think that I am being shadowed by spies. And I *do* think that my father is mixed up in it. But that's not the end, by any means." Humphrey was now looking at his tutor with an expression oddly compounded of desperation and malice. "What you called meeting oneself apparently involved in some obscure adventure. I've done that too. In fact, I saw myself this afternoon. It was terribly queer."

Mr Thewless felt rather queer himself. He recalled with a twinge of particular uneasiness his own momentary impression of a second Humphrey on board the train. He recalled too that in folklore there is no more certain presage of disaster than to meet oneself face to face—to meet what the Germans call one's *Doppelgänger*. And no doubt the superstition reflected some actual fact of mind. If Humphrey really believed that he had thus encountered himself his nervous condition must indeed be deplorable. "Nonsense!" Mr Thewless said loudly to the empty smoke-room.

"Actually, I ought to say that I *heard* myself—but I suppose it's much the same thing. It was in a cinema. And you were there too—more or less."

"*I* was there!" Mr Thewless's dismay was now tempered with indignation.

"You see, I didn't really go to the dentist's this afternoon. I took Beverley to see a rotten film called *Plutonium Blonde*. I dare say some people were quite amused. But with Daddy being the sort of person he is, I get quite enough about smashing the atom at home. And this one was just silly. There was a sort of tropical heroine, all bottom and breastworks——"

"Um," said Mr Thewless.

"And she had a revolver with a special bullet, so that in the end——" Here Humphrey suddenly paused. "Only we didn't

125

wait for the end. Because when I found that I was sitting next myself I got into a panic and bolted, dragging Beverley with me. She was terribly puzzled. And naturally I couldn't explain to her. She's quite, quite dumb."

"Of course, Humphrey, I am very glad that you are telling me all this. But are you quite sure that you were not acting rather extravagantly? You say you only *heard* this boy. And just because his voice sounded rather like your own——"

"It didn't. As it happened, I could be quite sure of that. Because, you see, this other boy had a lisp."

"Then if it was *not*——"

"But it *was*. You see, they whispered a bit—and chiefly about a gun. And the boy was Humphrey Paxton. And the man was his new tutor. And they were going to Ireland."

Humphrey paused again. The throb of the ship's engines vibrated in the stale air of the empty smoking-room and very faintly they could hear the slap of water against the hull. Mr Thewless found it necessary to speak. "I am afraid——" he began.

"I know." Humphrey appeared to be quite calm now, and he was momentarily at his most mature. "It must be a great worry having been landed with so imaginative a child. What do you think of the story so far?"

"I am more convinced than ever that we ought to be in bed." And Mr Thewless got to his feet with a firmness that somewhat belied his inner mind.

"But the really odd part is still to come." Humphrey remained obstinately curled up in his chair. "I mean about your being so right on all the things I fancy to myself. Didn't you say something about being imprisoned in dark, confined spaces?"

"Possibly I did. But I realise now that these things are not to be discussed with any advantage at present."

"Well, that was what happened in the train." As Humphrey made this announcement, he looked straight at his tutor, and Mr Thewless was aware of what was surely an almost hypnotic power in the dark glance thus directed upon him. Before it, indeed, he felt the need of bracing himself to a firm incredulity

—for had not some emanation or aura from the boy already wrought havoc in his own plain common sense that day? Almost Mr Thewless would have stopped his ears. But this was something that dignity made impossible, and Humphrey talked on.

"I imagined that I was imprisoned in a dark, confined space. *Very* confined. Would you expect it to be that?"

Mr Thewless, although he had for some time been moving in an intellectual fog, was nevertheless not without certain instinctive perceptions still. He recognised the irony; recognised that his pupil was making fun of him; and recognised too that in doing so Humphrey had found a sort of safety-valve for great emotional pressure. So he made no reply to the gibe, but simply knocked out his pipe and sat down again on the arm of a chair. The ship was now rolling slightly and the silence was punctuated by the intermittent creak of timber.

"It was when I left the compartment and went along to the lavatory." Humphrey's voice was suddenly casual. But at the same time it rose a note—and with an effect that Mr Thewless by no means cared for, since it suggested something like hysteria beneath the boy's malicious calm. "I can't tell you precisely what happened. I only know that I opened the lavatory door, and that it suddenly went dark, and that I was dizzy and quite powerless and being heaved or bundled somewhere—quite a short distance, I think. And then I found that I had been tied up—my hands, I mean—and packed into a box. It was a very frightening thing—well, to imagine."

Once more Mr Thewless was silent, but his heart was sinking. With a young mind so disordered as this what could possibly be done? At the end of this exhausting and tragic journey to Ireland doctors must be called and Humphrey be taken home. There was nothing for it but that.

"But then almost at once, and again without my really knowing how it happened, I was pulled out and set free. And a voice said: 'There's the lavatory. Stay in it till the train stops and starts again.' And I did. And there my—my imaginings ended. For the time, that is to say. Because, of course, one can't tell what to-morrow may bring." Humphrey reached for his gun. "And now that you know how right you were, I think we really had better go to bed."

Mr Thewless, although he had now for some hours been devoutly desiring just this acquiescence on his charge's part, nodded almost absently. Perhaps—he was doggedly thinking—perhaps it was not so *very* bad after all. The boy had undeniably a nervous intensity that made the communication of these fevered day-dreams an alarming experience. But, for all Mr Thewless knew, the actual confusion of fact and fantasy might be neither very uncommon nor very ominous in one of Humphrey's years. Was it not, indeed, rather more disconcerting that he himself, a mature man, should quickly have been drawn into an identical insubstantial world on board the Heysham train? And yet one point in Humphrey's rigmarole particularly worried him. The boy imagined not only that he had been *shut* up, but also that he had been *tied* up as well. And for some reason—the reading, perhaps, of one or another newspaper horror long ago—Mr Thewless regarded this as peculiarly unfortunate. Upon those who indulged in fantasies of fetters and bonds it was likely that the most dismal forms of madness would eventually pounce. If only, thought Mr Thewless, the boy had not persuaded himself of just *that*. . . .

Humphrey's hand had closed on the canvas-swathed gun. As it did so he winced slightly. "It still hurts, rather," he said.

"Hurts?"

"These." And Humphrey stretched out his arms so that the cuffs of his jacket shot backwards. And Mr Thewless's head swam as he looked. Round each wrist was the red weal left by a cord drawn tight.

"To-morrow," said Humphrey, "it may be dragons or giants. Or pirates or smugglers or torture by Red Indian braves. Or, of course, it may just be spy stuff all over again."

CHAPTER XI

IT IS PROBABLE THAT, had Mr Thewless's education been less extensive than it was, he could not have continued blind to the actual posture of his and Humphrey Paxton's affairs for so long as he did. To be well informed is not in itself any more certain a blessing than to be rich in material endowment; similar risks in the misapplication of one's resources have to be accepted in either case. And knowledge is really more dangerous than a bank balance. It will not stay put until we sign a cheque, but must ever, like an importunate child, be nudging us into an awareness of its existence, and encumbering us in whatever we may be about by tumbling at the wrong moment into the wrong place. Had a man of simple mind and circumscribed information rolled wearily into a bunk hard upon being afforded the spectacle of Humphrey's chafed wrists it is unlikely that he would have got out again next morning without a tolerably firm conviction that the boy had been manhandled. But it was not so with Humphrey's new tutor.

On the subject of Roman Britain Mr Thewless knew pretty well all that was to be known. In the field of School Certificate, Higher Certificate, Responsions and Little-go he was almost equally omniscient. And on an enormous number of other matters he had a smattering of information that was both reasonably accurate and reasonably up to date. One of these was morbid psychology. And of this species of learning it is particularly true that slender draughts intoxicate the brain—though whether we are sobered again by large drinking is a matter still perhaps a little in doubt. However this may be, Mr Thewless had undoubtedly read quite a lot about the freakish powers and vagaries of the human mind. It thus came about that early next morning, and as he peered out of his porthole at the mouldering pile of Carrickfergus Castle, there rose fatally into his field of consciousness the beguiling topic of Hysterical Stigmatisation.

In particular, Mr Thewless recalled, it is adolescents who are prone to putting up these strange performances. A young girl may be lying quite alone in bed; she will give a sharp cry of pain; and there will straightway be found upon her cheek or back the physical evidences of a bite or scratch or blow. But the mischievous spirits or goblins who are sometimes credited with inflicting these injuries have assuredly no objective existence, and the process illustrates nothing more than the mysterious power that a mind can exercise over the body it inhabits. And so it must be with poor Humphrey. If he was able to persuade himself that he had been pinioned he might well be perfectly able spontaneously to produce the stigmata that would support the fantasy.

As a logical approach to the facts involved there is little doubt that this could have been improved upon. But if the merit of a hypothesis is to be judged merely by the confidence it gives us in jogging through life's diurnal bewilderments it must be admitted that Mr Thewless's intelligence had functioned admirably. Walking down the gangway at Belfast, he felt in every sense that he was no longer at sea; and from this feeling of an adequate grasp of the situation he drew resolution to proceed with Sir Bernard Paxton's holiday plans undisturbed. That his young charge would eventually require the help of medical science was a fact upon which, unhappily, he could now feel little doubt. But to abrupt his journey in a strange town and to announce himself in some bleak consulting room as the itinerant and helpless warden of a demented schoolboy was a procedure at once uncomfortable to contemplate and unnecessarily drastic in face of the immediate situation. It would be altogether wiser to travel straight on to the Paxtons' relatives—persons of position and substance with whom the responsibility for any further decision might very properly be shared.

Meantime, he might, of course, send an immediate report to Humphrey's father. But Mr Thewless rather shrank from announcing to Sir Bernard—and that with the baldness required by telegraphic communication—that his cherished son had announced encountering himself in a cinema and later being dramatically, if briefly, bound and shut up in a box. Mr Thewless decided therefore to go straight ahead, and to support the harassments of the coming day upon a resolutely buoyant, nervous tone. In all this he must by no means forfeit his claim to the reader's sympathy. Nature had made Humphrey Paxton a decidedly odd child; circumstances had dictated that his revelations should be odder still; certain obscure purposes of his own had necessitated these revelations being partial and therefore singularly unconvincing. Moreover, Mr Thewless steadily remembered that this was Paxton's boy; that genius in its weakness had turned to him for help; and that his obligations in this sad and exhausting affair were by no means to be measured in terms of fifteen guineas a week. An inspector of the C.I.D. (Cadover, for example—who was at this moment still being pursued by uneasy dreams in his semi-detached villa at Pinner) or a physician professionally versed in those psychological labyrinths into which Mr Thewless had with an unwary amateurism been dangerously drawn: either of these might have been more immediately useful to Humphrey. But neither could have been any more conscientious according to his lights.

An air of cheerful confidence, however, proved at first not easy to sustain. Belfast, grimly utilitarian and shrouded in rain, was very little evocative of any gateway to the holiday spirit; it suggested rather a various detritus from the less appealing parts of Glasgow washed across the Irish Sea during the darker years of the nineteenth century. But this may have been an unfairly coloured view, since no city looks at its best when observed on a wet morning from a four-wheeler cab the progress of which irresistibly hints at a destination not in a railway station but in a municipal cemetery. Nor did Humphrey help in any ready uplifting of the heart, since he was silent, withdrawn, and apparently indisposed to favour his sceptical guardian with further fantasies. This, although in a sense reassuring, was depressing as well. Mr Thewless could not quite forget that Humphrey was, among other things, a *capable* boy. It seemed deplorable that his temperamental troubles (to put the matter mildly) should stand in the way of those activities to which capable boys are rightly dedicated. The mental dexterity that he had put into the business of identifying his new tutor at Euston, the precocious subtlety with which he had analysed a father's inner responses to adolescent behaviour in his son, the complex manner in which he had for a time checked his own irrational fears by an intellectually-conceived mockery of his tutor: how fast and far these abilities would take a properly conducted boy into the recesses of the Greek and Latin languages! Peering out through the rain at the Great Northern railway terminus, and feeling in his pocket for half a crown, Mr Thewless fell for a moment into a weak nostalgia. The images of former pupils rose up before him—chubby-faced fourteen-year-olds solemnly construing from the immensely remote world of Juvenal, of the *Alcestis*; children learned in particles, lisping faultlessly in Sapphics and Alcaics. . . . Mr Thewless glanced at Humphrey beside him—pale, mum, and refusing to be separated for a second from that shot-gun which he had been so anxious to repudiate less than twelve hours before. And momentarily he caught the dark glance of the boy—caught that slightly hypnotic gaze once more. It showed no response or recognition. In fact, it was fixed, Mr Thewless saw, upon some unseen goal or conception with quite as much concentration as any of those earlier pupils had ever brought to the ultimate mysteries of the Glyconic and Pherecratean metres. . . . Mr Thewless, feeling the first stirrings of obscure doubt rising in him once more, jumped hastily from the cab and contrived his customary efficient capture of a porter. Humphrey followed. The railway station spread before them a classical portico nicely painted to look like milk chocolate. On one side stood an immobile policeman of gigantic size proportionately armed with truncheon and revolver. On the other a placard, equally generously conceived, announced

LIFE IS SHORT

DEATH IS COMING

ETERNITY—WHERE?

And upon this brief glimpse of the cultural life of Belfast their train received them and they were presently hurtling west.

There was one other passenger in their compartment, and presently Mr Thewless was eyeing her with considerable gloom. For she was none other than that tiresome Miss Liberty to whose futile chatter over her spy story he attributed a good deal of his own and Humphrey's nervous follies on the previous afternoon.

They breakfasted together. This was by Humphrey's initiative and somewhat to the annoyance of Mr Thewless, who had planned to begin with his pupil a discussion—thoroughgoing but not unnecessarily solemn—on the nature and functions of deponent verbs. What—he heard himself asking Humphrey with a spice of harmless fun—was the difference between a deponent verb and the Prime Minister? Mr Thewless had achieved a good deal of success in his time along such lines as these. A deponent verb——

"Not the kipper," Miss Liberty was saying. "They say kipper or sausage; but if one waits, the sausage turns out to be egg and tomato as well. Not that I am an experienced traveller"—and Miss Liberty turned from Humphrey to Mr Thewless as if anxious that there should be no false pretences in the matter. "It is simply part of the advice that I was given before setting out by my brother, Sir Charles."

Mr Thewless bowed. Remembering that he had not been very polite to Miss Liberty on the previous day, he felt obliged to accept her advice himself—and this although kipper was a breakfast of which he was particularly fond. With suitable resignation, he watched the dish being borne away. A deponent verb *looks* harmless and passive——

"When travelling on the Highland railway with my dear father, Sir Herbert," Miss Liberty was saying, "we commonly obtained a luncheon basket at Kingussie. The cold chicken was sometimes a little tough, but the moment was a romantic one, all the same."

Mr Thewless made an insincere noise, indicative of imaginative understanding of this remote thrill in Miss Liberty's past. He had an uncomfortable feeling that the sausage, to the confusion of Miss Liberty and the discrediting of her brother Sir Charles, would prove to be only sausage, after all. This, of course, made it particularly necessary to continue being polite. "A journey into the Highlands, ma'am," he said, "must always be a romantic experience for an—um—capable child."

"Precisely so. And the west of Ireland, I am told, is almost equally beautiful. So I am so grateful for the kindness of my brother——"

"Sir Charles?" Humphrey asked.

Mr Thewless was appalled. That his pupil should be on the verge of lunacy was one thing. But that he should suddenly become ill-bred was quite another. And there had undoubtedly been mockery in the boy's tone. And yet there was something else as well. Into this dining-car there had crept a faint atmosphere which Mr Thewless found it impossible to define. It *felt* like conspiracy. But how could it possibly be that? Could Miss Liberty, like a deponent verb, be a wolf in sheep's clothing? The idea was patently absurd.

"*Precisely* so." Miss Liberty was helping herself with surprising lavishness to what had veritably proved to be sausage, egg and tomato. "It was my brother who was so kind as to suggest this holiday at Killyboffin. The inn had been recommended to him as satisfactory. So often in hotels nowadays one cannot be sure of well-aired beds."

Mr Thewless was peering through a window. The train had slowed down and on the parapet of a stone bridge he could read the inscription

PREPARE TO MEET THY GOD.

Now he turned back and regarded Miss Liberty with a heroic effort at pleased surprise. "Killyboffin? That happens to be where Humphrey and I are going too."

"How very odd."

"Very odd, indeed," echoed Humphrey, and gulped coffee. Perhaps because the train was gaining speed and rocking slightly, he gave a sudden squirm and splutter. "But then a lot of odd things do happen."

A sort of baffled uneasiness—now only too familiar to him—assailed Mr Thewless. He had the illusion of a momentary vivid penetration into the mind of this tiresome old chatterbox—and what he found there was a fixed determination to carry out some formidable task. But this was nonsense. It was a fancy hitching on to nothing whatever in the actual world; it belonged to last night's nightmare on the express. What was desirable was to finish breakfast quickly and announce a frontal assault upon the Latin language. A deponent verb comes up to you looking quite harmless; then it throws off its fleece. . . . Gazing through the window again in the direction of Lough Neigh, Mr Thewless frowned absently. What troubled him this time was a suspicion that Humphrey had in some way changed. He had planned a day in which his own cheerful common sense would do something to hearten this sadly possessed child; but now it was Humphrey's spirits which were in some odd way rising, while Mr Thewless himself was becoming a prey to irrational foreboding and gloom. Was it possible that the presence of Miss Liberty had some subtle effect on the boy? Or was there a relationship more definite than that? Was it possible, for example, that they had held some conference on board ship in the small hours of the morning; that Humphrey had poured out the pernicious fantasies by which he was beset; and that Miss Liberty, instead of insisting upon their true character as mere figments, had irresponsibly accepted them as gospel, thereby gaining the lad's confidence upon thoroughly reprehensible terms? If this were so, nothing, surely, could be more dangerous. For a time the boy's confidence might rise at finding himself seriously taken as the hero of an adventure story. But Mr Thewless knew only too well the sort of nervous reaction that was likely to follow. All this was conceivable, and it would explain that sense of conspiracy which he felt as rising about him.

Mr Thewless stared glumly at the remains of his sausage and then once more out across the landscape. The green and yellow fields were now flecked with sunshine, and a blue line of mountains lay far to the south. It was a deeply peaceful scene. The train rounded a bend and across a lush meadow a long whitewashed barn swung into view. Along its whole length it bore the words

BOAST NOT THYSELF OF TO-MORROW.

The habits of the Northern Irish, although godly, appeared scarcely gay. In Mr Thewless the sense of foreboding and bafflement irrationally grew; he had a feeling that he was being hurtled at sixty miles an hour into the threatening sickle of a vast question-mark formed by the bogs and mountains that he knew lay ahead of him. Humphrey and Miss Liberty were exchanging critical opinions on the works of "Sapper"—and were apparently proposing to treat these one by one, in chronological order. In desperation, Mr Thewless opened the local paper he had bought at the railway station. It contained circumstantial accounts of several funerals, each ending with the information that the highly successful catering had been carried out by Messrs Tiffin and Tiffin. He turned to the back page and sought a meagre refuge in much incomprehensible information on horses and association footballers. Near the bottom somebody had bought quite a lot of space and caused to be printed

THOU FOOL THIS NIGHT
THY SOUL SHALL BE
REQUIRED OF THEE.

Mr Thewless put down the paper, and as he did so Miss Liberty paused in her anatomy of one of the earlier exploits of Captain Hugh Drummond and smiled at him with maidenly cheer. "And soon," she said, "we shall be on this most entertaining little train."

But Mr Thewless's reply was a mere mumble. For with his intermittent and always disturbing intuition he had, as it were, looked clean through that smile. He had looked into the grey eyes of the lady. And what he there encountered he recognised instantly, although to the best of his knowledge he had never seen it before. It was the clear light of battle.

Those intuitions by which Humphrey's tutor was occasionally troubled by no means extended to any form of prescience,

136

and it is not possible that he can have foreseen the accident. Nevertheless, his heart undoubtedly sank a little further when he saw the entertaining little train to which Miss Liberty had referred. They encountered it after an indefinite wait at a junction during which they were subjected to a somewhat perfunctory Customs examination, and when it finally appeared it looked less like a train of any description than a stunted single-decker bus—or it would have so appeared had it not much more powerfully suggested one of the lower forms of organic life monstrously enlarged to some problematical but assuredly sinister end. Into the belly of this bug-like creature they were presently bundled, but not before Mr Thewless had cast a final lingering look behind. He possessed, it is necessary to admit, something of an urban mind; and all too plainly the entertaining little train spoke of a destination at the back of beyond. Moreover, at this point of the journey there ceased to be anything of that segregation of classes which the philosopher in him was accustomed to deplore but which the social man was apt to take as part of the order of nature. Three or four impoverished persons with bundles were already on board, and immediately behind him an embarrassingly undernourished old woman was singing in a dismal, surprising and Celtic manner—although whether for monetary reward or the pleasures of self-expression was obscure. Presently the driver appeared. He was a melancholy man lost in reverie—and almost equally lost in an immensely old suit of Connemara cloth, evidently tailored for one of the giants before the Flood. He sat down before the controls, eyed them with that flicker of interest which a person of abstract mind may evince before some unfamiliar material thing, and presently pulled a lever with every appearance of random experiment. The bug instantly coughed violently, shuddered as if unkindly roused from sleep, gave a loud angry roar, and then abruptly fell silent and motionless once more. The driver again pulled the lever, but this time nothing happpened at all. He tried several other controls with an equally negative result. Whereupon—but with the reluctance of one who is innately kindly—he reached for a large hammer, climbed down from his seat and proceeded to beat the bug violently about the snout. At this the bug, as if far advanced in some horrid masochistic perversion, contentedly purred. The driver climbed back into his seat and settled himself with an air of deep metaphysical abstraction. The bug continued to purr. After this nothing happened for quite a long time.

The bug purred and the August sun warmed both its entrails and that temporary ingestation represented by Mr Thewless and his fellow travellers. Further impoverished persons crowded on board, the majority carrying ill-wrapped brown-paper parcels or uncertainly clothed children. Somebody brought up a number of cardboard boxes and proceeded to hoist them on the roof; these apparently contained young pigs and were rather smelly. Humphrey and Miss Liberty were discussing some nice point in the character portrayal of their author's middle period. The undernourished woman had stopped singing and was talking unintelligibly and uncomfortably down Mr Thewless's neck. Probably she was soliciting alms. But as it was just possible that she was obligingly explaining some point of Hibernian scholarship germane to her minstrelsy he felt unable to take any action. Suddenly the purring deepened and the bug, without warning, shot off with a swaying and bouncing motion down the narrow-gauge line before it. At this the conductor, a fat boy with a squint who had been eating sandwiches at the back, showed much presence of mind by violently ringing a bell. Whereupon the driver, emerging in some degree from his abstract speculations, as also from his enveloping suit, looked about him in some perplexity and experimentally pressed a button. Immediately a siren whooped demoniacally in the bowels of the bug and amid a series of bumps and bucketings the creature made for the open country. Overhead the piglets in their cardboard boxes squealed in justifiable alarm. The undernourished woman continued to talk down Mr Thewless's neck, but her tone had changed and was now quite evidently one of imprecation against a monster of parsimony. A number of people ate oranges and close to Mr Thewless a small boy announced what was evidently a most implacable intention to be sick. Every-

138

where the greatest good-humour prevailed. From a wayside hoarding Northern Ireland took a Parthian shot at the unregenerate:

THEIR WORM DIETH NOT
AND THE FIRE IS NOT QUENCHED.

Through the early afternoon sunshine the bug trundled westwards and the landscape began to take upon itself with surprising fidelity the characteristics of those railway posters that celebrate the beauties of Erin. In the distance the mountains showed bluer and more blue; blue peat smoke rose from the whitewashed cottages; stacks of peat lay about the bogs or moved mysteriously down the lanes, superincumbent upon invisible donkeys. It was a natural scene in which poetry was steadily gaining upon prose, and Mr Thewless endeavoured, amid the perturbations still active within him, to assume that æsthetic mode of contemplation proper in the circumstances to a cultivated English traveller. The boy who had said he was going to be sick was sick.

The bug stopped at a little whitewashed hut and there was another customs examination. A pillar-box bearing the monogram of Queen Victoria had been painted a nice green. On the platform stood a policeman of normal proportions, and instead of a revolver and a truncheon he carried a copy of *Ben Hur* translated into Irish, which he was evidently studying for an examination important to his professional advancement. Mr Thewless realised that the imperial might of Great Britain lay behind him and that in front was the philosophic republic of Mr De Valera. He several times endeavoured to show his passport and was somewhat hurt to find that the authorities took no interest in it. The attention of the policeman and the Customs officer was entirely given to the piglets, which they examined with many expressions of admiration and surprise. Contrary to popular supposition, it appeared that a pig was almost as much of a curiosity in Ireland as an armadillo would have been in Elizabethan London.

The bug moved on—inexplicably on any merely mechanistic hypothesis regarding its constitution, since both the driver and conductor became aware of the fact only in time to race down the platform and leap on board as it rounded a bend and headed towards the Atlantic Ocean. For a couple of hours it purred and clanked from station to station, but these halts grew gradually more indeterminate in character as the afternoon advanced, and eventually it simply stopped whenever summoned to do so by agitated persons hurrying across an adjoining field. Once when the single track upon which it ran breasted a rise Mr Thewless was startled to see an identical bug rapidly advancing upon them in the middle distance. The driver, also by chance observing this appearance, called to the conductor, and the two engaged for some minutes in dispassionate conversation, bending curiously over the controls of the vehicle and pointing now to one lever and now to another. Meanwhile, the advancing bug hurtled towards them. The conductor made some suggestion which the driver upon consideration rejected; the conductor reflected and then urged some further argument; the driver, being plainly a man of open mind, agreed to give the suggestion a trial and depressed some object with his foot; with an agonising jolt the bug came to a dead halt. Some ten yards away the second bug had done the same, and the two appeared to eye each other balefully, much like two fleas that have been taught to simulate pugilistic encounter. The drivers and conductors, however, climbing out to meet upon neutral ground, debated the situation in the friendliest spirit over cans of tea and a cigarette; eventually the oncoming bug was coaxed by its crew to back for half a mile into a siding which had been discovered by the enterprise of a reconnoitring conductor—whereon the journey was resumed. One other hitch occurred about an hour later, when the bug came to a halt, baffled by a bifurcation of the line before it. And this occasioned the only flaw in the complete harmony of the afternoon's proceedings, for whereas the driver was in favour of taking the line to the left the conductor was obstinately wedded to the notion of taking the one to the right. Various passengers took part in the discussion, which presently re-echoed to a spirited bandying of the musical place-names of the district. Miss Liberty, hearing the driver several times enunciate in tones of disgust and repudiation the name of Killyboffin, joined in vigorously on the conductor's side; and it was this opinion that eventually carried the day.

The journey went interminably on. Apart from two or three silent men who sat at the back, conversaion was general on various points of crop and animal husbandry. A friendly farmer observing that Mr Thewless had nothing more entertaining to read than a novel by Mr Charles Morgan, insisted on lending him the current issue of the *Tullycleave, Derryness and Kinnoghty Recorder*, and from this he learnt that at Crockacooan on the following Thursday it would be possible to bid for three store heifers in forward condition, four dairy cows springing and in full milk, a slipe, three rundlets and a number of double and single trees. He was just speculating on the nature of a double tree when the train ran into the tunnel.

One short tunnel there had already been; traversing it had made Mr Thewless notice the absence of any form of artificial light in this primitive vehicle. One simply sat in the dark and waited. And this time the period of darkness was longer. It must be fully——

At this moment the thing happened: first a shattering jar; then a splintering crash and a tinkle of breaking glass as the bug lurched over on its side; then shouts, cries and—from somewhere at the back—a succession of spine-chilling screams.

It was a situation made all the more unnerving by the complete darkness which enveloped it. Mr Thewless, clinging with one arm to a seat which had reared itself up at an angle of some thirty degrees, stretched out the other in the direction in which he judged the shoulder of his pupil ought to be. "Humphrey," he called, "are you all right?" But there was too much noise for him to be sure if there was any reply. The driver and conductor were endeavouring to restore calm by each shouting at the top of his voice; children were dismally howling; overhead the piglets sustainedly squealed. In the restricted space of the tunnel the resulting reverberations were altogether bewildering, and it was not easy to decide whether what was involved was a major disaster or a largely baseless panic. Somebody struck a match and there was a momentary vision of sprawled bodies and scared faces. From the rear a man's voice called: "I'll get back along the tunnel and bring help"—and this was followed by a further shivering of glass, as of somebody breaking resolutely out of the coach. From the rear too the most agonised groans continued to come, and when another match was struck Mr Thewless saw that one man there was writhing as if in agony and another slumped in his seat, apparently streaming with blood. This last glimpse presented so clamant a call for aid that Mr Thewless began to scramble over the seats, the lessons of long-past first-aid classes reassembling themselves surprisingly in his mind. But he got no distance in this charitable endeavour. For in the darkness and continued confusion something struck him with unaccountable violence on the head and all consciousness left him.

He came to his senses knowing somehow that no great interval of time had elapsed. Nor had the situation greatly changed, except that he himself was now outside the coach and propped against the curved side of the tunnel. Here and there a torch flickered, but there was still more of impenetrable blackness than of light—as also more of turmoil than of order. It was clear, however, that some outside help had arrived. It must, indeed, have arrived with surprising speed, since almost the first object of which he was aware in a passing flicker of light was an efficient-looking stretcher upon which, momentarily unattended, a shrouded form reposed. And Mr Thewless felt a sudden cold fear. Could it be Humphrey who lay in sinister stillness there? The mere thought brought him staggering to his feet and he reached out towards the stretcher. As he did so another uncertain beam of light showed him Miss Liberty close by—Miss Liberty with her features set in swift calculation and with her arm oddly raised. . . . Unaccountably, once more Mr Thewless was struck on the head and was just aware of being gripped in strong arms as he fell.

When he recovered consciousness for the second time it was to discover that a throbbing which he had supposed to be the subjective consequence of his own battered cranium was in

142

fact the steady pulse of a powerful engine, and for a moment he had the confused impression that the bug, with that resistance to even extensive injury characteristic of lowly organisms, had again got under way. But this was an altogether smoother mode of progression, and some subtle report of the senses assured him that it was much more rapid as well. There was still complete darkness around him, but presently he discovered with great surprise that this was merely because he had his eyes shut. Opening them, he found himself to be lying on a stretcher in an admirably appointed ambulance, all chromium, white enamel, and antiseptic smell. Despite the warmth of the afternoon, a little electric radiator was thoughtfully burning, and above it was a tastefully arranged vase of flowers. There was a gay frieze of delightful nursery scenes, and perched at Mr Thewless's feet was an uncompromisingly hygienic but nevertheless cuddlesome teddy-bear. On the other side of the vehicle was a second, and empty, stretcher.

From all this there was only one reasonable inference. He had been badly injured in the accident and was now being borne away in an ambulance hastily requisitioned from some children's hospital. But it was odd that there was nobody else in need of similar conveyance; for example, there had been the two badly hurt men at the back. And what had happened to Humphrey? Even if he had escaped injury, what would be the consequence of these untoward events upon a boy so easily thrown off his balance?

Confronted by this thought, Mr Thewless realised that it was his first duty to ascertain the extent of his injuries and thereupon come to a determination as to what was best to be done. There being no nurse or attendant in the ambulance of whom to enquire, he decided upon a cautious exploration. Apart from a moderate headache and a decided tenderness on the top of the skull, he was aware in himself of no unusual sensation. He knew, however, that sometimes for a considerable interval after the sustaining even of grave injuries very little pain may be felt. But if sensation were delusive, movement could scarcely be so. Now, what was the worst that could have befallen him? The answer, he decided, was a broken

143

back. And, with a broken back, there was one thing assuredly that one could not possibly do: sit up. Bracing himself against some sharp agony, Mr Thewless made the effort to achieve this position. And immediately he found that he was sitting up with as little inconvenience as he experienced every morning in bed.

Mr Thewless moved a limb. He moved all his limbs. He twiddled his toes and twisted his neck. Then, as an after-thought, he vigorously champed his jaws, blinked his eyelids, and retracted the muscles of his abdomen. The issue of all these experiments was incontravertible. Whatever minor sprains or abrasions he might have received, he was by no means in the sort of condition that justified his thus being treated as a cot case and hurtled away from his young charge hard upon an alarming and dangerous experience. And as soon as he realised this Mr Thewless acted with vigour. "Stop!" he shouted loudly. "Please stop at once. There has been some ridiculous mistake."

Nothing happened. He called more loudly still, but again in vain. The hum of the engine must be rendering his cries in-audible through the partition separating him from the driver and anyone else in front. He therefore explored the back, and found only double doors which appeared to be locked on the outside. At the other end, however, and quite close to where the driver's ear must presumably be, there was what proved to be a sliding shutter—and this Mr Thewless opened with considerable relief. "Excuse me," he said politely through it; "would you mind stopping, and opening the door? I find that I have sustained no serious injury."

These remarks being, even if faintly surprising, eminently rational, Mr Thewless was a good deal startled to hear them received with a loud laugh. "Shut your trap, son," said a rough voice. "Hollering won't do no good. Sit down and play with yer bloody bear."

Mr Thewless was not unnaturally much shocked. It was evident that the driver, being accustomed to conveying children, had forgotten that upon this occasion he was dealing with an adult. But that sick children should ever be spoken to in such a way aroused his extreme indignation at once. "Stop the ambulance instantly," he said. "Your language is disgraceful, and you may be sure that I shall report upon it with the utmost severity to the proper authorities."

Again the driver laughed loudly. "Gawd," he said, "what a rum kid."

" 'Ere"—it was a second voice that spoke this time—"*is* it a kid? It don't sound much like a kid to me."

"Wot's that?" The driver was startled and jammed on his brakes. "Didn't yer have a look at 'im under that ruddy sheet?" The ambulance jolted to a stop. "Let's 'ave a look."

And a moment later the doors were flung open. Mr Thewless, boiling with indignation, jumped to the ground and confronted two surly and oddly uncertain men, who had not at all the appearance of hospital attendants. "Strewth!" said one. "'Ere's a go."

But the second appeared more self-possessed, and now presented Mr Thewless with an ingratiating smile. "You mustn't mind his language, sir," he said. "He don't belong at all regular with the ambulance; it's just that the regular driver's away like."

At this the first man growled what might have been an apology. When he spoke, however, it was in tones of indignation almost matching Mr Thewless's own. "Look 'ere," he said, "ain't yer tripes 'arf torn out? A'n't yer at death's door? Ain't yer a bleeding mess?"

Mr Thewless uttered a comprehensive denial of these charges. "I am perfectly well," he said sternly. "And I demand to know——"

"Then we ain't got no time to waste on yer. What d'jer mean coming joy-riding with them as 'is employed strikly on errands of mercy? Serious calls is wot we attend to. Come along, mate. And jigger off, yer silly old goat."

At this the two men leapt with surprising speed into their ambulance and drove away. Mr Thewless was left standing by the roadside, speechless with bewilderment and rage. All around him stretched an empty moor, now growing bleak and inhospitable in the late afternoon sunlight. Miles away, a single white spot on the horizon suggested some humble species of human dwelling. Further sign of life or habitation there was none. He examined the dusty surface of the road. No tracks were visible except those of the ambulance which was now growing small in the distance. It was only too evident that the back of beyond had veritably received him.

Doggedly he began to trudge towards the distant white speck.

CHAPTER XII

"No eggs! No eggs!! Good heavens, man, what do you mean by no eggs?" And, as one thunderstruck, Mr Cyril Bolderwood of Killyboffin Hall stared at Denis, the general factotum whom, in expansive moments, he was pleased to describe as his steward. Then less vehemently he added: "You did say *no* eggs?"

"It's a shameful fact, sir, that I'm just after discovering." Denis paused to remove a straw from his hair and drop it in his master's waste-paper basket. "But Mr Ivor had the last of our own for his breakfast surely, and now there's never an egg to be bought in all Killyboffin on account of the fish having come."

"God bless my soul!" Mr Bolderwood raised both hands in air with an expressiveness possibly indicating his long sojourn in Latin-American countries. "Do you realise, Denis, that here is Mr Ivor's cousin coming from London, where not the King himself has an egg to his breakfast except once in a way —and coming, mark you, with a tutor, Denis, a great doctor from the universities, no doubt—and you stand there and tell me the eggs are all gone from Killyboffin because the fish have come? Is it the tinned salmon in old Mrs Fallon's little window that have risen up in the night and sucked them dry, Denis? Now tell me that." And Mr Bolderwood, who prided himself on a manner of speech both feudal and familiar, sat down with regained composure and began to stuff an ancient pipe.

"Indeed and your honour knows it is no such thing, but

146

rather the live fish coming up the loughs in their millions like the stars of heaven and all the world's ships labouring after them from Hull and Narvik and Nineveh. And it's myself have seen boatloads of them coming ashore all morning, and taking Tannian's car and Donohoe's, yes and Michael Orr's old Ford too, and scouring the land to eat it up like the locusts, and ourselves in want of a simple dish to set before a fine lad from London itself, broad and fair and blue-eyed as he is, that none of us has ever had the joy of setting eyes on, and him Mr Ivor's own cousin." Denis paused on this. He found a rhetoric based upon uncertain memories of his grandmother distinctly exhausting to keep up. But since his cosmopolitan employer liked to play at being surrounded by old Ireland, and was prepared to pay for the illusion, Denis did his best to get the atmosphere right. "Isn't it a hard case, your honour, myself and yourself to be treated——"

"So that's it!" Cyril Bolderwood had risen again and walked to the window of the long shabby room he called his study. "Steam trawlers, eh? And rascals off them wandering the countryside buying by day what they haven't already stolen by night? Why don't the police see to them? Why doesn't the *garda* act?"

"Indeed, sir, he well might." Denis shook his head. "And yet it would maybe be beyond reason to expect a poor lad like Shaun Cushin, with a great examination in the Irish before him that would tax the bottomless learning of the Taoiseach himself, to concern himself with chasing after a rabble of foreigners and gaoling them for stealing a goose or a hen or a handful of eggs. Unless"—Denis added as an after-thought—"they should be your honour's own, indeed."

Mr Bolderwood was now staring thoughtfully at a curl of smoke which rose presumably from one of the offending trawlers in the little harbour beyond the village. "If we can't have eggs——" he began, and abruptly broke off. "What the devil is all that noise about?"

Killyboffin Hall was a large, bare, rambling building, Georgian in a bleak way and falling down at the corners. The lightest breeze, on gaining entry through its many cracks,

147

crevices and broken panes, became mysteriously transformed into a gale that sobbed and moaned through its lofty rooms, stirring the dust from shadowy cornices and immemorial hangings, and making the worn carpets rise and fall in the long corridors. It was the sort of house in which, in the small hours, boards start from worm-eaten joists, and ancient wicker furniture creaks in shrouded rooms, and invisible fingers are at play upon doors and windows. That the Bolderwoods were positively obliged to live amid such a *décor* nobody very seriously believed, for clearly it was old Mr Bolderwood's whim thus to assimilate himself with impoverished landowners upon whom such conditions were obligatory, and the fancy was licensed by sundry tortuous but indubitable bloodties, with the nobility and gentry of the region. Life at Killyboffin, then, had superficially every appearance of all the discomforts associated with genteel penury, and had Sir Bernard Paxton gained any inkling of this eccentric humour on the part of his kinsman he would certainly not—prizing life's material surfaces as he was inclined to do—have sanctioned the expedition upon which his only son had recently embarked.

One consequence of the somewhat bare condition of the mansion was the tendency of noise in any volume to gain resonance as it travelled from room to room, and to propagate itself through a complex system of echoes. It was a phenomenon of this sort that was disturbing Mr Bolderwood now. "Denis," he repeated, "what the devil is that?"

Denis considered. "It might be the half-Ayrshire, your honour, got unbeknownst among the turnips, and Gracie and Billy and the lad Pat and the dogs——"

"Stuff and nonsense, man! It's coming up the kitchen stairs —and whoever heard of a half-Ayrshire doing that? But here's Mr Ivor. Ivor, in heaven's name——"

Ivor Bolderwood, a mild young man behind large round glasses, had entered his father's study by a door at its far end; and at the same moment a confused rout of persons had burst in opposite. One of these latter, a stout woman in an apron, appeared to possess some power of articulate speech, and her voice presently rose clear of the babel around her. "The terrible disaster that it is!" she cried. "And the poor lad nigh at the end of his long journey and all—alas! that Killyboffin should see such a day."

To these words a general consenting murmur arose from Mr Bolderwood's other retainers. And Denis, although without any notion of what all this betokened, judged that some more specifically Celtic reaction would be appropriate. "Ochone," he cried with great satisfaction, and began swaying his body in a rhythmical manner from the hips. "Ochone, ochone!"

"Hold your tongue, man!" Ivor Bolderwood spoke with a decision unexpected in one whose eyes gleamed so vaguely from behind their expanses of glass. "Now, Gracie, why——" But here the young man stopped, his glance having fallen for the first time upon another of the intruders. "Billy, weren't you told to be off to the station long ago?"

"And indeed I was, Mr Ivor." The man addressed took a step forward, acknowledging the presence of his employer as he did so by pulling at a forelock. "And I'm after driving back this moment with the terrible news of the great disaster to the train. And sorry I am that it's without the poor young gentleman that I've returned here."

"A disaster to the train!" The elder Mr Bolderwood paled. "You don't mean the train on which my nephew and his tutor were——"

"Indeed he does, sir." The woman called Gracie spoke again. "A great and terrible accident in the tunnel it has been, and the mangled bodies and severed limbs strewn far under the wide heaven, and the cries of those in their agony like to be heard from here to Sligo."

"But this is too ghastly to believe." Mr Bolderwood looked in consternation at his son, whose perturbation was equal to his own. "And is the poor boy——"

"The poor boy, indeed!" Denis was no longer to be restrained. "The fine lad that was to be coming amongst us, triumphant and brave, to be no more than one of a dark line of corpses crying shame upon the railways of Ireland!"

"And the learned man that was with him to be less even

149

than that, by far and far." Gracie had risen and raised imprecating hands against the heavens. "For no morsel of him have they pieced to morsel in all that dolorous field."

"Not with all the labour of all the doctors that be there now with all their fair and shining instruments," said Denis with conviction. "But thanks be to God we can do better for the boy. For with a stitch here, and maybe some hay or tow thrust in there, he can be laid neat and decent in his coffin and it shipped at no great expense to his sorrowing dad in London. And no trouble on the way except it may be a bit rummage, reverently undertaken, in the Customs sheds of Dublin."

At this Mr Bolderwood produced a large coloured handkerchief and mopped his brow. "Am I to understand," he cried, "that my nephew is *dead*?"

Billy, who was chiefly addressed, made a motion with his head which contrived to be at once vigorous and completely ambiguous. "As soon," he began, "as ever the train got into the station——"

"Got into the station?" It was Ivor Bolderwood who exclaimed this time. "And how the deuce could the train get into the station when it had had a terrible accident in the tunnel?"

"Indeed and why should it not?" Billy was innocently surprised. "The great disaster was safely over, praise God, and what should the train do but arrive where it was intended?"

"It's enough to drive a man out of his senses!" Mr Bolderwood's voice rose in despair. "Haven't you been telling us, you abominable rascal, of mangled bodies and severed limbs and dark lines of corpses and—and doctors and surgeons by the bevy. And now you——"

"But indeed, your honour, there was an ambulance." Billy produced this with a good deal of triumph. "There's five or six of them that was on the train to swear to it—although others will yet be denying of it, to be sure, since it was gone it seems almost as soon as come."

"There was an accident—but not so bad that the train couldn't continue on its way." Mr Bolderwood had advanced and was grasping Billy sternly by the lapel of his coat. "And there was an ambulance—but it saw no reason to stay long. Now, what of all the rest of this outrageous nonsense? Was *anyone* killed? Was *anyone* injured?"

"Or"—and Ivor Bolderwood intervened sharply—"is anyone missing?"

Billy threw up admiring hands—thereby dexterously freeing himself from his employer's grasp. "There, now!" he said. "It's a great intelligence that your honour's son has, and a great pride that he must be to his father. For there were three strangers at the back of the train, it seems, and they the most sorely wounded of all. Screaming in their agony, they were, and the blood all about them as deep as fish-pools, while the others, as it appeared in the end, were no more than shaken and bruised. And when all that great fear and panic was over it was seen that these three had vanished entirely, and with them the learned man that was your honour's nephew's tutor. And this same that I'm after telling you is but another proof that there was an ambulance there surely, for how else could the wounded men have vanished? And the tutor, Christ help him, must have been taken as at death's door too."

"Then it comes to this." Ivor Bolderwood turned to address his father, who, wrathful and bewildered, still confronted Billy. "The accident resulted in three strangers and Mr Thewless being injured and taken away in an ambulance. That is bad enough, although not nearly so bad as all this excited chatter suggested. But where is the boy?"

"Exactly so." The elder Mr Bolderwood was now trembling with mingled anxiety and irritation. "Where is Mr Humphrey, you blackguard? Why haven't you brought him home? Do you realise how—how *important* this is?"

"And that we are responsible," Ivor added, "to his father?"

"There, now!" said Denis indignantly. "And can't you answer his honour with some mite or drop of reason, Billy Bone, instead of blathering, God help you, over every irrelevant thing?"

"And causing the limbs to drop and the blood to flow," cried Gracie, "from untold Irish souls, when there was no mischief but to three poor creatures from the North, and

151

maybe to the young lad's tutor, which is a person of great learning, God be praised, but of small consideration either among Christian folk or gentry?"

Under this general reprobation, Billy Bone shifted uneasily from one foot to the other. "Should I not be sparing his honour's feelings," he demanded of the company at large, "and waiting some more seemly time for telling him that his nephew has gone off with a woman in Tannian's car?"

"Gone off with a woman? Stuff and nonsense!" The elder Mr Bolderwood threw up his arms in despair. "Why should Mr Humphrey do a fantastic thing like that?"

"And why should he do anything else?" Billy was bewildered. "With the tutor that was set at guard over him laid low in an ambulance, and a fine woman in her perfumes and her pearls and her rich and rustling garments waiting for him in Tannian's great car, and himself a young heretic without fear of priest or purgatory or the blessed St Patrick——"

"Lunacy—utter lunacy!" Mr Bolderwood's manner wavered between incredulity and apprehensiveness. "Do you ask me to believe that a—a woman of this character should be waiting in the wilds of Killyboffin on the chance that a railway accident might incapacitate my nephew's tutor?"

Ivor Bolderwood had strolled to the window and was staring out at the wisp of smoke rising from the hidden trawler. Now he turned back and looked at his father soberly. "To me," he said, "the unlikely touch is Tannian's car. One would expect the equipage of such an adventuress to match the perfumes and the pearls and the alluring limbs."

Mr Bolderwood looked at his son in some surpise. "But surely you can't think——"

"Well, the boy *has* vanished. And something odd *does* seem to have happened on the train. I begin to wonder if we quite reckoned with what we might be taking on." He glanced round the circle of his father's retainers. "*Paxton pere*," he said, "*n'est-il pas tres riche et tres célèbre? Peutêtre on trame l'enlèvement de l'enfant.*"

The element of play-acting commonly discernible in the elder Mr Bolderwood quite evaporated under this dire hint.

He sat down heavily and without the intention of creating an effect. "You disturb me," he said. "You disturb me very much."

Ivor's eyebrows had dipped beneath his glasses in a thoughtful scowl. "The tutor—this Mr Thewless—sounded extremely respectable. But, of course, there might have been a second adventuress waiting to nail *him*. She might have lurked in the tunnel. She might have been disguised as a beautiful nurse and laid on with the ambulance."

The elder Mr Bolderwood looked momentarily relieved. "You ought not to make these jokes," he said. "I am naturally worried; naturally very worried indeed."

"If, of course, this Mr Thewless who has travelled with the boy is the genuine Mr Thewless. We can't really be sure. . . . Ah—that may tell us something!"

This exclamation was occasioned by the shrill ringing of a telephone bell in a far corner of the room. Ivor Bolderwood made for it, but not before he had ejected his father's retainers with the gesture of one who drives sheep expertly through a gate. He picked up the receiver. "Yes," he said, ". . . yes. This is Ivor Bolderwood speaking. . . . No, he hasn't turned up yet. As a matter of fact, we have become a little anxious. One of the servants says he has gone off with a lady. . . . No, I didn't say there had been something shady. I said that we are told he has gone off with a lady. . . . Yes, we are certainly going to enquire at once. I hope that you yourself. . . . Dear me . . . *dear* me! Yes, indeed. A most alarming experience. . . . Good lord! Extremely careless. . . . Certainly a stiff letter will be the thing. Can we send the car? . . . I see. Yes, we look forward to it. . . . Yes, we will start a search now . . . You think it will be all right? I am so glad. It will allay my father's anxieties. . . . A prank? Quite possibly. . . . Goodbye."

Ivor Bolderwood put back the receiver and turned to his father. His eyebrows had risen expressively over the rims of his glasses. "Thewless," he said. "Thewless, as you may have guessed. There really was some sort of accident in the tunnel. He was hit on the head."

"In the accident?"

"It sounded to me more like *after* the accident. And then he was put into an ambulance—so there really was an ambulance —and driven away. Apparently it was a *children's* ambulance. And when the people in charge of it discovered that *he* was not a child they more or less dropped him like a hot potato and disappeared."

"Well I'm damned!" The elder Mr Bolderwood looked doubtfully at his son. "And was he terribly upset when he heard that Humphrey hasn't turned up?"

"Not a bit of it. He says it must be some boyish prank."

"Bless me! And does he think being carried off in an ambulance was a boyish prank too?"

"He considers that it was careless—really unpardonably careless. He is going to write a letter about it to the local authorities."

"It is certainly a sort of thing that must be stopped." Cyril Bolderwood frowned. "But, my dear Ivor, this is most disturbing—positively sinister, indeed—whatever this fool of a tutor thinks of it. The lad may be in the hands of Lord knows what set of gangsters or professional kidnappers at this very moment. This Thewless must be a confoundedly casual chap."

"He didn't give me quite that impression." And Ivor Bolderwood stared at the telephone as if that instrument might be capable of throwing light on the matter. "He struck me as a man who was almost irrationally determined to deny that the universe holds anything dangerous or surprising."

"An admirable temperament! I wish I could feel the same."

Ivor Bolderwood shook his head. "I didn't feel it was a matter of his temperament. The learned tutor is in some rather abnormal state of mind. His ordinary way of taking things may be quite different."

"Well, it's our way of taking things that is the question. What the devil are we to do?"

"Make sure that the excellent Thewless isn't right, and that the boy's disappearance isn't, in one way or another, a mare's nest. After that—well, we must send a wire to Bernard Paxton and call in the police."

"Oh dear, oh dear!"

"But do Irish rural policemen believe stories of kidnappers and beautiful decoys? I doubt it." And Ivor Bolderwood, disregarding his father's evident perturbation, placidly chuckled. "It would be better—yes, decidedly better—to rescue the boy ourselves. Don't you think?"

"I think I'll get the police station now." Cyril Bolderwood rose with sudden resolution and approached the telephone. "They may at least tell us something like the truth about the train. . . . Whatever is that?"

From somewhere beyond the precincts of Killyboffin Hall there had come a sound as of the ragged firing of small-arms. It drew nearer and presently disclosed itself as being in the nature of a death-rattle from some internal combustion engine.

"Tannian's car!" exclaimed Ivor. "Perhaps it's the adventuress come to do a deal with us." He strode to the window, threw it open and leant out. There was a moment's pause and then his laughter floated back into the room. "It's the lady, sure enough. But she's fifty, if she's a day. And she's brought the boy with her."

Cyril Bolderwood produced his handkerchief and once more mopped his brow. "Bewildering," he said, "really bewildering. One doesn't at all know what to make of it. And—do you know?—there isn't a single egg in the place."

CHAPTER XIII

THE VARIOUS ANXIETIES to which Mr Thewless had been subject since accepting the guardianship of Humphrey Paxton had indeed produced very much the effect divined by Ivor Bolderwood over the telephone. He was, he assured himself, a commonplace person who had undertaken commonplace employment. Law, order and security surrounded him as they had always done, and the only disturbing factor in the situation was the lurid and infectious imagination of his pupil. The affair of the ambulance had certainly been a little out of the way; but this was all the more reason for his being on his guard against treating it as Humphrey would do—as a springboard to some alarming fantasy. Even to write that stiff letter of complaint might be to make too much of the incident. The Irish, after all, were known to be a somewhat erratic people, and the mistake that had been made, although perplexing and vexatious, was not serious. Much more disturbing was the fact that Humphrey, although uninjured in the affair in the tunnel, had made another of his foolish disappearances.

And Mr Thewless (who had found little difficulty in hiring a car which was now carrying him comfortably towards Killyboffin Hall) remembered with mortification the absurd suspicions he had harboured upon the occasion of Humphrey's vanishing on the Heysham train. Those suspicions had not even held any coherency among themselves. For instance, there had been that muddled idea that the boy travelling with him was an imposter—an idea upon which he might positively have acted (to the vast detriment of poor Humphrey's nervous balance) but for that fortunate flash-back to the Velasquez in Sir Bernard Paxton's library. But now the whole of that bad twenty-four hours was behind him; the life of a country-house in this remote region could scarcely be other than tranquil; and once Humphrey had turned up again a quiet and wholesome routine could be established. Unless, indeed, the house-party assembled by Sir Bernard's cousins was of an order so large, brilliant or—abominable thought!—rackety as to make quiet and study difficult.

But for the moment, at least, complete tranquillity was possible. Mr Thewless's pipe and tobacco had come safely through his adventures; he employed himself with them comfortably now, while he surveyed a countryside which was quite unfamiliar to him. Ahead were occasional glimpses of an ocean the deep blue of which was beginning to take the glitter of the declining sun; and here and there, too, he had seen cliffs and headlands which hinted at a rugged and deeply indented coast. Behind and on either hand stretched gently undulating country, intensely green, divided by stone dykes into fields and paddocks that grew larger and more ill-defined

156

as they climbed from the valleys towards the higher ground. Sparsely threaded on invisible tracks that ran diagonally up and down the hills were the low white cottages which were almost the sole sign of human occupation. Their doors, windows and chimneys were so disposed as to make them strongly suggestive of sentient beings, crouched with wide eyes and pricked ears to mark the intruder. Twice the car had passed the burnt-out shell of a large mansion amid abandoned gardens, and Mr Thewless's driver took it upon himself to explain that this state of affairs dated from the Troubles, and was the work of persons whom he, the driver, held in the strongest reprobation; whom he regarded, indeed, as possessing a reach of wickedness quite beyond even the common large tether of humanity. Mr Thewless, having a strong persuasion that his informant had himself been a handy man with a firebrand, supposed that this political attitude was not unconnected with the amount of the fare he should presently be expected to pay. Perhaps (speculated Mr Thewless, thoughtful for his employer's pocket) the Bolderwoods would have some idea of what was reasonable. Two shillings would certainly be an adequate tip.

At this moment the car swung sharply and the driver announced that they were on the drive to the big house. Mr Thewless would not have guessed it, but looking back at what appeared to be a cart-track he discerned that they had passed the ruins of a small lodge. These were unblackened by flame, and the mere product, it was to be conjectured, of the effluction of time. The car took another bend and the house was before them. Mr Thewless looked at it with some surprise. For here too time seemed to have been let play almost unimpeded. The mansion, although it was not actually ruinous—having recently received, indeed, a sort of token restoration in the form of much amateurishly applied white paint—was not such as Sir Bernard Paxton's manner would have prepared one to expect. It contrived to suggest the idea of an immemorial and settled possession, of the confident tenure that comes only with generations; but at the same time there appeared to be whole wings and floors that were deserted, so that the life of the whole place conveyed the notion of a gentle peripheral decay. This effect was enhanced by a long balustraded terrace along the line of which were disposed sundry groups of statuary so drastically decayed as to display little more than a tangle of lower limbs, human and brute, from which an anatomist might possibly have reconstructed the various super-incumbent dramas now missing. Behind this somewhat mournful detritus of classical culture a woman was moving about in what appeared to be the motion of feeding hens.

When he had recovered from his first mild surprise at these unexpected appearances, Mr Thewless was distinctly pleased. There was unlikely to be anything rackety or pretentious here. It seemed to be a very good setting, indeed, for that labour of rehabilitation, both nervous and scholastic, to which he and his charge were dedicated. And, even as he made this reflec-tion, Mr Thewless found further reassurance in an eminently quiet domestic scene. Below the terrace, and upon a large space of ground midway in character between a lawn and a hayfield, an elderly lady and gentleman sat beneath an ancient coloured umbrella the shade of which had crept away from them with the sinking sun. Beside them on a wicker table a silver tea equipage of considerable complication suggested an ordering of things at once sober and substantial. Some fifty yards beyond, and on the farther side of a low hedge, were two other figures whom Mr Thewless could at first distinguish merely as those of a younger man and a boy. These were bent over some object presently invisible; they straightened up and Mr Thewless heard a dull report; their conference was re-newed and in a flash its nature became clear. The boy was being instructed in the use of a shot-gun—that same shot-gun which he had been disposed violently to repudiate at Euston. Humphrey had turned up.

Perhaps because he was more relieved than he was prepared to acknowledge, Mr Thewless paid his fare without enquiry. He was then led, by a female servant markedly more disposed to hospitality than deference, across the decaying terrace and into the presence of the persons beneath the umbrella. He had only time to remark, with a twinge of obscure misgiving, that

158

the lady was none other than his old acquaintance, Miss Liberty, when his attention was commanded by the volubility of his host.

"My dear sir, I'm delighted to see you safe—most delighted. Gracie! bring another pot of tea. . . . Yes, very pleased indeed and I hope you're not unduly fatigued. Dinner, woman—dinner? Hold your tongue and do as you're told—am I to be dinnered in my own house when I choose that it shall be tea-time still? . . . I think you know Miss Liberty. She took charge of Humphrey, you know—a nice lad, Bernard's boy, and intelligent, I'd be inclined to say—took charge of him, you know, and they went off to search for you in Tannian's car. But here you are, after the rascals have done their damndest, eh?"

"Done their damndest?" Mr Thewless was disturbed.

But Mr Bolderwood largely laughed. "No animus, of course; nothing directed against you in particular, my dear sir. But first they let fly at you with a railway accident and then with this odd ambulance affair, eh? It's their stupidity, you know. All the Irish are intensely stupid. Charming, of course; full of poetry and often extremely industrious; religious too—positively religious to a fault." Mr Bolderwood paused for a moment, and Mr Thewless conjectured that he was proposing to supply this last statement with some larger theological context. But all he did was to take breath the more effectively to shout across the length of the terrace: "Gracie, send out another fruit cake! And tell that woman to stop feeding the fowls." Mr Bolderwood turned this time to Miss Liberty. "Positively," he said, "I won't feed the fowls if the fowls refuse to feed me. Would you believe, now, that there's not an egg in the place, and that they won't even send up a dozen —not a dozen, mark you!—from the village? And on a day, as Ivor there would tell you, that I distinctly had it in mind to order an omelette for dinner. By the way, I hope you'll stop for a meal?"

During these wandering remarks, Miss Liberty had been studying Humphrey's tutor with a good deal of attention—and this with a frankness making the latter feel faintly like an object exposed behind plate-glass. But now the lady rose and drew on her gloves. "Thank you," she said, "but I am afraid I cannot accept your most *kind* invitation. Not, Mr Bolderwood, that I will claim to feel a stranger, or in any way unintroduced, after the *curious* circumstances in which we have met and the most friendly reception you gave me. When Humphrey was parted from Mr Thewless as a result of the mishap in the tunnel I felt it right to make what enquiries I could, and then to bring the boy on to his destination. But now I must find my inn. It is said to be most *comfortable*. Indeed, it was strongly recommended to my-brother, Sir Charles. Personal recommendation is most important, do you not think? And now I propose to walk to the village, and nobody is to accompany me a single step."

Delivering herself of this command, Miss Liberty paused as if for a final survey of the scene. Ivor Bolderwood, unaware of the arrival of Mr Thewless, had wandered the length of some fields away, but the occasional pop of the shot-gun told that the boy's education was proceeding. Further off in the same direction could be seen an arm of the sea, and beyond it a promontory running out and up to a commanding eminence from which cliffs dropped sheer to the water below. At this Miss Liberty pointed suddenly and with a decisive finger. "There must be a very fine view from there," she said to Mr Bolderwood.

"View?" Her host's gaze went somewhat vaguely after her finger. "Oh, yes, capital—really capital."

"Particularly in the morning." Miss Liberty was now critically taking her bearings by the sun. She turned to Mr Thewless. "Say at ten o'clock."

"I beg your pardon?" Fleetingly—he was by now decidedly fatigued—Mr Thewless was aware of something dropping softly into the depths of his mind.

"The shadows," said Miss Liberty. "The shadows over the bay must be just right then. Mr Bolderwood, I quite envy you living amid such beauties of Nature. *Good*-bye."

And Miss Liberty, having shaken hands with some ceremony, walked composedly away.

This departure was the signal for Mr Thewless to be shown to his room—an operation which Mr Bolderwood directed in person, and which involved the services of a surprising number of assistants. The factotum Denis was present in something of the position of an interpreter, reiterating and augmenting the sufficiently considerable volubility of his employer. The lad called Billy Bone bumped about with suitcases. Gracie, having thumped the bed upon which the guest was to repose himself, with results very little to her satisfaction, fell to re-making it amid loud exclamations of indignation and shame. Two further maids appeared with large jugs of hot and cold water, and proceeded with such concentration to the mixing together of these in a basin that Mr Thewless had an alarmed feeling that these maidens, with a positively Homeric simplicity, intended themselves to wash him down there and then. This sense of mild personal insecurity was further increased when an enthusiastic youth, in feature disconcertingly like the traditional Irishman celebrated on comic postcards, slipped deftly behind him and neatly stripped him of his jacket—while at the same moment another lad, possibly a twin to the first, threw himself on the floor and seized Mr Thewless by a leg, although with no more hurtful intention, as it presently appeared, than of depriving him of his shoes and socks. Mr. Bolderwood, meanwhile, stamped about the apartment, tugging at curtains which came off their rings, and knobs which came off their drawers, and cupboard doors which came off their hinges. The whole effect was like a page by Smollett or a print after Rowlandson; and Mr Thewless was rather sleepily aware of it as being—although by no means displeasingly—somewhat factitious in character. It was evidently a turn which this retired South American commercial magnate (for Mr Bolderwood, he recalled, was really that) pleased himself with putting up. And although Mr Thewless would certainly have preferred running water, decent seclusion, and drawers from which there was some prospect of extracting shirts and ties without exhausting operations with pocket-knives and shoe-horns, he was nevertheless quite prepared to take this harmless feudal fantasy in good part. Besides, he reflected, it might amuse Humphrey.

Presently, however, Mr Bolderwood brought down the curtain abruptly on the scene by driving his retainers with something approximating to sudden physical violence from the room. Mr Thewless rather expected that he would follow, leaving his guest to pursue his own occasions until summoned to dinner. But Mr Bolderwood simply seated himself comfortably on the faded cretonne of a window-seat—gaining himself thereby a pleasant bath of evening sunshine—and prepared to keep his guest company during his ablutions. "Soap?" he said. "Yes, I see the rascals have remembered soap. Our ways are very informal at Killyboffin, very informal indeed. But I assure you, my dear sir, that we are very glad to see you. And I like cousin Bernard's boy. Ivor and he are going to get on admirably. Ivor has a good touch with lads. For my part, I look forward to a very pleasant time while you are with us." Mr Bolderwood paused, and it appeared to his companion, peering at him from amid an abundant soapy lather, that some shade of doubt momentarily clouded his ingenuous brow. But this instantly explained itself. "If it wasn't for the eggs," said Mr Bolderwood. "Did you ever hear of so outrageous a thing? And when we had positively planned an enormous omelette. I greatly fear that for dinner now we shall have to fall back upon stelk. Do you awfully mind?"

Mr Thewless, reaching for a towel, murmured some inarticulate civility. Conceivably stelk was some very considerable delicacy which his host was heralding with modest disclaimers. But somehow it did not sound altogether promising.

"But, of course, we might have boxty." Mr Bolderwood brightened. "Gracie's boxty is very eatable, very eatable indeed. And you'll agree that that's more than can be said for boxty as a general rule."

Mr Thewless was again inarticulate. He did not think he would care for boxty—whether Gracie's or another's—and moreover he felt a scarcely rational apprehension lest Humphrey, also disliking it, might be prompted to some demonstration as with Lord Buffery and the cream jug. He was casting round for some means of changing the subject when his host himself did this with some abruptness. "I say," he said, "that old girl—do you think she's all right?"

"All right?" It took Mr Thewless some seconds to realise that this question, which had broken from Mr Bolderwood in a manner betraying considerable inner anxiety, referred to his late travelling-companion. And even when assured of this he was quite at sea as to its bearing. It was his first thought that the lady's morals were being brought to the question; then it occurred to him that it was perhaps her social acceptability, and that Mr Bolderwood was fearful that accident had brought him into too familiar contact with a person of insufficient consideration. But these were both suppositions so absurd as to be untenable. "I really don't know much about her," he said. "But, one way and another, she had a good deal of conversation with Humphrey."

"That is what I gathered. Did she talk——?" And from his patch of sunshine, Mr Bolderwood looked in sharp interrogation at Humphrey's tutor.

"I thought she talked a lot of dangerous nonsense."

There was the effect of a good deal of stored-up irritation in Mr Thewless's tone. For a moment Mr Bolderwood appeared to consider it on that basis. "Ah," he said.

"Spy stories," said Mr Thewless, "and stuff of that sort. In ordinary circumstances it would, of course, be harmless enough. But in this particular case——"

Here Mr Thewless hesitated. He was a man who, even when tired, continued to act from delicate feelings; and it went a little against the grain to announce so soon, even to one in whom confidence might quite properly be reposed, his discovery of his pupil's infirmities. In this situation Mr Bolderwood, with a nice tact of which one would not have suspected him in his feudal moments, took the initiative. "Yes," he said, "I gather that Humphrey is a little difficult. A pity in so capable a boy."

"Exactly!" Mr Thewless was much pleased by this perception. "The lad is thoroughly capable—which is no more than one would expect of his father's son. Moreover, he is very attractive. Oddly young for his years at times, and yet at

163

other times with a streak of disconcerting precociousness. But thoroughly nice." Mr Thewless paused, it may be, fleetingly surprised by the decided character of his own sentiments. "There is no doubt, however, that Humphrey can day-dream himself into some rather alarming world of romantic adventure, with nervous consequences that are by no means desirable. And I was a little annoyed with Miss Liberty—although I don't doubt she is a well-meaning woman enough—for encouraging him. When there was this little hitch in the tunnel, and I was taken off under some absurd misapprehension in that ambulance, it appears that she got hold of a car and drove about the country with the boy looking for me. Heaven knows what melodramatic nonsense they stuffed into each other's heads. And fancies of that sort propagate themselves rather easily." Mr Thewless paused. "As a matter of fact, I must confess to have got a little fanciful myself."

If Mr Bolderwood was at all interested in this tentative confession, his sense of civility prevented him from betraying the fact. "I quite follow you," he said, "about what is desirable for the boy. We have, of course, heard about him from Bernard. A little apt to do undisciplined and alarming things."

"He threw a cream jug at Lord Buffery."

Mr Bolderwood received this information for what his guest designed it—a humorous touch on the situation which at the same time staked out a claim for forbearance should any such small untoward incidents occur at Killyboffin. "I'm afraid," he said, "that we shall have no distinguished targets of that sort. But I can find Humphrey plenty of common-or-garden ones. I have a dozen rascals about the place for whom the experience would be thoroughly wholesome. Don't, by the way, think of taking that dinner-jacket off its hanger. Our habits are of the simplest here from month's end to month's end."

By this time Mr Thewless had got used to the engaging familiarity of his host, who sat by him while he changed for all the world as if they had been at school together. So he now responded with unwonted warmth. "I look forward to my stay with you all the more. Going round doing private tutoring

164

as I do, I get a little tired of formal households." He smiled.
"Nor would they suit Humphrey. I have an idea that Sir
Bernard's rather magnificent manner of living may have
rather an oppressive effect where his son is concerned."

"Quite so." Mr Bolderwood was now looking in some
absence of mind out of the window, rather as if he had
detected in the grounds below an illicit attempt to feed the
disgraced Killyboffin poultry. "Hence, no doubt, the running
away."

"The running-away?" Mr Thewless was startled.

Mr Bolderwood chuckled. "Just something that Ivor tells
me cousin Bernard mentioned about our young handful—that
it wouldn't be surprising if he cut off to sea or joined up with
a circus. I suppose boys still do these things from time to
time."

"I see." Mr Thewless, finding himself a pair of house-
slippers in a suitcase, was dimly aware that, in fact, he didn't
quite see. "Well, we must make sure that we are not landed
with anything like that."

"Most certainly we must." Mr Bolderwood was at once
properly emphatic and charmingly amused. "Although, with
exploits of that sort, one never knows, does one?"

"Never knows?" Despite his tardy tea, Mr Thewless was
feeling hungry as well as tired, and the combination made him
stupid.

"Something was put in my head. *Captains Courageous*, and
that sort of thing. I imagine that Humphrey has been a little
fussed by his father—I don't intend any serious criticism of
Bernard, I need hardly say—and been brought up in an
atmosphere of wealth, and formality, and at the same time of
abstract and intellectual preoccupations rather depressing to
a young mind. A bit of an escapade, and a bit of roughing it,
might actually do him a world of good. Of course I may be
quite wrong—and you, my dear fellow, have infinitely more
experience with lads than I. It need hardly be said that we
shall entirely rely upon you for the regulating of Humphrey's
ways during your stay."

This last was altogether a proper declaration. On the

strength of it, Mr Thewless was quite prepared to accept in a cordial spirit his becoming his host's dear fellow a little early in the day. And now Mr Bolderwood got to his feet. "If Humphrey did cast loose," he said idly, "it would be a considerable comfort that he has a brain to deal with things."

Mr Thewless, had he not been engaged in brushing his hair, would certainly have accorded this proposition an emphatic nod. He recalled his pupil's story of the blackmailer—a story which he was still disposed to regard as a little island of true report in the ocean of the unfortunate lad's imaginings. And he decidedly agreed that if a child must be rum he had better be brainy as well.

"You must tell us about your routine; when you want to work with the boy and when you want him taken off your hands. Ivor will be able, and most willing, to give him quite a lot of time. They seem to be getting on very well already. Steady work, plenty of absorbing occupation out of doors— shooting, swimming and that sort of thing—and, above all, the sense of a quiet, ordered life." And Mr Bolderwood smiled benevolently on his guest, altogether the understanding and sympathetic host. "Yes," he repeated, "a quiet, ordered life." He glanced at his watch. "Damnation!" he shouted—and charging at Mr Thewless's door, flung it open with the utmost violence, and proceeded bellowing angrily to the staircase across the corridor. Here, hanging hazardously over the battered elegance of a Georgian balustrade which looked as if it had suffered a good deal of Bolderwood impetuosity in its time, he fell to upbraiding the negligence and unpunctuality of his retainers after a fashion which the notable resonance of Killyboffin Hall rendered startlingly effective. Moreover, the cry was presently taken up by Denis somewhere below, and this impudent proposal to transmit rather than receive his master's displeasure so irritated Mr Bolderwood that his own vociferations were redoubled. Mr Thewless was aware of a rather startled Humphrey peering out of the room adjoining his own, and then of the quiet voice of Ivor Bolderwood apparently composing and expediting matters below. Ivor

166

seemed to be without his father's disposition to put on squire-archal turns. Mr Thewless, as he made his way through the din in order to have a little conversation with his pupil, felt that the son of the house might turn out to be someone to rely upon.

CHAPTER XIV

THERE SEEMED TO BE NO reason why Humphrey should have been taken by surprise, since Mr Thewless had most meticulously knocked on his door and waited to be called upon to enter. But Humphrey, who, since making his own reconnaissance, had sat down at a small desk by his window, had it seemed responded automatically, with the result that his tutor came upon him making a flurried attempt to thrust an exercise book into a drawer. The drawer, since it was a true Killyboffin drawer, resisted the attempt. Whereupon Humphrey, with considerable presence of mind, dropped the exercise book on the floor, edged it with a deft toe beneath the carpet, and turned to Mr Thewless with a charming smile. "Hullo," he said. "I'm so glad to see they didn't handle you too roughly. Although they *must* have hit you on the head."

"I was certainly knocked unconscious for a time, my dear Humphrey, when things began falling about us in the tunnel. If it suits you to think that some villain was involved—why, I see no substantial reason why you should not do so."

As Mr Thewless delivered himself of this indulgent speech it struck him that here was precisely what *did* suit Humphrey. The boy was clearly surrounded still by his delusions; his eye and cheek spoke of considerable excitement; and at the same time he looked in much better trim than his tutor had yet known him. Moreover, Mr Thewless could feel a new element —it was a sort of easy benevolence rather reminiscent of Mr Bolderwood—in Humphrey's attitude to him. The boy was no longer disturbed by the fact that his tutor was sceptical; he gave the impression of rather liking him that way. At the moment Mr Thewless was given no leisure to be more than briefly puzzled by this, since Humphrey was very wholesomely intent upon proceeding to dinner. He had changed circumspectly into a dark suit; an insufficiency of soap and water was seemingly not among his numerous personal indisciplines; at the moment he nicely displayed the extravagantly scrubbed and mildly cheerful features which are the orthodox insignia of the well-conducted public schoolboy. Mr Thewless, heartened by this sight and auguring well from it for much dutifully conned French and Latin in the coming quiet and ordered life that his host had promised, fell to teasing Humphrey about his immoderate expectations from the meal they were awaiting. It was Friday, he pointed out, and what had been projected was an omelette. But owing to the ill-regulated conduct of the Killyboffin hens nothing except boxty was likely to meet them below. Humphrey must by no means expect a whopping steak, misled by his insufficient erudition into supposing the word in any way connected with *bulls*; rather that peculiar species of sea-fish sacred to Hermes, the *box* or βοαξ, so named because of its unfishlike ability to emit a short, plopping noise, gave the true derivation of the word. They would undoubtedly find that boxty was in every sense a wholly fishy dish.

With such gamesome talk as this, immemorial to his kind, did Mr Thewless presently conduct his charge downstairs. An evening breeze had risen, blowing in from ocean; its effect upon the respectable antiquity of Killyboffin was to set a hundred soft tongues whispering, a thousand tiny creatures moving, all around one in the bare, pervasively dilapidated house. Mr Thewless again remarked that it was a place of considerable size. Everywhere corridors ran off in a dimness of white walls and faded cream paint, with here and there the dark rectangle of an oil painting in which troops of hunters moved obscurely through Italian landscapes which time or the varnish bottle had umbered to a cavernous gloom. The house, moreover, had this peculiarity: that its contents, so soon as one should stray in person or in glance from, as it were, certain narrow channels leading from various inhabited corners to the living-rooms of the family, were for the most part swathed and sheeted after the fashion of large establishments from which the owner has taken his departure for the time. Mr Bolderwood had among his fancies, it appeared, that of living like a caretaker in his own rambling halls, and this although the confused multitude of his retainers would surely have been adequate to the dusting and polishing of the mansion several times over. Moreover, some past Bolderwood had owned a taste in statuary; another had collected armour; a third had been interested in grandfather clocks. All these objects, in common with the chairs, benches, tables and the like which lined, after the common fashion of ornament rather than utility, the broad corridors of the house, were swathed in a white sheeting from which one could have puffed the dust in passing. The effect could not well be other than spectral. It was as if, in addition to the vociferous Denis and his rout, the place owned another body of inhabitants, who waited, shrouded and silent in the gathering dusk, the stroke of some hour that should release them to their own nocturnal offices. Nor indeed did their silence appear entire, since the wind as it sighed through Killyboffin had the effect of prompting them to sinister confabulation, the result of which was already an uneasy twitch and stir in their enveloping garments.

Mr Thewless, when he remarked this rather uncanny effect, glanced in some anxiety at Humphrey. But at the moment, at least, the boy made nothing of it. He had paused, driven by hunger though he professed to be, by a window on a broad landing, attracted by an equal prospect of sea and mountain there revealed. The gentle declivities by which Killyboffin Hall was surrounded already lay for the most part in shadow, but, on higher ground beyond, the level light of late evening was still brilliant upon emerald fields, white or pink cottages and, in the farther distance, dun bogs scarred by the darker brown of peat cuttings. Here and there along the dykes and hedges that demarcated the tiny fields lay inexplicable streaks and splashes of colour—orange and crimson and ultramarine —much as if, casually but to a happy effect, an artist had scattered his brightest pigments over the picture.

"Wool," said Humphrey. "Isn't that it? They dye it them-selves and put it out like that to dry. And look! There's an old woman boiling something up in a cauldron. That must be wool too. And those girls are taking it from her and carrying it on their heads in baskets. I've seen that in Italy. They're taking it to those others to wash in the stream. And—I say!—just look at the hillsides. You'd think they were so empty, and yet there are people all over them. And in those same gorgeous colours too."

Mr Thewless looked, and saw that all these appearances were as Humphrey had remarked. Everywhere on the hill-sides, and to distances that were almost remote, one could pick out slowly moving specks of brilliant colour.

"There's always something happening in an Irish country-side."

It was Ivor Bolderwood who spoke; he had come up behind them and was looking mildly out through his large glasses. Humphrey turned to him with an alacrity from which Mr Thewless gathered that the young man had substantially gained his pupil's confidence. "Are these people very poor?" Humphrey asked.

Ivor nodded soberly. "Very poor indeed, most of them. They have to go miles and miles to the bogs where they can cut peat, and not all of them have even a donkey to bring it home on. And you will see them gathering seaweed as the only manure they can afford for their patches of potatoes. Still, they dye the cloth they make for themselves in those brave colours, and they know a lot of stories and poetry and songs. Some of those bright, moving specks are thinking of no more than their suppers, I expect—as you and I are doing." Ivor paused and chuckled as Humphrey faintly blushed. "But the minds of others are moving through old, old poems that nobody, perhaps, has ever written down—poems about kings and heroes and all the sad and splendid things that beautiful women have brought into the world."

"Is that really true?" Humphrey was round-eyed. "Could I go among them, and would they tell me, and could I put it in a book?"

Ivor Bolderwood laughed. "A good many people have tried to do that. And there is a difficult language you would have to learn before you could hope to understand a great deal. But I think some of them might tell you something."

Humphrey glanced from Ivor to his tutor, and Mr Thewless thought proper to offer an interested and approving murmur. Here, he judged, was a vein of interest altogether more wholesome than anything represented by the boy's current reading, or by the matters on which he conversed with Miss Liberty. "We shall certainly," he said, "try to get into conversation with some of them."

"So long as they don't suppose you to be folk off the trawlers." And Ivor pointed in the other direction, where from their present height they could just see the masts and funnel of a vessel anchored some way out from a little pier. "They dislike the way the foreigners, who don't speak even English, often enough, come and eat out the country. But some of these sailors are interesting folk too. There's Viking blood in some of them, and presently they will be off in their dirty little ships to the places from which their ancestors sailed to harry Ireland. In quite a short time that tub out there may have rounded the North Cape, and instead of these tiny Irish fields and cottages the sailors may be seeing the sort of things the Ancient Mariner saw: icebergs and the aurora borealis—or, at this time of year, the midnight sun."

> "And ice mast-high came floating by
> As green as emerald."

Humphrey, now staring out to sea, quoted the lines shyly but in a glow of pleasure. "But don't you think the bit about the moon is the best? *The moving moon went up the sky*——" He broke off suddenly. "Hullo, here's something else. And—I say! —isn't she wizard?"

Round a precipitous headland which bounded the scene— the same from which Miss Liberty had conjectured that there must be a superlative view—there had appeared a vessel which Mr Thewless, unversed in maritime matters, could have defined only as an outsize motorboat. An affair of gleaming

171

white paint and flashing brass, its thrusting bows, flowing lines and flattened stern suggested formidable speed and power, while the scale upon which it was built seemed indicative of a craft built for blue water. Mr Thewless looked at it with mild but genuine interest, Humphrey with an enthusiasm which this time was a little conventional, Ivor Bolderwood in swift and knowledgeable appraisal. "She's certainly rather grand," the last-named said. "We usually get only the most modest pleasure-craft bothering about Killyboffin." His fingers drummed for a moment on the window-pane. "Well, we had better go down, or Denis will have the triumph of announcing dinner before we're all there, after all." He turned pleasantly to Mr Thewless. "I do hope that you will get more amusement than annoyance out of our way of things here. We can at least make some interesting expeditions. The pre-Celtic antiquities are numerous, and I have always wanted to go over them with an authority."

Mr Thewless was pleased. That an amateur in Roman archæology was competent to pronounce upon the monuments of prehistoric Ireland was assuredly something that young Ivor Bolderwood was much too well informed to suppose. But the success of this sort of compliment lies all in its manner, and at the end of his exhausting day (or what he supposed to himself to be its end) Mr Thewless found himself sitting down to dinner with feelings of considerable pleasure in the society of his hosts.

Nor, he presently discovered, was the dinner itself such as to depress the spirits. Although the boxty was certainly in evidence, it was given more prominence by the elder Mr Bolderwood in his conversation than by Denis as he handed the dishes; and Mr Thewless was more aware of the excellence of the salmon and the perfection of the hock. His host, it is true, was still much troubled about the eggs, and supposed that for breakfast it was impossible that they should have anything but siot or skirlie-mirlie. Ivor, while he refrained from disputing this, pointed to the sustaining fact that in four days they would undoubtedly be eating grouse—and grouse,

172

moreover, which they should owe to Humphrey's rapidly increasing skill with a shot-gun. And at this Humphrey, who not much more than twenty-four hours before had been repudiating with vast humanitarian indignation the suggestion that he should slaughter living things, and who after that again had been clutching the same weapon as a resource against imaginary spies and assassins, produced in high pleasure the modest disclaimers proper in well-mannered persons of his age. Mr Thewless felt eminently satisfied, and his various meaningless alarms, together with the absurd but harmless conduct of the men with the ambulance, altogether assumed their proper proportions in his mind. He had discovered that Killyboffin was on the telephone, and he had thus been able to send a telegram to Sir Bernard Paxton, informing him of the safe arrival of his son. And when he considered Humphrey's present equable state, and remembered the sort of dire intelligence which at one time he had been persuaded it might be necessary to despatch to his father, he saw how much he himself must at one point have been thrown off his balance. Humphrey, it was true, was still going to be nervously disturbed and thoroughly difficult from time to time; Mr Thewless stood in no doubt as to that. But Ivor Bolderwood was going to be an excellent person to take part of the strain; already he was absorbing the boy's interest with well-informed talk about remote places and peoples; he was much what Mr Thewless himself aspired to be: simultaneously instructive and entertaining.

Nevertheless, Mr Thewless, despite his own sense of nervous relaxation, presently found himself wondering whether Humphrey was not up to his tricks again. There are children in whose presence small objects are liable to drop inexplicably off the mantelpiece, or to levitate in air and glide quaintly to another corner of the room. But in the presence of his pupil, Mr Thewless had come to believe, it was rather the furniture of the mind that was apt to suffer disconcerting small displacements; and he was by no means certain that something of the sort was not now beginning to tinge the consciousness of his elder companions. It was possible, again, that the boy had produced this effect not merely telepathically but by some direct communication to Ivor Bolderwood during their first ramble with the shot-gun. Perhaps he had assured his newly-found cousin that during his journey from London he had been the interesting centre of sundry alarming melodramatic adventures. And perhaps Ivor, abundantly sensible as he appeared to be, had been a little shaken by the odd conviction which Humphrey had the trick of importing into his fantasies.

It was certainly true that Ivor, in spite of his competence as an entertainer, was unable to keep some part of his thoughts from straying elsewhere. It was as if he felt intermittently impelled to fine calculation on some state of affairs altogether unforeseen. Perhaps Humphrey had indeed told him a vast deal of nonsense and he was debating with himself whether the boy's tutor was likely to have received the same absurd confidences; and, if not, whether he was the sort of man with whom a difficult situation might usefully be discussed. And this reading of the matter Mr Thewless was for a time the more inclined to in that he had very markedly the sense of being appraised. Miss Liberty herself, in fact, fixing upon him her wholly enigmatical eye, had scarcely given him this uncomfortable feeling more strongly. He was reminded that he was, after all, a mere substitute for Captain Cox, that favoured young man whom some intimate bereavement had removed at the last moment from the scene. It was natural that his hosts should be disposed to wonder whether Sir Bernard Paxton's second choice was a reliable man for his job.

But this chastening reflection was presently replaced by another. It became evident as Mr Thewless's perceptions sharpened themselves under the material recruitment afforded by Mr Bolderwood's table that if considerations of this sort were active in Ivor's mind so too were others of a different order. To what might be termed the atmospheric effects of Killyboffin—the genius of the place for disconcerting suggestions of murmured colloquy, stealthy movement, and all the imponderables commonly associated with edifices of much greater antiquity—the young man must be abundantly inured.

It was natural, when the night wind, flapping the worn carpets in remote corridors or tinkling somewhere in abandoned candelabra, suggested the rapid tread and clinking accoutrements of some army of invading dwarves, or the rattle of some mouldering upper casement sounded like a discharge of small arms, that Mr Thewless himself should feel a certain irrational disposition to glance over his sholder. But it was surprising that Ivor Bolderwood should indefinably betray a similar tendency, or convey, by a certain wariness of regard upon door and window, an obscure apprehension of physical insecurity. A poet, Humphrey had declared, should keep a sword upstairs; Ivor's manner, even as he conversed absorbingly about the Sahara and the Caribbean, betrayed some sense that it might be useful to have one under the table. And at this a horrid doubt came to Mr Thewless. He feared that Ivor—whose talk, after all, hinted at an imagination romantic in cast—might, despite his appearance of eminent good sense, prove to be such another as Miss Liberty—one with whom he would have to wrestle in the task of keeping cobweb and chimera out of Humphrey's head.

But at least it was different with the elder Mr Bolderwood. Despite the strain of fancy revealed in his manner of life at Killyboffin, his mind appeared to be of a reassuringly solid cast, and the only disturbance to which it was at present subject was one still connected with his recalcitrant poultry. A fourth glass of hock had produced in this matter something like the dawn of illumination, and it was becoming clear to him that he was confronted, not with an unnatural and unseasonable continence on the part of the creatures concerned, but simply with a new and monstrous instance of the worthlessness and dishonesty of his retainers. It was his misfortune to be subjected by these to every species of robbery and extortion, and now they were taking the very eggs out of his guests' mouths—doubtless to sell them at unreasonable prices to the black marketeers, smugglers and bandits by whom the whole countryside was now overrun. Not since the heyday of the Troubles, indeed, had a wellnigh universal lawlessness so prevailed; housebreaking had become common and arson might be expected to spring up again at any time. For two pins he would return to South America or settle in some atrocious part of Surrey.

This comparatively harmless talk was for the most part directed to Mr Thewless. Humphrey, engaged with Ivor, clearly gave no heed to it. And thus dinner passed comfortably enough. It was followed, as a preliminary to packing Humphrey off to bed, by a stroll upon the terrace. Mr Thewless found the ritual a trifle chilly, and he judged that the tumbledown statuary, dimly revealed by a moon now in its last quarter, was depressing rather than picturesque. Behind the house the sough of the ocean could be faintly heard; sparsely on the hillsides, and to an effect of great loneliness, there gleamed a yellow light from cottage windows; periodically the beam from a lighthouse on some adjacent headland swept over the uppermost story of the house and passed on like a hunter's noose that has failed to snare its prey. Humphrey was delighted with the effect, and at this Mr Thewless found himself being foolishly relieved. The truth was, he realised, that he had fallen into the way of being unnecessarily apprehensive as to what might alarm his pupil's sensibilities and precipitate undesirable imaginative repercussions. He was the more startled, therefore, at the sudden starting up of what might well have proved disastrous in this regard.

The Bolderwoods, father and son, had fallen behind together for domestic discussion, and Mr Thewless was about to make some remark to Humphrey about the possibility of one day visiting the lighthouse that was at play above them, when the voice of the elder Mr Bolderwood was heard clearly behind them in tones of characteristic incautious exasperation.

"Bless my soul, Ivor! You don't mean to tell me that the imbeciles have put the boy in the haunted room?"

Mr Thewless, appalled by this luckless stroke of fate, glanced swiftly at Humphrey and saw that mischief had indeed been done. The boy looked thoroughly alarmed. But in a second Ivor had overtaken them, and laid his hand on Humphrey's shoulder with a cheerful laugh. "Humphrey," he said, "would give quite a lot for the chance of sleeping in a haunted room!

But, as a matter of fact, I rather want to move him to the one next my own. Shall you mind, Humphrey? It means that we can slip out quite early with the guns, and nobody need be disturbed."

"Excellent!" Mr Thewless had the wit instantly to back up this deft sparing of his pupil's *amour propre*. "I should hate to be wakened up by Humphrey and his gun bumping about together next door to *me*. And perhaps you will be able to bring something back for breakfast."

Ivor laughed again. "To eke out the skirlie-mirlie? Perhaps we shall. Well, come along, and we'll make the move now."

And at this the party returned to the house and, without calling upon menial assistance, transferred an evidently relieved Humphrey to his new quarters. There he was bidden good night, and Mr Thewless was carried off by his hosts to desultory conversation and a generous provision of Irish whiskey in Mr Bolderwood's study. At eleven o'clock Mr Bolderwood announced that he proposed to lock up the house.

This proved to be an occupation of some labour, and began with the securing of a door which shut off the servants' quarters—an out-of-the-way proceeding sufficiently explained by Mr Bolderwood's whimsical conviction of the unreliability and dishonesty of those who attended him. There was then much bolting of other doors and securing of windows—and this again was unremarkable in one who believed the countryside to be alive with robbers. Mr Thewless, however—although by this time thoroughly sleepy, slightly fuddled and only intermittently attentive—was mildly surprised when his host proceeded to make a thorough search of the house. In this operation, which was rendered considerably more troublesome by the fact that the only artificial light at Killyboffin was supplied by oil-lamps and candles, Mr Bolderwood was assisted by his son with rather more vigour than was necessary simply for the purpose of humouring an eccentric parent. Whether the proceeding was customary, and with a rational basis in the apprehension of robbery, or whether it was a matter of the tiresome imaginative aura of Humphrey Paxton at work once more, was a question that Mr Thewless was now much too tired to entertain. When the Bolderwoods had satisfied themselves that reasonable security reigned at Killyboffin he took up his candle, bade his hosts good night, and took himself thankfully to bed.

CHAPTER XV

IT WAS THE HEALTHFUL custom of Mr Thewless to sleep with his window open to its fullest extent. When he had undressed, therefore, he extinguished the lamp which had been burning in his room, drew back his curtains, and threw open the casement. The waning moon was hidden in cloud and the night was almost completely dark; he had the sense, rather than the perception, of standing at a considerable elevation, and he remembered that what was commanded from this aspect of the house must be a view of the sea. A single light was visible at a distance not easy to determine; presently he distinguished that this was faintly reflected in water; and it occurred to him that it might well represent a riding-light on the motor cruiser noticed by Humphrey before dinner. There was still a chilly breeze, and Mr Thewless climbed without more ado into bed. He had been not without fears, reasonably bred by the marked unreliability of the furniture around him, that the night might bring discomforts of its own. He found, however, that the bed was in excellent order and soothingly sheeted in the finest linen. As he tumbled in, he became aware of a dim radiance gliding smoothly across the ceiling of his room. It must be the faint reflection of the beam from the lighthouse that he had previously remarked as touching the upper part of the house. The effect was too slight to be disturbing. Within a minute Mr Thewless was asleep.

It would have been no more than fair had his late vicissitudes earned him a full night's oblivion. But his undisturbed sleep was of short duration, and was succeeded by uneasy and perplexing dreams. In these he was himself at first the only living participant and he moved amid a décor which his waking consciousness—as we have seen, nicely informed in

178

such matters—would have assured him reflected the alarms and dismays which had attended a singularly frightening episode of his career undertaken jointly with his mother some fifty years before. Painful progressions through narrow tunnels, terrifying drops through space, sudden assaults upon eye and ear by unanalysable lights and sounds, the dread presage of unknown modes of being: all these things, in a confusion somewhat suggestive of the best modern music, formed as it were the overture to his nocturnal drama. And then it was as if the curtain rose and slowly, with a careful regard for the sluggish understanding of the audience, the actors appeared one by one. The first of these was Mr Thewless himself, aware—and surprised, but only midly so, at his awareness—that he was no longer very substantially Mr Thewless, since he had assumed the vastly more distinguished role or identity of Sir Bernard Paxton. Mr Thewless having become Sir Bernard, and having gained thereby an insight into Sir Bernard, remarked that Sir Bernard (who was himself) was by no means so impressive a spectacle when viewed from within as he (Mr Thewless, that was to say) had found him when viewed from without. In particular he was prone to behave in an indecisive and timorous fashion when confronted by heights. And this was the position now. In a vast, void darkness Thewless-Paxton trod falteringly the brink of some unimaginable precipice. Far below shone a single light dimly reflected in dreadful waters; to a sickening plunge towards this he felt himself irresistibly impelled; his head swam, his knees gave way beneath him and he fell. But from the darkness a strong arm stretched out and held him and, turning in air, he recognised that his preserver was Humphrey Paxton, who was his son. Again he trod the precipice, the boy holding his hand and guiding him as he went, and presently their path through darkness began to rock and pulse beneath them. It was a path no longer, but the corridor of an express train, its outer side cut away to expose them to the hurtling night, its inner giving upon a series of compartments through the glass of which there gibbered and mowed monsters and prodigies in endless sinister diversity. But in every compartment too sat

179

Ivor Bolderwood—always in the same corner an Ivor Bolder-wood, his glance composed and direct through his large round glasses, in his lap a bowl of boxty from which he ceaselessly fed the horrors around him with a long-handled wooden spoon. But whether Ivor was master of the rout or whether he was in their thrall Mr Thewless could by no means determine as the boy hurried him onwards down the interminable train, his lips parted and his eyes, bright with challenge, fixed upon some distant and shrouded goal.

The dream seemed interminable: always the monsters, always an Ivor, always the swaying corridor beneath the feet. Once Mr Thewless turned his head and behind him saw the bearded man with pebble glasses, in his hand a bludgeon raised and prepared to strike. But even as Mr Thewless shrank in anticipation of the blow that bearded man was transformed into Mr Wambus, swathed and powerless in his bandages, like a corpse in some old picture. Once—and once only—the dread monotony of the teeming compartments was varied, and Mr Thewless glimpsed the solitary figure of Miss Liberty, a volume by Sapper in her lap. But her face was blank and sight-less; or rather—he realised with a chill of sudden horror—it was no face at all, but simply the dial of a clock from which the hands had been wrenched so as to render it useless.

And now the unending train was devouring not only space but time as well; it was hurtling at such speed through æons of time that Mr Thewless recognised in a rhythmic sweep of light and darkness about him an actual procession of nights and days. And suddenly he knew the destination of the train. It was hurtling towards the sun. This was the goal upon which the eyes of the boy who still guided and supported him were set; ahead was nothing but empty space, with that vast con-flagration at the end. And then it was before him—burning, incandescent light. Mr Thewless felt the leap and lick of its vast tongues of flame upon his brow. He woke up.

Mr Thewless woke up and on his retina there glowed and swam a single orb of orange fire. He stared at it and instantly, from its voyaging place a thousand millions miles away, his mind made a wonderful leap at objective fact. Somebody had shone an electric torch in his face. Hence the sun as terminus to that unending journey; hence now this fading spot of colour on his brain. And this realisation was followed by another almost as immediate. The swift procession of nights and days through which his dream had moved as over a chequerboard of darkness and light had also been physically determined. It was dark now; presently there would pass over his ceiling the faint illumination from the lighthouse. In this illumination it would be possible to *see*.

Yet long before that tiny wash of light swept into the room he knew by some sufficient instinct what would be revealed by it. Watchers stood beside his bed, waiting in absolute stillness to know whether their inspection had aroused him. Mr Thewless kept his eyes shut and opened all his ears. A soft breathing was unquestionably distinguishable on either side of him.

The humble creatures that turn immobile at danger, and whom not even a thrusting stick or nudging toe can stir to any sign of life, have no monopoly of this primitive notion of self-protection. Mr Thewless had a very strong impulse simply to lie still, keep his eyes shut, and trust that the mysterious presences would depart. Indeed, this was less a proposal of his mind, a plan or craft to act on, than simply something that was happening to his body as it lay. Cautiously he endeavoured to flex a knee and was by no means convinced that he had the power to do so. He wondered if he could even open his mouth, and he remembered those worst nocturnal terrors of childhood in which there is reft from one the power of calling out.

And Mr Thewless endeavoured to seek security by returning into his dream. In his dream there had been safety amid innumerable hazards because . . . yes, because he had been in the charge of Humphrey Paxton. And suddenly, with an agility altogether surprising, Mr Thewless leapt out of bed. For Humphrey Paxton was *his* charge; he was responsible for the safety of the boy; and to hesitate in the face of undefined danger was to cling ignobly to the topsyturvy realm of sleep. It might be by his own bedside that threatening figures hovered. Nevertheless, he knew himself to be a person of no

181

consequence, and if they did so hover there this was merely incidental in some way to a design against the boy. Therefore it was the boy's safety that was to be seen to.

Thus did Mr Thewless for the moment bring wisdom from his dream. He leapt from his bed, aware of startled movement on either side of him, and by some paranormal sense of direction also dredged up from sleep, precipitated himself across and out of the room. In an instant he was at the next door, and as he opened it and entered the dim illumination from the lighthouse swept across it. It was, of course, empty and the bed undisturbed; his mind in prompting him to sudden action had missed a step, and he had forgotten about Humphrey's having been moved to another part of the house. He paused irresolutely, and as action failed him fear returned. There *were* people in his own room. It was a testing moment—and the more so because he saw before him a rational yet surely craven plan. The door on which his hand now rested had a key on its inner side. In an instant he could lock himself in, and from the refuge thus obtained raise a loud alarm. In a sense this was even his wisest, his most responsible, course. For if he returned to encounter the intruders alone it was very possible that he might be instantly and silently overpowered, and the villains might then achieve with impunity whatever further mischief they proposed.

But as these sensible considerations presented themselves to Mr Thewless's mind something altogether more potent and primitive stirred in his blood. Sapper, it might be said, and not simple sapience took control; a glorious anger sang suddenly in his ears; he took a deep breath and marched back to his own room. The corridor which he had briefly to traverse was for the moment sufficiently lit through some skylight to make observation possible to his sharpened sense. Nothing stirred in the long vista it presented. The intruders must be awaiting him in his own room still.

Mr Thewless belonged to a clerkly caste whose immemorial weapon has been words. As he took the half-dozen further steps that would confront him with the enemy he absurdly tested out on his inner ear some form of words that would confound them. He would point out that they had been detected, that the household contained a considerable number of able-bodied men, that firearms were available to these and—since prevarication was surely permissible in a situation like the present—that the police had already been summoned by telephone. But at the same time as he prepared this mere logomachy he had the good sense to wish himself possessed of a poker or even an empty bottle. And in default of anything of the sort, he clenched his fists in a manner suggesting itself to him as the right posture for pugilistic encounter and walked into his room.

He was standing in the middle of it and nothing had happened. The glint of light came and went, revealing seeming emptiness. He walked bodly to his bedside and lit his candle. Still nothing revealed itself. He searched, and satisfied himself that he was alone. And at that, feeling slightly giddy, he sat down on the bed.

Deep in the mind there is a clock that never goes wrong. Hypnotists can exploit it as an alarm, enjoining one to blow one's nose at four twenty-five next Thursday. Of this instrument, which is said to work with particular nicety during sleep, Mr Thewless was still sufficiently possessed to have an instinctive assurance that the interval during which he had been in Humphrey's late room was insufficient to have permitted anyone to escape down the corridor. He stood up and had a second look under his bed. He crossed to the window and satisfied himself that no creature not possessed of wings could have departed that way with any hope of an unbroken neck. And at this he sat down again upon his bed, possessed by a new alarm. The nature of this may be guessed. He feared that his imagination had been playing tricks with him—and doing so with more resounding success than any substantial sanity would have allowed. He was now resigned to believing himself highly susceptible to melodrama viewed as a sort of infection or plague, and even to the hypothesis—nebulous but nevertheless haunting—that he and his pupil were in some degree of *rapport* in matters of the sort. Yes, that would be it. Humphrey had been having a nightmare on the lines upon which his fantasy commonly ran, and the shadow of it had fallen upon himself at the other end of the house. But at least Humphrey, whether or not he too had actually awakened to the conviction of lurking presences, had not made night hideous with his alarms; and Mr Thewless was thankful that he had himself at the critical moment at least managed to refrain from doing this. Assuredly it had all been a figment. The only thing to do was to go to sleep again.

His candle afforded only the most feeble illumination, but when he turned to light the oil lamp which had stood at the bottom of his bed he found that in his hasty rising he had overturned it and knocked it to the floor. This was both tiresome and embarrassing, as was also the evidence of an extreme of terrified violence with which he must have acted. For his bed was in quite surprising confusion, its various furnishings tumbled around it and a heavy mattress, of the kind comfortably constructed with an interior springing, dragged cornerwise to the floor. This he now set about remedying, an apparently simple if vexatious task which presently revealed itself as as unexpected difficulty. At first he made considerable progress, only to find upon scrutiny that he had employed as an under sheet what was demonstrably some species of linen coverlet. To leave matters so disposed might be to excite surprise and even ridicule in Mr. Bolderwood's domestics in the morning. He therefore started again. But this time he could find no sheets at all; the candle was burning unnervingly near its socket; and for a moment he paused between irritation and discouragement.

In this pause his conscience stirred. If it was indeed true that his recent alarming experience was no more than a sympathetic response to some nightmare or even hallucination of Humphrey's was it not his duty to inform himself as to the boy's condition now? That Humphrey had raised no outcry was a fact capable of a distressing equally with a reassuring interpretation. Indeed, the fact that this abnormal experience had come to his tutor as some sort of message from another mind was surely an indication of that mind's having been perilously disturbed. And Mr Thewless had a sudden and vivid picture of the unfortunate child, prone to believe in sinister powers intent to shut him up in dark, confined spaces, lying strained and motionless in a bed round which he believed these powers to have gathered for a final onslaught. Humphrey's removal to another part of the house had not left him altogether happy—not because he judged Ivor Bolderwood other than in every way reliable, but because it was to himself, after all that the boy had been confided, and it was he, again, who was best acquainted with the distresses to which he was liable.

There was, then, nothing for it. He must go at once and see how Humphrey was getting on. If the boy proved to be peacefully sleeping there would be no harm done. And Mr Thewless, taking up his stump of candle in his holder, opened his door once more. As he did so, he remembered *why* Humphrey had been moved out of his first room. It was because he had unfortunately been let overhear the elder Mr Bolderwood remark that it was haunted.

Had Mr Thewless been asked if he believed in ghosts, he would have replied at some length, and in a fashion altogether philosophical or scientific. But all this would have boiled down to the statement that he *did*. Supernatural appearances were for him, in theory, an essentially harmless and highly interesting class of phenomena, for long—most unfortunately— merely vestigial in human experience, from an intelligent study of which it might be possible to draw important conclusions on the growth and structure of the human mind. Thus if manifestations of this order lurked in Humphrey's late room; if it had been anything of the sort that had intruded upon himself; if, out in the corridor now, forces aside from the common order of Nature waited patiently for any move Mr Thewless might make: if these things were so the circumstance was to be regarded essentially in the light of a "find." A philologist who stumbles upon some substantial vestige of a dying language, or an anthropologist who peers over a rock and surprises some last rehearsal of the immemorial ceremonies of a vanishing tribe, presented—again in theory—a fair parallel to Mr Thewless's situation now. And yet he did not feel quite like this. Killyboffin Hall showed several aspects to the world, and if the one predominant among these was benign, being represented by the cheerful irascibility and muddle of its owner, there was yet another which was distinctly inimical to the easy poise of highly educated persons. The mere manner on which the winds blew through the place, and the diversity of odd acoustic effects they produced, were things in themselves discomposing. The recurrent washes of faint light through this upper story, like an infinitely distant reflection of the flicker and flare of some infernal bonfire, brought another sense into the service of unsettlement. And again—for by this time Mr Thewless had got himself fairly into the corridor—there was the powerful tide of suggestion that seemed to sweep in from the untenanted quarters of the house, from the vistas of shrouded objects—or, better, forms that every branching corridor and open door revealed. Into one of these—it was some piece of sheeted statuary which, unaccountably, he had not noticed before—he almost bumped as he turned left from his room and addressed himself to the task, not altogether simple, of making his way to Humphrey's new quarters.

There was a staircase to go down and presently another to ascend, with some stretch of corridor intervening and at either end. But he was now, he believed, thoroughly awake, and he set off confidently enough. If his wandering disturbed his hosts he might look a little foolish, but it was reasonable to suppose that they would accept his explanations sympathetically. And at least there seemed to be no possibility of a tiresome encounter with wakeful servants, since one of Mr Bolderwood's whims had effectively barred these from the main part of the building. He advanced, therefore, with his candle-stick held before him, his free hand shielding as effectively as possible its uncertain flame. He had, he presently discovered, forgotten to bring his matches, so that an extinguishing puff of wind might be awkward unless he cared to go back and remedy the omission. But this he found himself obscurely disinclined to do. And the candle, for that matter, seemed not vital to him, for all along this corridor, and over the stair-head which he now glimpsed dimly before him, there

still through sundry uncurtained windows played the intermittent gleam from the lighthouse—as also, he now noticed,
a steady and yet more tenuous illumination which spoke of the
waning moon as having emerged from cloud.

All this was almost cheerful. Nevertheless, Mr Thewless, his
recent experiences having been as they were, would have been
insensitive indeed had he not powerfully owned an impulse to
peer warily about him as his bare feet (he had not paused for
slippers or dressing-gown) felt cautiously over the expanses of
worn carpet which he trod. First there was a line of large
pictures so darkened that they might have been windows
giving upon a starless night; his candle as he passed fleetingly
conjured from their lower margins, above the dull gleam of
tarnished gold frames, marble steps, the nether folds of flowing
draperies, broken lances and abandoned armour, here and
there a human limb splayed out in some martial disaster or,
it might be, voluptuous excess. These appearances were un-
alarming in themselves; yet their suggestion of violent matters
transacting themselves just beyond his present circumscribed
field of vision was not without its effect upon Mr Thewless,
and irrational apprehensiveness would doubtless have gained
upon him again even had it not been for the sudden appearance of the dog.

It was a creature that swept him back at once into that world
of prodigies within which his railway journey had for a time
submerged him; this less because of its evident ferocity as it
stood suddenly and solidly before him than because of its
unnatural size. It was a dog quite as big—and that in the
sense of quite as *tall*—as Mr Thewless himself; and it seemed to
have sprung from nowhere in this silent house and to be
regarding the pyjama'd figure before it much in the light of
a wholly unexpected nocturnal snack. In this crisis Mr
Thewless's brain worked very well. From the size of the
animal he concluded that it was extinct; if it was extinct it
was stuffed; and a stuffed dog needs no collops. Nevertheless,
the intellectual conviction that he was merely in the presence
of a pretty museum specimen of the ancient Irish wolf-hound
did not altogether end the matter. There was a glint in the

creature's verisimilar glass eye that almost defied the reassuring voice of reason; and it was from the moment of this encounter that Mr Thewless looked not merely about him but *behind*. The stuffed hound remained harmlessly immobile, but it had done its work.

Mr Thewless looked nervously over his shoulder, and the motion bred the instant suspicion that he was being followed. This too was something against which reason's voice spoke loudly enough. Certainly there was no occasion to suppose that anything *physical* was following him, since he had concluded that, in the first instance, nothing physical had been involved. Moreover, the light was for the moment adequate for a careful inspection, and there was demonstrably nothing in the long corridor behind him except the now foreshortened pictures, and the stern of the stuffed dog, and a number of those sheeted objects—statues, armour or whatever—which were pervasive about the house. Mr Thewless paused for a moment to convince himself of the folly of this latest feeling; then, without again turning his head, he marched on to the head of the stairs he must descend.

But now his ears were only all too open, and Killyboffin was suddenly alive for him with whisperings, soft footfalls, muffled groans and all the hackneyed gamut—as he desperately told himself—of conventional supernatural solicitation. He had only, he felt, to allow credulity another inch to its tether and there would at once be added to these the final banality of dismally clanking chains. He was at the stair-head; a half-turn was topographically essential to his further progress; *one* more look behind, therefore, he might venture without too gross a capitulation to his own senseless doubts. Arguing thus, he looked—and the result ought to have been wholly reassuring. The corridor was empty still; only the same objects met his scrutiny. And yet he was at once—and as he had not yet been—alarmed. There was a sense in which this new trepidation could not be called baseless, since he was convinced that it was occasioned by some specific fact. But what this was he was unable to determine; turning face forwards once more and taking his first step downstairs, he was aware only of the uncomfortable fact of water creeping in a chill trickle down his spine. And at the same time there seeped into mind an anecdote of the most extreme inconsequence. It was that of the bishop who, glancing into a field, remarked casually that it contained a hundred and eight sheep—a circumstance presently verified by the computations of his curate. The point of the story, as Mr Thewless knew, lay in the fact that the number of objects that the normal mind can instantaneously enumerate is five. But if the point was tenuous the application was more so, and by the time that he was half-way down the first flight of stairs the mental image accompanying this odd reminiscence had been replaced by a melting succession of others, dredged up from childhood, in which, behind unfortunate persons benighted in dark forests, there peeped and crept maleficent goblin bands.

Almost, he saw himself presently in panic flight through the sleeping house; and it was as a rudimentary test of self-control that he now stopped by the staircase-window as if to look at his leisure into the night. But this pause was more definitive than anything that had happened yet, so absolute was the sense it brought him of other entities pausing too. Yes, behind him *they* had stopped because he had stopped; and when he moved on *they* would move on too.

To allow his apprehensions to crystallise in this way around a pronoun so consecrated in a popular consciousness to expressing the menace of the unknown was, he very well knew, a step towards disintegration steeper than any he now trod again to reach the lower corridor. The wind—although he had a sense that, outside, it had almost died away—continued to prowl the house, and only the more eerily because now its operations were to be apprehended only by the tip of the senses. If the pattering footfalls were softer it was because, at some sinister crisis, they were approaching with additional stealth; if the breeze no longer flapped at one's pyjamas it was the more possible to feel it as the chill breath of some sepulchral phantom on one's neck.

Gaining the lower corridor, he found a deeper darkness. Here the sweep of the lighthouse was without effect, and only the faintest glint of moonlight percolated through a line of windows on his right hand. His candle, now all but guttering, had become vital to him; were it to go out he could only grope. For some yards he pressed forward rapidly—but not too rapidly, lest the little flame should be extinguished by the wind of his own speed. The corridor was much like that above, with the same embrowned paintings and shrouded statuary and ranged furniture along the walls. Once more he stopped and looked back. And this time it was as if he had caught the presences in the act, for his eye had surely glimpsed some suddenly arrested movement, some swiftly frozen gesture, in the short vista behind him. Again he thought of the bishop and the sheep, and this time the association tentatively explained itself. Had he—all instantaneously, with the speed of the unconscious mind—computed the number of the objects dispersed behind him, and found that they held no tally with a similar unconscious computation made upon his previous traversing of the ground? He was moving forward again before this speculation, in the circumstances highly creditable to his intellectual vitality, had fully formed itself in his mind; when it had done so he took some steps further and this time swung round with all the speed he could contrive. The issue of this manœuvre, which precisely reproduced the ancient playground game of Grandmother's Steps or Fox and Geese, was at once successful and completely disastrous. It was successful because the shadowing presences did not on this occasion freeze into immobility with adequate speed—so that indeed, were the game being played according to the rules, Mr Thewless would have achieved the decisive stroke of returning them to their "base." What in fact he saw was two sheeted figures, entirely ghostly after the prescriptions of Christmas pantomime, hastily assume the postures appropriate to objects of statuary shrouded after the bizarre Killyboffin fashion. This untoward spectacle, as it were inverse to those which gratified Pygmalion and liquidated Don Juan, he had no opportunity to probe, for the disaster attendant upon his whirling round was as decisive as it was inevitable. His candle went out.

190

Were Mr Thewless's adventures in the hands of what is called an atmospheric writer, it might be possible to credibilise a fact which, as matters stand, can only be baldly stated. Killyboffin in the small hours had now wrought upon Humphrey Paxton's tutor to such a degree that, while retaining considerable power of rational thought, he was lamentably confused about the probable nature of the entities behind him; about the order of being, as it may be put, to which they belonged. Had he been convinced that they were human marauders, mere breakers-in such as his host was apprehensive of, the problem presented, even if uncomfortable, would have been comparatively simple. Correspondingly, had he kept clearly in focus the concept or theory of supernatural appearances, he would have been able to regain something of the poise of the open-minded, the speculative man. But all that Mr Thewless could now predicate of the forces behind him was this: that they stood for Danger.

But the peril was whose? For Mr Thewless, standing as he was in darkness and with his enemies creeping up behind, the achieving of this question was what the thoughtful reader will already having recognised it as being: a signal triumph of the mind. Were he being pursued with intent to silence him before an alarm could be given, this could have been done long ago—and with greater advantage while he was still substantially remote from the other occupants of the mansion. If on the other hand, the constitution of his pursuers was such that they were without the power to command physical agencies, and must work their malign will by a mere operation of terror upon the mind, they would surely do better to bar the way between Mr Thewless and the moral support which he would gain by making his way to his friends. It seemed not their object, then, either to offer him direct violence or to lead or drive him into the prescriptive hazards of precipice, flood or bog. They were, in the strictest sense, trailing him. They were, and with all the unobtrusiveness at their command, keeping him in view until his present pilgrimage through the house was completed.

In other words, Humphrey was the quarry. Mr Thewless

did not, it must be repeated, at all clearly formulate the quarry of *what*; nor did he, standing with his extinguished candle while the house muttered and whispered around him, endeavour to relate this conviction to what had hitherto been his overriding sense of the total situation in which, with the boy, he had involved himself. He simply knew that it was the boy that was threatened. And he knew that this knowledge, held securely as gospel for the time, imposed upon him a complete reversal of his present plan. For it was a clear inference from what had been revealed to him that these sinister powers were without knowledge of where Humphrey was now lodged. They had penetrated to—or was it conjured themselves into apprehensible shape in?—the haunted room from which Ivor Bolderwood had caused him to be removed; failing to find him there they had taken a cast next door and so disturbed his tutor; they had now divined the injudicious purpose by which that tutor was at present actuated, and proposed simply that he should lead them where they wanted to go. There was thus for Mr Thewless only one course consonant with the safety of his charge. He must turn round in the darkness now enveloping him; march, or grope, straight past, or upon, his adversaries; and so return to his own room.

In this formidable posture of his affairs it would be ungenerous to say that he was frightened; what chiefly confronted him was the rudimentary business of getting his limbs to obey the entirely unequivocal dictates of his will. For in this episode of nightmare (and it did occur to him, indeed, positively to wonder whether he might not, in point of ultimately comforting fact, be at this moment simply if unsoundly asleep)—in this episode of nightmare he found himself for a struggling moment circumstanced as in certain veritable nightmares of long ago. In these, which drew their material, he had been accustomed to believe, from an early and soon exhausted interest in the mechanism of the homely "tram," he had been wont to find himself, at sufficiently awkward moments, rooted to the ground as if by the agency of some magnet powerfully reinforced by electrical means. And this was his situation now. Neither his right foot nor his left was prepared to accept the hazard of detaching itself from the worn carpeting to which it was clamped. Mr Thewless, in the fullest sense of the slangy phrase, was "in a fix."

What came to his rescue was the decidedly chilly quality of the night to one attired exiguously for slumber. Mr Thewless sneezed. And at this the charm was miraculously broken. He found himself advancing, with what confidence was possible in a medium between the Cimmerian and the Stygian, in the direction that he wished to go. From the mere fact of this, unpromising though in some aspects it seemed, there was more than a grain of confidence to be extracted; and this less desperate mood was now reinforced by more factors than one. He had the impression that in the darkness in front of him his tergiversation was the occasion of perturbed conference; of a whispering suggesting that, whether his adversaries were creatures in or out of nature, his so decided move had, at least for the moment, "got them guessing." Moreover, it occurred to him that his candlestick, being of the massive and ornamental rather than of the utilitarian or dormitory kind, was by no means rendered entirely useless to him by reason of the temporary desuetude of its primary function. By reversing it in his grasp so that its heavy base was at a farthest remove from his hand, and exalting in air the makeshift bludgeon thus achieved, he could provide himself with what, for one without the opportunity of choice, was a fortuitously accorded weapon to be thankful for.

Mr Thewless, then, retraced his steps with some firmness, although to guide him he had now only the dim outlines of the row of windows on his left, together with a slightly more substantial radiance percolating down the staircase which he must climb. Nevertheless, it was in the nature of the transposition that had taken place that of anything of occult or other significance to be seen he should now have a substantial and unintermittent view. And in a moment he did become aware, upon the evidence of certain swiftly gliding silhouettes across the line of the windows just mentioned, that the enemy was in retreat before him. It was feasible, by rising only a little to the imaginative occasion, to frame it that he was now

193

the hunter and these the hunted. And at this he felt within himself a certain mounting exhilaration which was yet not an index, perhaps, of any very reliable emotional tone. Indeed, Mr Thewless, had he known it, was approaching very near a point of complete nervous exhaustion. There would have to be but one further turn of the screw—the revelation, say, of a Parthian strategy in the apparent debacle before him—altogether to upset such balance as, through the course of his trials, he had hitherto very creditably attained.

And of this now marginal and precarious nature of his resistance the passage of the staircase was an immediate index. He pressed up it boldly, but amid a physical distress having the effect of rendering each tread some two feet high. It was steep, it was gigantic, it was interminable; and, moreover, he acutely felt the possible advantage which, in point of any sudden assault, the retreating creatures might gain from their superior position on the incline. And again—and this assuredly was more ominous—he derived no satisfaction from the reflection that he was climbing steadily into a lesser darkness; into what was, comparatively speaking, a medium of light. It was clearly within our friend's recollection that the upper corridor upon which his own room lay admitted through some system of skylights considerably more of whatever mild moonlight lay without; and, moreover, that the periodic illumination from the lighthouse lent fleetingly to the scene a quality of which the only description at once compendious and fair would be one free of any hint of inconvenient tenebrosity. In this simple thought there ought to have been gratification enough. The entities which, whether preternatural or merely sordidly criminal, could scarcely be regarded as other than thoroughly sinister in their nocturnal intentions, and which, having—as he somehow fleetingly and all obscurely knew—assumed the protective covering of his own impudently ravished sheets, had pursued him far into the recesses of the mansion, he was now —by a mere assertion, it might fairly be said, of his own perilously stretched but yet supervalent will—pressing triumphantly back to what, at least for him, had been the very *fons et origo* of their existence. This was surely decisive success, and by its token he ought to have been eager for whatever final *éclairissement* might now be achieved. But this was not at all the way in which Mr Thewless's mind found itself working. At any moment now there might indeed be something clearly to be seen. But Mr Thewless was with a definiteness unparalleled in his remotest recollection without the shadow of list to see it.

But now this curious episode in the Paxton affair, of which the present chapter has stumblingly attempted a rude chronicle, was nearing its term. Mr Thewless had reached the topmost stair, and his knees were trembling. Nevertheless, he now attempted and achieved what he had not hitherto ventured upon: he ran. The door of his own room was open and visible before him; he had only to gain it, bolt it behind him, and tumble into a bed which, whether sheeted or not, offered a sufficiency of bedclothes of rougher integument to permit of his gaining the species of somewhat infantile security now with a quite resplendent candour uppermost in his mind. He ran— a swift glance having delusively assured him that the corridor was as void as he could hope. But even as the goal was within his grasp this assurance was betrayed, and one of the creatures of his long struggle—whether of design or through some hasty miscalculation of the line on which he stood— appeared hard before the doorway, barring his path. At this Mr Thewless perforce looked indeed—and what he saw was a shrouded figure hurriedly assume the posture, sufficiently hinted beneath an enveloping sheet, of some placidly posed Apollo of the Phidean age. It was a grotesque revelation beneath which Mr Thewless felt his nether limbs turning shamefully to water; and it is once more a mark of his quality that he now decisively acted in the very terminal moment in which action was possible to him. The candlestick which he still bore as a bludgeon he turned incontinently into a missile which he hurled with all his residual force at the figure before him. At this the figure gave a yelp of pain—a yelp swiftly overtaken in Mr Thewless's ear by a roaring as of great waters. Mistily he saw the figure stagger, the sheet drop away and then—for a brief flash, whether of revelation or hallucination—the swimming, melting, fading features of the man with the beard and the pebble glasses.

Even at this juncture he cannot altogether have lost consciousness. For, mingled with painful and massive auditory phenomena assuredly subjective in origin, he heard shouts, running footsteps, breaking glass, a violently closing door, glimpsed the elder Mr Bolderwood, red-faced and brandishing a revolver; glimpsed too the younger Mr Bolderwood, pale, swiftly calculating, similarly armed. These things faded, and he next knew that his head was being raised on a small, taut arm. He opened his eyes and saw that it was Humphrey who supported him—supported him much as in his dream an interminable æon ago. The boy was looking down at him with compunction, with amusement innocent of all malice. Mr Thewless felt that things had passed off not too badly and that he might reasonably go to sleep.

CHAPTER XVI

WHILE THESE SIMPLE PASSAGES of melodrama were transacting themselves at Killyboffin Hall, Detective-Inspector Cadover had been pursuing a plodding investigation into the murder in the cinema. He had failed to find any short cut to the identity of the dead man by way of the young lady with whom he was accustomed to dine confidentially at Smith's. For the degree of confidence involved in this particular satisfaction of certain of man's simpler needs had not extended to the communication of a surname and address; and when the clue of the casual letter referring to a scientists' son had failed him Cadover was no further forward than at the moment of his first glimpse of the young man's formidably anonymous corpse.

He had recognised this over his breakfast; recognised it with an insistence that spoke of his obscure sense of some special urgency in the affair. Nothing was less his inclination than to sit back and wait the event, even although his experience told him that this was now the course that the cinema case was most likely to pursue. His night's perambulations had been a sharp disappointment; in such subsidiary clues as remained to his hand he had very little faith; in all probability the next stage of the matter would be represented by somebody's turning up to claim the body. This always happened. It was remarkable—Cadover reflected over a somewhat inattentive communion with his wife at the breakfast-table—how hard it was in a civilised community to disappear without fuss. Taken in the mass, we have come to hold life extraordinarily cheap—far cheaper, surely, than any culture since something dimly Sumerian or Babylonian. We scrap a generation by violent and costly means, and very soon it is the cost and not the scrapping that troubles us. But let the loneliest old woman vanish from her garret and presently the local police station is besieged by a throng of her intimate acquaintance demanding an instant dragging of the local ponds. Only there is a time-interval in these disappearances; and one of the longest gaps, Cadover knew, is apt to occur between the disappearance of just such a person as his present corpse suggested and the emergence of a body of enquiring relatives. For young men of the sort either have, or by their mothers, sisters or wives are apprehended to have, impulses liable to take them regrettably out of the family circle from time to time. The awkwardness produced by this—by the lurking suspicion that the missing man may, in the vulgar phrase, be enjoying a night, or series of nights, on the tiles—had often, in Cadover's experience, occasioned deplorable delay in the enquiries made by devoted persons into the disappearance of entirely blameless men. Human beings can be as inhibited by shyness before the very gates of death as before the door of a strange house to which one has been casually bidden to a party. About the young man of military appearance shot dead at the showing of *Plutonium Blonde* questions would almost certainly be asked. But they were unlikely to be asked for several days yet.

How, then, was Cadover to proceed? He summoned his available information—which consisted, in effect, of the scanty letter received by Miss Joyce Vane and the yet scantier entries in the dead man's diary. The picture to be built up from these documents was not remarkable for detail. The young man had engaged himself as a private tutor to take a boy to Ireland. The address to which they were going was unknown but might possibly incorporate the word—or fragment of a word—*Hump*. There was a substantial probability that it lay somewhere within the extensive area served by a series of wandering light railways of which the starting-point was the junction of Dundrane.

Next, the boy in question was the son of a scientist. This scientist was eminent either in the field of atomic physics or in some more or less related field which casual and uninformed reference might so name. Was anything else known of him? Cadover frowned. In the space in his new diary appropriate to Thursday—the day, that was to say, on which he had died —the prospective tutor had written the words *gun for boy 1.15*. This might, of course, refer to some quite inexpensive weapon —say, an air-gun of one of the well-known popular makes. But against this reading there had to be set one of the two entries immediately preceeding; the one that read *N.I. police re guns etc*. The suggestion here of Customs regulations to be complied with, as also the season of the year, pointed to substantial designs upon the game birds of Ireland. The probability, then, seemed clear. The eminent scientist had delegated the new tutor to buy the boy a shot-gun.

Cadover reached for *The Times*—in the advertisement columns of which, at this time of year, there would certainly be a number of such weapons offered for sale. And presently he was confirmed in what he had supposed. Sporting guns were uncommonly costly in these days. Moreover, private tutors could not be altogether inexpensive. So here was something else that might reasonably be inferred about the unknown scientist: he was a person of some substance. And at this Cadover recalled Sir Bernard Paxton, whose style of living would here have fitted him so nicely into the picture. Unfortunately, Sir Bernard had proved a most abysmal blank, and in this he had been at one with two other comfortably circumstanced savants whom Cadover had interviewed on the previous night: Lord Buffery and Sir Adrian Ramm.

What more was there to go on? On the apparent eve of his departure, and at the seeming instance of his future pupil, Miss Vane's nameless friend had been persuaded to visit a cinema; and in that cinema he had been killed. Now, although many tutors, private or otherwise, are undoubtedly moribund, a positively dead tutor is of no use at all, and can certainly not be employed to take a small boy to Ireland. It seemed likely, therefore, that the particular small boy involved was not in Ireland now, and that inquiry at Dundrane or beyond would yield no very immediate result. For with the death of the tutor the Irish project had surely fallen through.

But where, then, was the boy now? This initial question raised a series of others of a complexity which, until now, Cadover had not quite fully realised. Had the boy left the cinema before his tutor was killed—or at least unaware that he had been killed? Was this scientist's son at home somewhere in London now, in a household merely perplexed by some unexplained hitch in a holiday plan? It was difficult to see any plausibility in this. Moreover, it took no account of another factor which now leapt at Cadover as of sudden immense significance.

The dead man's visit to *Plutonium Blonde*—there was his own word for it as given in his note to Miss Vane—had been something urged upon him by his new pupil. And *Plutonium Blonde* was assuredly the only film then in London during the showing of which a member of the audience could be shot, or otherwise violently despatched, without the risk of instant alarm; the only film, certainly, to combine a moment of absorbing suspense with an ear-splitting inferno of sound. Was the whole Irish proposal, then, bogus—the means, simply, of establishing a relationship whereby the unfortunate young man could be fatally lured into a certain cinema at a certain hour?

Cadover inspected this proposition carefully, and there came a point at which he had to boggle at it. That point was simply the proposed purchase, or acquisition, of the gun. If the boy was only a decoy, and the proposal to take him to Ireland a mere figment, this business of getting him a gun, Cadover felt, would simply not have happened; to have suggested it to the victim, and thus to have put him in the way, presumably, of

199

enquiring after such a weapon, would be a useless bringing into the notice of sundry shop people a situation for which as little publicity as possible would be desired. Moreover, the whole supposition, further considered, seemed fantastic. To invent an eminent scientist, and provide him with a son who must be taken to Ireland, because it was for some reason necessary that a commonplace young man should be murdered, was a course of things too laboriously oblique to be sensible. And that an actual scientist of eminence should be involved in such a design, and should employ either an actual or a pretended son to further it, was surely a scheme of things equally fantastic. Cadover on the whole was disposed to believe in the scientist, in his son, and in the authenticity of some proposal to send that son to Ireland in the company of the man whose death he was now puzzling over. But from this it seemed to follow that it had been a boy innocent of any evil design who had accompanied—nay, persuaded—the doomed man into the cinema. On this supposition, how could any sense be made of what had followed?

There had been talk of two boys. And here Cadover got out his notes of the day before and propped them against the coffee pot. There had been talk of two boys—and there was some indication, moreover, that five persons in all had been in some degree involved in the affair in the cinema. Three seats had been booked together; to occupy the first of these a woman had arrived independently; to occupy the other two the dead man had arrived along with a fifteen-year-old boy. Subsequently, and before the discovery of the body, the woman and the boy had left unnoticed. But there was this to be remarked: that the boy upon his arrival had struck an usherette as being, in fact, not quite the sort of boy that he was holding himself out to be. This, of course, the usherette had announced only after the perpetration of an interesting murder. It would be folly to give weight to it. But it would be a graver folly to ignore it entirely.

Next, there were the remaining two of the five seats somehow concerned. From these, which had been booked independently, there had come out, apparently before the murder, and also before it was possible to have seen the main film through, a lad and a girl. The girl had been cross and bewildered; the lad had been hurrying her away. And the grand fact about the boy who was thus seen leaving the scene with a girl was a singular point of similarity he bore to the boy who was earlier seen to arrive upon it with the man who was killed. In an age in which many English public schools have dispensed with so much as a cap both the boys who had come under observation were sporting bowler hats. That the boy who came with the man was the *same* who had left with the girl was a hypothesis which, as soon as one peered into the matter, presented considerable difficulty. Suppose, then, there were indeed *two* boys. The identical style of their headgear was scarcely to be explained by the obvious supposition that here were two friends from the same school attending a cinema in each other's company, since it appeared certain that they occupied seats independently booked. On the other hand, it by no means followed from this last fact that the boys were in no significant relationship the one with the other. Coincidence might have brought them together with some immediate result thoroughly germane to the mystery.

It was after this fashion that Cadover's mind ploughed slowly forward as he presently made his way to Scotland Yard. In recognising that the casual and the causal might have been bewilderingly at interplay in the cinema, he had an instinctive feeling that he was getting a first grip on the case. He knew comparatively little of what had happened at the Metrodrome, but it was enough to enable him to suspect that *too much* had happened; that the episode had taken on some complication it was not intended to bear. But along with this persuasion there grew up in his mind another to which he found himself equally disposed to attend. In any mental picture of the affair that he attempted to conjure up, or that came to him involuntarily as he essayed a more abstract dealing with it, he found that the predominant feature was the two boys with their several bowler hats. They balanced the composition like a pair of identical twins in comedy, dodging now one and now the other out of the wings to the diversion of a bewildered audience. Or, better perhaps, the evocation was of farce; of one character with a false beard impersonating another character with a real one. And surely that was it! Cadover, reaching his room at length and hanging up his own bowler hat, concluded that some element of impersonation would be found to lie near the heart of the mystery.

He knew what he had to do; what were the several lines, none of them particularly promising, that he must now take up. But for a time he sat doggedly driving his brain through any further inches of the thickening tangle that it could be made to go. Say that the dead man had arrived with the "real" boy—with him on whom the bowler hat sat native and of right. And say that disposed hard by was some young criminal similarly provided and—it went without saying—similarly clothed *in toto* and of stature and feature colourably the same. Suppose that the genuine youth could presently be lured for a space from his seat, so that the other could then slip into with the effect of the first returning to it. The intended victim, on whose other hand there already sat a woman already implicated in the affair, would then be nicely isolated between enemies.

Considering this, Cadover impatiently shook his head. It ignored far too much. It ignored that strong likelihood of some element merely coincidential in the situation suggested by the independent booking of the seats in groups of three and two respectively. It required, moreover, that the "real" boy should not return to the seat he had vacated. In fact he must be supposed (unless, indeed, it was to be imagined that he, too, had met with violence) simply to leave the cinema and take no further interest in what happened there. Through this, by dint of certain rather fantastic propositions, it was possible in part to see one's way. For example, leaving his seat for a time, the boy might be given some urgent message, or confronted with some attractive proposition, which would indeed take him straight from the cinema. But—and Cadover glanced at his watch—yesterday's evening papers were now some thirty hours old and to-day's morning papers sucked dry on the breakfast tables. The murder at the Metrodrome was national news, and under that alliterative title bade fair to be a nine days' wonder. Unless this hypothetical innocent lad was also an uncommonly frightened one something ought to have been heard of him by now.

Patiently, then, Cadover retraced his mental footsteps to the point at which the theory of some impersonation had first opened before him. Take it the other way. Take it that it was the boy arriving with the dead man who was the impostor. And remember that this was a supposition sharply congruous with the social consciousness of the usherette who had believed herself to have detected something spurious about him! Cadover drew a long breath. Suppose that the tutor, perhaps newly engaged, had not in fact met his future charge until this visit to the cinema. There was nothing in the note to Miss Vane to conflict with that. Indeed, the note described the boy as "sounding a bit of a handful all round." At the moment of writing, in fact, he had *not* met the boy. And with a boy who was a handful—resentful or distrustful, perhaps, about the arrangements proposed for his holidays—might not going to a cinema together have been hit upon as a means, so to speak, of breaking the ice? The tutor, then, comes to the Metrodrome and thinks he meets his charge. But actually he meets an impostor, and presently he is seated between this impostor and a woman who is also in the plot. And meanwhile the genuine boy has been persuaded, say, to play a prank; to be present nearby in the company of a girl-friend. For a crime is to be committed and the genuine boy to be implicated. But just before the deed is done the genuine boy somehow takes the alarm, hurries out with his friend, and is now perhaps at home, panic-stricken, and explaining the disappearance of his tutor-elect in the best way he can. . . .

Cadover's career would not have been the success it had did he not possess, mingled with qualities merely solid and reliable, a streak of genius that could, on occasion, run up such effective imaginative constructions as this. But equally—a fact of which he was abundantly aware—he would have come many more croppers than he had, had he not known with what extreme caution to proceed upon them. Moreover, any confidence he might have felt in his theory was in this instance conditioned by a troubled sense of something which he found peculiarly difficult to define. The notion of impersonation had really gripped him more than it should—or rather it remained in his mind as requiring attention which, in all this of the bowler-hatted boys, it was not really receiving at all. Already he had felt in this affair the haunting hint of some tenuous pointer by a hair's breadth fatally missed. And here was a similar feeling assailing him now. What the police detective chiefly needs is rather less a formidably developed power of inferential reasoning than the "fine ear" upon which the successful physician also relies. And now Cadover's ear was just failing, or so he believed, to achieve some discrimination essential to the analysis of his problem.

He turned back to the dead man's diary. It was the point, after all, at which the criminals had slipped up. Potentially, it had been a very bad slip indeed, for had the diary been a little less new, a little more informative, their hope to prevent or delay identification of the body would have been frustrated from the start. And, even as it stood, the diary perhaps still represented the chink or crevice through which a first leverage could be obtained on the blank wall before him.

Smith's 7.30. That had led to Miss Vane, and Miss Vane, for the time, to a dead end only. He turned to the next entry:

Bolderwood
Hump

Here was something that could be investigated either swiftly or slowly. Within a couple of hours, that was to say, he could have a policeman on the doorstep of every known Bolderwood in Great Britain, Northern Ireland and Eire, asking for any light they could throw upon the Metrodrome murder. But this might well be to sacrifice some virtue of surprise, and such enquiries should perhaps be preluded by confidential investigation in each case. Certainly the first thing to do was to hunt the directories for any Bolderwood in any way associated with a Hump; should such a one be discovered a very formidable battery would be turned upon him at once.

Cadover pushed a button on his desk and spent some time delegating this task to assistants. And then he considered the two definitely Irish entries:

N.I. police re guns etc

and

Light railway from Dundrane.

Neither of these entries seemed very hopeful. The second appeared to be a mere memorandum, casually written, of how the latter part of the proposed journey was to be accomplished. One does not reserve seats, or book ahead, on an Irish light railway. There was nothing, then, in this, except a general pointer to a certain tract of country. Nor did the first of the entries suggest anything in the nature of preliminary correspondence; it was merely a reminder of certain formalities to be complied with—formalities, Cadover suspected, which, during a tourist season, might not be very strictly maintained. What the entry did give was this: that the "Ireland" referred to in the dead man's letter to Miss Vane did in fact mean Eire and not Northern Ireland. It was for the purpose of taking guns into Eire—or rather of being permitted ultimately to take them out again—that some application was necessary or desirable to the Northern Ireland police. Here too Cadover set certain enquiries on foot. Then he turned to the final entry —the one which had already been prominently in his mind.

gun for boy 1.15

One did not note in quite this way an intention to *hand over* a gun; the reference must definitely be to *acquiring* one. And if the figures represented a time of day—as almost certainly they did—then there was surely some significance to be attached to them. A quarter past one is a slightly out of the way time to go buying an article the choice of which requires considerable deliberation. It means either an unusually early luncheon or an uncomfortably delayed one. But the fact that the entry was for the previous day suggested an obvious reason for this. The dead man's programme had been full. And if

205

written out it would have read something like: *meet boy—quick luncheon—buy gun—Metrodrome in time for Plutonium Blonde—Irish boat train.* For the letter to Miss Vane, it had to be remembered, definitely named Thursday as the young man's proposed day of departure with his pupil. About this, of course, there might have been some later change of plan. But on the whole it seemed likely that about the entire affair this was the signal fact: the fatality in the cinema had taken place on the very eve of the Irish project.

Suppose, then, that a shot-gun had actually been bought round about one-fifteen. What had happened to it? Where had it been, this last-moment purchase, while the people who had bought it were in the cinema? There seemed to be two possible answers. Either it had been sent to some private address in order to be put with other baggage, or it had been sent to a railway terminus to await the travellers there. And if Cadover was right in thinking that no journey to Ireland could well have taken place, then, in the latter eventuality, the gun might be in some railway "left luggage" room still. There was a fair line of investigation in this, but it was one in which success would probably come more quickly at any other season of the year. Guns, in the second week of August, were decidedly on the move. It was true that King's Cross and Euston no longer presented the spectacle—astonishing to the itinerant foreigner caught in the whirl—of a whole social class equipped with such weapons, and migrating, together with an infinitude of crates, hampers, trunks, upper servants and privileged dogs, to the remoter corners of the kingdom. Nevertheless traffic of this sort was still considerable, and a single gun would be hard to trace.

The occasion of purchase was a good deal more immediately hopeful. Considering it, Cadover indeed concluded that he had been taking too gloomy a view of the merely waiting part that might be imposed upon him. Again the season was a factor. The columns of *The Times,* for example, had shown him a good many people wanting to buy or sell sporting weapons, and the gunsmiths would similarly be doing a brisk trade. So again it was possible that a single purchase might take a little time to track down. Nevertheless, it could almost certainly be done, since one cannot walk into a shop and buy a shot-gun with the casual anonymity natural to the purchase of a pair of gloves or a packet of cigarettes. Indeed, Cadover, although not well versed in such matters, suspected that a good deal of ritual would accompany the acquiring of fresh property of this sort. He judged it likely that a man's gunsmith would hold something the same position—that of a species of paternal toady—as a man's tailor. But would the dead man *have*, in that sense, a gunsmith? He was not, presumably, a person of any great substance; nevertheless, this was one of the likelier points at which he would be tied on to the tail of privilege. He had looked just that type. *Gun for boy*, then, meant, most probably, his bringing some special knowledge or connection of his own to bear; this more probably than his acting, namelessly and unnoticeably, as agent for the boy's father.

But would the gun, for that matter, be bought in a shop at all? Cadover was beginning to reach an age in which, every now and then, he had to hitch himself back into the present; and for a moment he had forgotten that nowadays neither gloves nor cigarettes nor shot-guns are simply to be had for the asking. Almost everything is in short supply at one time or another; and sporting equipment is particularly likely to be so at the start of the shooting season. But on this one could get assured information quickly. Cadover picked up his telephone and rang the first large firm of gunsmiths to come into his head. It was as he supposed. They took the gloomiest view of being able expeditiously to supply a weapon suitable for a boy of fifteen or sixteen.

Gun for boy 1.15. The man who made this confident note could not have been on any sort of waiting list for a suitable weapon, since his engagement to accompany a pupil to Ireland had not been more than a few days' old. It was, of course, conceivable that he was somewhere the particulaly privileged sort of customer for whom wanted articles are, in fact, produced. Alternatively, he might simply have chanced to know that some acquaintance of his own had an appropriate gun to dispose of. This second possibility Cadover eyed askance

207

for a moment; it would be a circumstance that would pretty well destroy such hopefulness as there was in this approach to the case. But the tutor's likeliest manner of proceeding, after all, lay yet to explore; and Cadover sent for a file of recent newspapers. "Articles for Sale" was his quarry, and he kept a particularly sanguine eye upon the personal column of *The Times* once more. The old agony advertisements, he reflected, were not quite what they had been when they delighted Sherlock Holmes; nevertheless, there must be a little drama, and a great deal of oddity, hidden behind some of them still. . . . Every now and then he scribbled in his notebook, and as he did so his spirits rose. As he had anticipated, a substantial— yet not too substantial—body of people had been holding themselves out of late as having sporting guns to dispose of. To question them meant another pilgrimage much like that of the previous evening, and Cadover debated whether to put a team of men on the work. He decided once more to keep the matter in his own hands, thrust his notebook in his pocket, and reached for his bowler hat.

It will be recalled that the portion of our narrative now being offered to the reader is retrospective in cast. While Detective-Inspector Cadover is thus stepping out of Scotland Yard, with that heavy tread recalling his beat of long ago, the unknown boy with whom he is concerned, and the substitute tutor whose existence he does not suspect, are transferring to the light railway at Dundrane, with the greater part of their adventures yet before them.

CHAPTER XVII

IN ESTIMATING THE COURSE and tempo of the enquiry lying before him, Cadover had neglected a consideration that ought to have been sufficiently obvious. Persons with sporting guns for sale are commonly persons owning other sporting guns as well, and having a predisposition to put these into use in the second week of August. Working systematically through his list of advertisers, he found himself seeking a surprising number of people who were now out of Town. As he abandoned none of these until he had obtained from them by telephone or telegram, or through the agency of local police, particulars of anyone who had bought, or considered buying, the weapon they had advertised—and, moreover, as many of the replies received involved the instigating of further enquiries for which several assistants had to be briefed—the shades of evening had fallen as he drew towards the end of his list.

Now he rang the bell of a small flat in Hampstead. The house was retired and shabby, and its conversion into a dwelling adequate for several households had been carried out uncompromisingly on the cheap. A seedy retired major, Cadover speculated, who had felt a powerful urge to raise the price of a crate or two of whiskey. The door opened before him. "Does Mr Standage live here?" he enquired.

For a decayed sporty major, if such there was to be, was not yet visible; Cadover found himself regarding, in a gloom not very convenient for precise observation, a sombrely dressed woman in late middle age, who appeared to look back at him with completely expressionless eyes. "I am Mrs Standage," she said; "and I live alone. Will you come in?" She let him past and closed the door. "This way, please." And she led the way into a room on the left.

Here it was darker still and Cadover waited for his conductress to turn on the light. But the lady—she was emphatically that, and the more evidently in being a person from whom all other species of emphasis had drained away long ago—merely motioned to a chair and herself sat down with a straight back which seemed to speak uncompromisingly of a merely business occasion. "I think I ought to tell you at once," she said, "that I have had an offer. An offer from a clergyman."

Cadover, who was weary, had for a moment a confused impulse to offer congratulations, as if what had been confessed to him was the prospect of some imminent matrimonial success. His perception of the folly of this left him just presence of mind to repeat, "A clergyman?"

"For use in his parish hall. And I should, of course, be very pleased to think of the instrument as being employed for what would be, virtually, purposes of piety. Two of my uncles were archdeacons." Mrs Standage paused, but not from any consciousness of irrelevance. "Unfortunately the offer he was able to make was far from meeting my mind in the matter. Perhaps you would care to try the touch and tone."

Glancing round the room, Cadover saw that what was being offered to him was the species of instrument known as a baby grand. "It looks very nice," he said politically. "But I have not, as a matter of fact, come to buy a piano. I must explain to you that I am——"

"Then it's the rug." Mrs Standage, who kept her eyes fixed somewhat unnervingly over her visitor's left shoulder, spoke with a shade of chagrin. "Unfortunately, it is already sold—as was to be expected, I'm afraid. So fine a Persian rug would scarcely remain on—on the market long. But if a small Aubusson carpet would suit your needs equally well——" Here she broke off, as if aware of salesmanship of a somewhat too precipitate order. "You may wonder why I should be anxious to dispose of things of such excellent quality—heirlooms, as they might be called. The fact is that I have had somewhat to contract my living quarters of late, and I am above all things fond of *space*. This is the sole reason for my having decided to part with something here and there."

"I see." Cadover barely did see, for the dusk was now deepening rapidly. But the room in which he sat, in addition to being faded, seemed already singularly bare; and by his head he could just detect a square patch on the wall from which a picture must recently have vanished. He was in the presence, in fact, of dire poverty in one of its most distressing forms. "But you must understand," he said gently, "that I have not come to buy anything you still have to sell. I am a detective-inspector of the police, and I have come to make enquiries about something you have already sold. I mean the shot-gun which you advertised about a week ago."

Mrs Standage bowed, and it could be seen that a faint spot of colour had risen to her cheek. "I beg your pardon," she said stiffly. "The misunderstanding was due entirely to my own carelessness. And any questions you have to ask I shall, of course, answer if I can. I hope I have not been culpable. It did cross my mind that formalities unknown to me might attend the—the disposal of firearms. The gun belonged to my late husband."

"Quite so." Cadover was infinitely soothing. "But I don't think you will find us raising any questions of that sort."

'It was taking up room." Mrs Standage appeared to feel this a little tenuous and to cast about in her mind. "And falling over. It made me decidedly nervous. I was not assured that the mechanism was entirely safe. So it appeared best to sell the weapon and be rid of it."

"You acted very wisely, ma'am. Firearms can be extremely dangerous to those unfamiliar with them." Cadover paused on this vacuous sentiment and then plunged decisively. "And the gun suited the boy?"

"The gun suited the boy very well. He was delighted with it. It pleased me to feel that my husband's old companion was going to give such pleasure."

For almost the first time in the cinema affair, Cadover felt a strong leap of hope within him. "And the offer made—um—met your mind in the matter?"

"Entirely so. I had rung up my solicitor, an old friend with whom my husband used to go rough shooting, and he suggested a fair price."

"I see. And that figure was——?"

"Thirty pounds."

"The purchaser gave you that?"

Mrs Standage's curiously absent eyes appeared for a moment to waver. Then she smoothed out a fold in her dress. "He gave me," she said, "thirty-seven pounds ten shillings. I had to bear in mind that solicitors are conservatively inclined. They don't quite realise how everything goes up and up." For a moment Mrs Standage's voice wavered as her eyes had done. "And they *do* go up and up, as I have some occasion to know."

"I am glad that you made a fair bargain. There might have

been some danger of the gun's being too heavy for the lad. Perhaps it's being just right persuaded the purchaser not to hesitate."

"That was precisely the way of it. I know, as I have said, little of such things. But my husband was a small man—a *very* slightly built man, although full of fire and courage—and his gun was in consequence a light one. That was why the Captain bought it at once."

"He was an Army man?" Cadover leant forward in his eagerness. "His name was——?"

"He told me his name, of course—and his late regiment as well. But—do you know?—they have entirely slipped my memory."

"My dear ma'am, this, I must tell you, is a matter of the utmost gravity. It is essential that I should learn this man's name at once. Did he not write out a cheque? Did he sign any sort of receipt?"

"Neither, I fear." Mrs Standage was visibly distressed, and Cadover was convinced that it was not her intention to attempt any form of concealment. "He was entirely a gentleman, and no record of the transaction appeared to be necessary. He paid me in cash."

"I see. Now, in such a substantial sum there were no doubt Bank of England notes? Five-pound notes, for example?"

"He had only pound notes—Treasury notes, are they called? I remember his remarking that people are so reluctant to take larger notes nowadays—because of the Germans having forged so many, I think he said—that he never carried them."

"That is most unfortunate." And Cadover heartily cursed this further example of the dead man's circumspection. "It means that, almost certainly, the money cannot be traced. Will you please make some effort to recall his name?"

Mrs Standage made a nervous gesture with her hands. "I am ashamed to be so stupid," she said. "But it was so commonplace and unmemorable a name! And, indeed, so was the young man himself—although entirely a gentleman, as I have said. Or was it *because* he was entirely a gentleman? There are so many ways in which a gentleman *should* be unnoticeable."

"No doubt." Cadover successfully concealed more than faint exasperation at this speculative social dictum. "Well, what about the boy? Was he called anything?"

"Certainly. His name was Humphrey. And he addressed his companion as 'sir.' I conjectured that their relationship was that of pupil and tutor."

"I think your conjecture was entirely accurate. But I should be better pleased to have the fellow's surname—better pleased by a long way."

For several seconds Mrs Standage was silent. "Do you know," she said at length, "that I think it had something to do with rivers or boats?"

"That is something—indeed, it's a great deal. He wasn't just Captain Rivers, by any chance—Captain Peter Rivers?"

Mrs Standage shook her head. "Decidedly not."

"Or Captain Banks?"

"Not that either."

"Shipton . . . Shipway . . . Seaman?"

"None of these."

"*Steer?*" Cadover was irrationally hopeful. "Captain Peter Steer?"

Mrs Standage oddly hesitated. "No," she said presently; "his name was *not* Steer either. No doubt it will recur to me in time."

"Well, for the moment let us take up another point. Did these two simply walk away with the gun?"

"No. They had some engagement that would have made that course inconvenient. The Captain asked if he might use my telephone, and he rang for a messenger, who came and collected the gun shortly after they had left."

"I see." For a moment Cadover gloomily confronted the blank wall that again seemed to have raised itself between him and his quarry. It was now almost dark in Mrs Standage's drawing-room. No doubt the lady's reluctance to turn on the light arose from a wish to conceal from her visitor the extent to which it had recently been depleted through the agency of public advertisements. But—perhaps under the influence of disappointment—Cadover's sense of delicacy in this matter had worn a trifle thin. He rose, switched on the light himself, and advanced upon the depressed gentlewoman before him, holding out a copy of the police photograph of the dead man. "Will you be so good," he asked, "as to tell me if this is the person who bought your gun?"

Mrs Standage did not move, and she appeared to ignore what was presented to her. When she spoke, it was very slowly. "I am afraid, sir, that I cannot be of further help to you."

"I realise that you have done your best. But please look at this carefully."

"It is useless, sir. I must bid you good night." And with even more dignity than she had yet shown, Mrs Standage rose and smoothed her dress about her.

"Useless——?" Cadover looked squarely at the lady, and the indignation that was in his tone died away upon his lips. For he saw that the woman who stood before him was blind. This was the explanation of the obstinately darkened room, and of what had seemed the absent gaze over his shoulder.

"I gather that you now realise my disability." And Mrs Standage smiled faintly. "And you will realise that I can give no description of persons who have never been visible to me. Let me show you out. I have—just at present—no servant in the house."

There seemed nothing to say. Cadover stuffed the useless photograph into his pocket and walked behind his entertainer. His tread, he uneasily noted, was loud upon bare wood. Somewhere in the house an Aubusson carpet might remain. But from this room any floor-covering had disappeared—inch by inch, as it were, through the attenuated digestive system of the blind owner. With the help of the personal column of *The Times* she would nibble her way through what remaining possessions she commanded. And after that? Well, she might end up by being badgered by just such a conscientious constable as Cadover had once been for hawking matches in the streets.

Mrs Standage's shabby front door was opening before him. He was suddenly resolved not to let his commiseration and embarrassment stand in the way of a final effort. "You say that the fellow's name calls up in your mind associations of rivers and boats. Well, what *are* your associations with such things?"

"It is difficult to say. I have never had anything in particular to do with them. It is an odd thing to have come into my head."

"There must have been some associative process at work." Cadover was obstinate. "You sold him"—he barely hesitated—"your husband's gun. Did your husband have anything to do with rivers and boats?"

"I don't think he did." Mrs Standage's voice was strained and weary. "And you make me feel it was wrong, indelicate, avaricious, to sell——"

"Nonsense, ma'am!" Cadover felt that to be brusque was to be kindly here. "You must keep going—keep your end up —as you can. I admire you for it."

"Thank you." The voice in the near-darkness beside him trembled. "And my husband, I say, had little to do with boats and rivers—or little since before I knew him, in his Cambridge days."

"He rowed at Cambridge?"

"No. He was too light to row. But he coxed his college eight." Mrs Standage paused. "And that is it," she said quietly. "The name of the man I sold the gun to was Captain Cox."

Captain Peter Cox. He was not in the London telephone directory. Although presumably a soldier, he was not, and had never been, in the Regular Army—and this, it seemed, would mean an indefinite number of hours' delay in getting anything about him out of the War Office. He had, at least in his own name, made no booking of a sleeping-berth or the like between London and Ireland. He belonged to no London club. He had not recently been in any London hospital. . . . Cadover, doggedly intent on beating to it, if only by an insignificant interval of time, the machine which would undoubtedly now disclose the dead man's history, found himself

215

once more working into the night. At half-past ten he was brought news that a certain Cyril Bolderwood was a substantial landowner at a place called Killyboffin in the west of Ireland. This opened a new line and what looked like a definitive one. Here was almost certainly the man whose name Captain Peter Cox, not many days before being shot in the Metrodrome Cinema, had confided to his pocket diary. And he was on the telephone. . . . Cadover, haunted, as he had been from the start, by a feeling that in this obscure affair time was not to waste, let his hand hover over the instrument on his desk. But caution stayed him. Do that and—as he had discovered more than once—you can never tell what you may be giving away to whom. The case was beginning to move, and when that happens the first essential is that the movement should be controlled. Very obscurely, an imperfect pattern was forming itself in Cadover's mind—and cardinal in this was a notion of the species of crime into which his investigation had started to wind. And now there was no question of his holding everything within his own hand; of his plodding round on his own ex-constable's feet to peer at every point for himself. A whole posse was working under him. And other instruments of public order and security—robust infants merely godfathered by the venerable sage represented by Scotland Yard —must be asked if they had anything to say. . . . At midnight Cadover went to get himself a cup of coffee.

The place never sleeps, for none would sleep securely in their beds if it did. Cadover brushed past two colleagues, their heads together over a plate of ham rolls.

"To me," said one of these, "it sounded like *hump*. And the poor devil could get out nothing else."

Memory tugged at Cadover. It brought him up with a jerk, like an actual tether. And as he thus stopped in his tracks the second of his colleagues spoke. "It explained itself a minute later; if you'd stopped you'd have heard. *Humphrey*. That's what he was trying to say. Something nasty on his conscience, if you ask me."

Cadover sat down abruptly. Coffee slopped in his saucer. He returned it carefully to the cup and stretched out a still trembling hand for a sandwich. "Would you mind," he asked, "sharing the joke?"

The first of his colleagues glanced up at him. "Hullo, Cadover—hard at it keeping London pure? Poor old Hudspith was the chap for that."

"Or solving horrid murders in ducal halls?" The second man chuckled. "Appleby's mantle must fall somewhere, one supposes. And you, my dear Cadover——"

Cadover, holding his sandwich suspended in air, stretched out his other hand in a clutch suddenly as compelling as the ancient mariner's. "Seriously," he said, "what was that about *Humphrey* and *hump*?"

"Certainly nothing by way of a joke to share." The first man spoke soberly. "I expect the poor chap's dead by now."

"Nasty specimen called Soapy Clodd." The second man put down his cup. "Teen-age blackmailer, of all filthy trades. But he's got it now. Groaning in casualty. And any minute he'll be howling in hell. I hope it's hotter than the coffee they manage in this blasted cellar."

Cadover, like one to whom has been granted a sudden mystical assurance of revelation, momentarily bowed his head. But, being economically disposed, he made the same motion serve for a gulp at his own coffee. "Listen," he said. "There's something odd here. It sounds like linking up with an affair I'm busy on now. Tell me about it."

"There's very little to tell. They'd been after this fellow Clodd for a long time, and at last they had enough for a fair chance of a conviction. So they picked him up. And then he bolted, made a run for it, and found himself underneath a bus. If you go up now—and if he's not, as I say, dead—you'll hear hear him moaning away about Humphrey Somebody—one of his victims lying particularly heavy on his conscience, I suppose."

And Cadover went up. Tiled walls, glass shelves, chromium plate, the smell of ether and iodine: it was a chamber that had seen a large number of bad ends and a few surprisingly good ones. And, clearly, there was soon to be another end now. Soapy Clodd was a grey, contorted face on a pillow; a single skinny arm over which a police surgeon bent with a hypodermic syringe. His eyes were closed. There was the sweat of agony on his forehead; it collected in the wrinkles there and ploughed tiny furrows in the dirt.

"He'll have another period of consciousness soon." The surgeon spoke impassively. "And then he'll be out of it. He doesn't look as if life had enriched him, poor devil—or he it. Give me a call." The surgeon went out. Cadover and an orderly were left together by the bedside.

Cadover stood motionless and absorbed. He remembered the coincidence of his driver's having remarked this wretched creature Clodd on the previous night. Was he really a fragment of the puzzle? If so, there seemed only one place into which he could be dropped . . . and yet it was a place into which he would not properly fit.

A long time passed and still Cadover waited, obscurely compelled to the conviction that he was not wasting time. And at length the dying man's eyes opened. Cadover sat down beside the bed. "Clodd," he said distinctly, "what about this Humphrey?"

A faint indrawn breath was the immediate answer, and Clodd moved his head uneasily on the pillow, as if straining to hear something that came to him from very far away. Words formed themselves upon his lips—they were faintly blue—but no sound came.

"Humphrey," said Cadover loudly. "Speak up."

"They're after him, the bastards." Clodd's was a barely audible whisper. "They're after my boy."

"Your boy?" Cadover was disconcerted. "You have a son · called Humphrey?"

"'E was *my* boy—not theirs." Weak indignation breathed in the dying man's voice. "And a fine lad, too. Couldn't arf write you a narsty letter, 'e couldn't—though I sez it that's a bit of an 'and at it myself. 'Beware'—that's wot 'e wrote me. And just a kid with no proper eddikation. Couldn't even spell. 'I'll 'ave yer put in goal,' 'e wrote—just like that. A good one, that was. 'I'll punch yer bleeding nose,' 'e wrote. I tell yer, I didn't arf like young 'Umphrey. But I'd 'ave got 'im in the

218

end, same as I've got lots with more spunk nor 'im. Then them blurry bashtards come along. What's their gime? That's what I'd like to know. Two lots of them, there were, and both up to something dirty over that poor kid. Made me sick, it did."

"Two lots?" Cadover bent forward eagerly. "You're sure of that?"

"I tell yer I was working that kid 'ard, and there wasn't much I didn't see. Two lots of crooks—narsty common crooks —up to something against that poor kid. And one lot 'ad a kid of their own. 'Opped out of a car, 'e did, and ran after the young chap was going to be a tutor or the like, and I'm blarsted if 'e didn't 'old himself out as 'Umphrey 'imself. And me listening down an area steps. Thought it might do me a bit o' good. 'Are you my new tutor?' That's what the common little crook said, bold as brarse. Blurry himpersonation in broad daylight, that's what it was. I arsk you, what's the police coming to? Sitting back on their great be'inds while we pays taxes for them through the nose."

"Who are these people? What is this Humphrey's other name?" Cadover spoke gently now, as if afraid that a vehement word might send Soapy Clodd a fatal second too soon to his last account.

And, plainly, the dying man did not hear. He lay quite motionless for a long time—only something, a sort of darkening or filming, was happening to his eyes. At last his voice came in a whisper even fainter than before. "Hashamed of nothing I say or do . . . hashamed of nothing I say or do."

It was, Cadover thought, a singularly strange profession for such a man. But a moment later he realised that it was quotation to which he was listening again.

"And there's not many as writes that, there ain't. . . . 'Hashamed of nothing I say or do. . . .' And then a flourish, as you might call it, at the end. . . . 'Umphrey. . . . 'Umphrey Hedwyn 'Onyel Paxton."

Cadover turned from the bedside and ran. Big Ben was tolling one of the small hours as he reached the open air and tumbled into his waiting car.

CHAPTER XVIII

Driving fast through deserted streets, Cadover at first asked himself the wrong question. Why should the eminent Sir Bernard Paxton wish to conceal the truth about his son's holiday plans? Had the boy, who had been for some reason regarded as a likely victim by the blackmailer Clodd, been involved in trouble so serious that his father had judged it necessary to safeguard his imminent escape from the country by telling a pack of lies? And had the trouble, in fact, been something very serious indeed—the sort of thing that might lead to a man's murder—and had there been an elaborate plan to baffle pursuit by creating a false Humphrey to lay a false trail? It was a hypothesis leaving a dozen questions unanswered, but it lasted Cadover through his brief dash across the West End of London and was in his mind still as he pressed the front-door bell at the top of Sir Bernard's stately steps. All patience had for the moment left him; the little button under his thumb was entirely inadequate to his feelings; he regretted that he could not prelude the stiff questions he was about to ask by tugging vigorously at a more primitive device calculated to make a much greater row. Probably, indeed, he would by this present means rouse nobody. And he was about to make night hideous by hammering loudly on the door—it would have pleased him to make with one of his stout boots a decided impression on that too pristine paint— when the offending barrier vanished before him and he found himself confronted by the butler whom he had encountered on the previous night. The man looked at him without visible surprise, and made no demur when he marched past him into the hall.

"I am Detective-Inspector Cadover. Rouse your master, please, and say that I must see him at once on a matter of the utmost urgency."

The man bowed imperturbably. His dignity was by no means disturbed by his having just scrambled out of bed; perhaps—Cadover inconsequently thought—it was fortified by a dressing-gown entirely appropriate in its sombre splendour. "Very good, sir. Will you please step into the library?"

It was, Cadover remembered, the Spanish room. He entered it and the door closed softly behind him. He waited.

He waited for perhaps five minutes, not displeased at having this interval in which to arrange his ideas and calm down. But presently he found that he was far from calming down; on the contrary, he felt an obscure pricking of impatience and even alarm. The house was quite silent. He listened in vain for a footstep, for the soft opening or closing of a bedroom door. He got to his feet and prowled. He stared at a picture confronting him from the end of the room. And as he did this there came back to him powerfully the first occasion upon which, tenuously but hauntingly, he had experienced the feeling of something eluding him that he ought to have held. Something that somebody had said . . . something that somebody had *failed* to say . . . a single word that had not been spoken. . . .

Velazquez. That was it. The owner of this splendid thing had said it was there because of its likeness to his son. And then—as if by way of placing it—he had said that it was an old picture—very old indeed. It was a remark absurdly wide of anything that could, in its context, be uttered by a person of genuine cultivation in such things. And Cadover had missed it. He had missed the moment at which a monstrous and daring imposture had given itself away. And here was why the notion of impersonation had haunted him in some connection other than that of the two lads with the two bowler hats. Sir Bernard Paxton, the owner of this august and sleeping mansion, was one on whom he had never yet set eyes. Sir Bernard had not told fibs about his son. Somebody else—having more colour as an eminent scientist than as an owner of Old Masters—had done that for him.

Cadover strode to the door and threw it open. The hall was in darkness. He brought out a pocket torch and let its beam play until it picked out the light switches. He flicked them on and an aggressively imposing world sprang into being around him. It was like one of those exaggeratedly spacious halls in the movies, with a great curving staircase on which female stars might display their gorgeous gowns or alluring nether limbs. Cadover glanced rapidly about him and discerned, among the numerous expensive and exotic objects displayed, one of homely domestic use, yet of proportions so noble as to be not inadequate to its surroundings. It was a gong—such a gong, it might be supposed, as had once thundered down the remotest corridors of some vast Tibetan lamasery. And Cadover, perhaps because his vanity was wounded at having been egregiously fooled, was prompted to have his moment of drama out of this plodding and harassing affair. He picked up the gong stick and plied it with a will.

The effect exceeded even his exasperated expectation. It was like being himself the stone cast into a still pool; great waves—and they seemed of sheer, quintessential energy rather than of mere sound—pulsed and beat outwards from him in widening circles. When he paused, laying a hand on the great bronze disk to still it, he was aware of numerous doors being thrown open, and of alarmed feet running, in some remote quarter of the house. That, no doubt, was the servants—or what was left of them. But he was aware, too, of something else. A light had flicked on at the head of the staircase, and a single tall figure stood there regarding him. And suddenly Cadover heard over again, on his inner ear, all the gloriously outrageous tumult he had just created. But it had shrunk to a tiny, foolish and impertinent noise. *This* was Paxton. There could be no doubt about that.

"Who are you, and what the devil do you mean?"

The words were such as any indignant householder might have used. They were accompanied, moreover, by the thrusting forward of an object altogether familiar to Cadover's experience: namely, an automatic pistol. But for a full second longer, and as he laid down the gong stick, he preserved the simple sense of a unique event. He had never before looked straight at genius, and he might never do so again.

"I am a police officer, and I have taken the quickest means I could to rouse you to a matter of extreme urgency."

For a split second the tremendous presence that was Sir Bernard Paxton wavered. It was, Cadover saw, unreadiness, irresolution; it was certainly no sort of uneasy conscience. And the impression was instantly gone. The tall figure half turned to some invisible corridor down which several pairs of feet could be heard hurrying. "Go back to your rooms," he said in a level voice. "Tell the women that there is no danger of any sort. It has been"—and his glance came back to Cadover—"a mere prank."

The footsteps died away, and as they did so Sir Bernard came steadily down the staircase. He looked hard at Cadover, the pistol still in his hand. "Your credentials," he said briefly.

Cadover showed them. Sir Bernard looked at them for what they were worth. It was still the man he was sizing up. "Please come into my study," he said. Cadover followed him and was presently aware of light-coloured walls, Chinese paintings, glowing lacquers. Sir Bernard faced him squarely. "Well?" he asked.

"I called here last night to interview you on a matter that might concern the safety of your son. I was shown into another room—I think, your library—and there I was interviewed by a person who purported to be yourself."

"I see." Very quietly, Sir Bernard Paxton turned aside and sat down. The movement, Cadover realised, covered the instant intellectual comprehension of a totally unsuspected danger. Because that danger touched his son, the man was shaken to the depths by it. But he was certainly not going to make an outcry. "Jollard—my butler?" he asked.

"It was your butler who received me, who told me to come back at a certain hour when you would be available, and who then ushered me into the presence of the impostor. Afterwards, he showed me out."

"And I came downstairs and saw him do so." Sir Bernard spoke sharply. "I called out to him and he told me I forget what. Well"—and he looked dryly at Cadover—"you have not been the only fool."

Cadover accepted this as it was offered. "I was the bigger fool of the two. I ought to have got the hang of it before I rang your front-door bell to-night. As it is, your butler—Jollard, did you say?—has shown us a clean pair of heels. Have you had him in your service for long, Sir Bernard?"

"Six months."

"And he has been in a position of some trust—or, at least, responsibility? He would be able to take, and appear to transmit, messages . . . that sort of thing?"

"Certainly. He appeared an efficient and reliable man, although I cannot say that I greatly cared for him. And now" —and Sir Bernard Paxton drew a long breath—"if there is anything in all this that really concerns my son, we had better have it from the beginning, and at once."

"Very well, Sir Bernard. I understand that you have an only son, Humphrey? And that you recently engaged a tutor to take him to Ireland?"

"I engaged a Mr Thewless, a most reliable and experienced man."

Cadover took out his notebook and made a jotting of the name. "Thank you. Did you, in the first instance, try to engage anyone else?"

"I engaged a Captain Peter Cox, who was highly recommended to me. Unfortunately, he has been prevented from taking up the post by an unexpected death in his family."

Cadover stared. "It would altogether surprise you, Sir Bernard, to learn that the unexpected death was his own?"

"It would, indeed. But all that I received was a telegram, which is no doubt evidence of the poorest sort. See for yourself." And with some deliberation, yet with a visibly trembling hand, Sir Bernard Paxton fished in a drawer of the desk beside him. "Here you are."

Cadover took the slip of paper held out to him and read it grimly. "Certainly," he said, "it was a sudden death that disqualified Captain Cox. We seem to have a bit of a joker to deal with." He thought for a moment. "So when you received this you fixed things up with Mr Thewless instead?"

"Precisely so. And Mr Thewless and Humphrey consequently left together for Ireland late yesterday afternoon—or I should say late on Thursday afternoon."

"This Captain Cox, Sir Bernard—did he ever, so far as you know, see Humphrey?"

"He did not. When he called on me, Humphrey chose not to show himself. He is a somewhat difficult boy."

"Would it be possible that he was put up to not showing himself by Jollard—I mean by way of a joke?"

Sir Bernard looked surprised. "It is not inconceivable. The man was at times a little too familiar with Humphrey. But I doubt if the boy liked him very much." He paused, squaring his shoulders. "Come," he said. "Let me have it, please. What has happened?"

"So far, I know only a little of what has happened, sir—and much of that is a matter of conjecture or inference. But I figure it out like this. When this Captain Cox left your house after accepting the post you offered him, he was accosted by a fifteen-year-old boy who gave himself out to be your son. The impression conveyed, I suppose, would be that your son, having been shy or coy while Cox was in the house, had now run out after him on a sudden impulse. Cox had no reason to suspect that anything was wrong, and he was probably rather pleased. And there and then, I suspect, they made two engagements. Humphrey, I think, was to have a gun?"

"Captain Cox suggested it, and I thought it quite proper. It was arranged that he should make the purchase."

"Then I think he communicated this intention to the boy, and they arranged to meet some time after noon on Thursday. The second arrangement was that they should go on to a cinema, and after that set straight off on their journey. And now I have to tell you that the object of this extraordinary deception was an extremely sinister one. What further communication with you Captain Cox judged himself to have had, I cannot, of course, tell. Jollard and the telephone might account for a good deal there. But the final result was this. Cox entered that cinema—the Metrodrome—believing himself

225

to be in the company of your son. And he never came out alive. He was shot, at close quarters, during the showing of a film called *Plutonium Blonde*. Meanwhile, you had been persuaded by this telegram that he had withdrawn from his engagement to you, and you arranged to employ Mr Thewless instead." Cadover paused. "It is clear, Sir Bernard, that this crime must have been designed to gain one of two possible objects."

"Quite so." Sir Bernard Paxton was now very pale, but it was evident that he had been thrown into no sort of mental confusion. "The criminals may have wanted to ensure that Thewless should go with Humphrey, or they may have wanted to ensure that Cox should *not* go with Humphrey. And now I think we had better put through a trunk call to Ireland at once."

"No, sir." Cadover spoke gravely. "I am afraid I cannot answer for that as being in the best interest of your son's safety. It is essential that we should try to get the whole matter clearer first."

Sir Bernard Paxton, who had stretched out his hand to an instrument on his desk, let it fall again to his side. "For the moment," he said, "I will abide by your judgment. What can I tell you more?"

"Tell me, please, in just what circumstances your son did leave."

"It was arranged that he should meet Mr Thewless at Euston. His baggage was sent on there in the morning. I was extremely hard-pressed with work, and I said goodbye to him about eleven o'clock. He was to go to his dentist, he told me, in the afternoon, and then direct to the station."

"I see." And Cadover paused again, thinking hard. "Tell me, Sir Bernard, has Humphrey begun to interest himself in girls?"

Sir Bernard Paxton looked startled. "Why should you ask?"

"For one thing, your boy was apparently being pestered by a very unpleasant character called Clodd. And Clodd makes a speciality of blackmailing adolescents who can be persuaded

226

that they have something shameful to conceal in matters of that sort. Incidentally, we must be grateful to Clodd, but for whom I should not be sitting here now."

Sir Bernard Paxton's fingers drummed nervously for a moment on the desk in front of him. "For some time I have had suspicion that Humphrey has formed a friendship with a girl—a girl, that is to say, who would not normally be within —um—his own circle of acquaintance. Indeed, it is a matter in which I have naturally felt considerable anxiety."

"I see." Cadover, although his ideas in the field now being discussed were certainly not lax, paused to reflect that Sir Bernard's evident habit of anxiety over Humphrey, and his equally evident inability to find time for joining in his son's occasions, made a combination about as fatal as could be. "But there is another indication here. Tell me, sir—did Humphrey by any chance mention to you this film called *Plutonium Blonde*?"

"He expressed a wish to see it. I believe I discouraged him, although it was not a matter upon which I should wish to be coercive. From the reviews I had judged it to be a film dealing in a cheaply sensational way with what is, in fact, a shadow of unimaginable calamity impending over our civilisation— and this, moreover, disgustingly glamourised through the superimposition of crude sexual solicitations."

Cadover made a sympathetic noise. These, decidedly, had been his own sentiments. At the same time he had a sort of sympathetic glimpse of the unknown Humphrey Paxton, subject to this polysyllabic disapproval when proposing an afternoon's mild excitement at the flicks. And this perception brought a touch of impatience into his voice now. "I have some reason to believe that your son did not go to his dentist on Thursday afternoon, and never intended to do so. He took an unknown girl to see *Plutonium Blonde*. And, by an extraordinary coincidence, he found himself sitting next to himself."

"I beg your pardon?"

"He found himself sitting next to the pretended Humphrey Paxton, or as near as made no matter. There was *himself*, and

227

there was the Captain Cox who had sent a telegram walking out on you. Your son and his friend then left the cinema in a hurry, and just before Cox was murdered. And now, sir, a question about which I am very anxious indeed. Have you heard from Humphrey since?"

Humphrey's father took a deep breath. "You appal me," he said. "But certainly I have heard—or rather I have heard from Mr Thewless. He wired to me late yesterday, Friday, evening, that he and Humphrey had arrived safely at Killyboffin."

"You realise that this Mr Thewless, if he is indeed now safely with your son, is so only as the result of a criminal conspiracy that has involved deliberate and callous murder?"

For the first time during this strange interview something like helpless bewilderment showed for a moment on Sir Bernard Paxton's face. He passed a hand over his tremendous forehead. "It is unbelievable!" he said. "I cannot conceive of such a man—patently the most harmless of mortals, interested in Roman archæology and other trifling branches of learning —being involved in complex conspiracy and atrocious crime. There is simply no sense in it, Inspector—no sense in it at all."

"That is just what I want to be assured of." And Cadover, in whose solidly buttressed veins a strong tide of excitement and anticipated triumph was beginning to pulse, leant eagerly forward. "Your every instinct assures you that this Mr Thewless is, in fact, precisely what he appears to be: a reliable, conscientious, and entirely harmless—well—pedagogue?"

"I am seldom impressed by the promptings of intuition." Sir Bernard, for the moment, appeared to mount some invisible rostrum as he spoke, so that it occurred to Cadover that he too, in the days before his present towering eminence, had owned to the pedagogic trade. "I am simply offering you the judgment of considerable experience as digested by an obstinately rational mind. And I say that Thewless is no other than he appears to be."

"So far, so good." And Cadover nodded. "Would you say that he would be a good man in a tight place?"

And this gave Sir Bernard Paxton pause—something, Cadover reflected, that had not happened hitherto. His extraordinary eyes—and Cadover had up to this moment scarcely noted *how* extraordinary his eyes were—seemed to shoot off into infinite space. "I don't know. I am rather inclined to think that it would depend on the degree of tightness involved. In a *very* tight place I imagine that Thewless might be a very good man indeed." And suddenly Sir Bernard smiled—and his smile was, after its fashion, as overwhelming as his most penetrating glance. "But here we are landed with intuitions, after all."

"We are landed with Captain Cox." In Cadover's eyes too there was now a very respectable gleam. "For remember our two propositions. If the crime was not a matter of *getting* Thewless, then it was a matter of *excluding* Cox. Now, why? What do you know about him? And what was your impression?"

"He was recommended to me by reliable friends as having a way with boys. His intellect was plainly negligible. He was commonplace and colourless. He had won the Victoria Cross."

"I see. And would you say that that was the complete picture?"

"It gives us a line." Sir Bernard was cautious. "With Cox about, anyone openly threatening Humphrey's safety might have been assured of a broken jaw."

Cadover pounced. "You had reason to be anxious about Humphrey's safety?"

For a second Sir Bernard hesitated. "I happen," he said, "to be a wealthy man—almost what passes for a very wealthy man in times like these. That is an accident of birth. And by another accident of birth, seconded by what self-discipline I have been able to achieve, I myself happen to be a man whose work is vital to the safety of this country."

"Quite so, sir." Cadover was mildly confused. If it is possible without slight absurdity to remind a policeman that one is a genius, Sir Bernard Paxton had achieved the feat. But there seemed a slight indecency in obliging him to do so. "Then it comes to this. The criminals with whom we appear to be concerned may have killed Cox because he was a person likely to be formidable to them. Not formidable in the sense that he had a penetrating intelligence, but simply as being of unflawed courage and possessing a powerful straight left. Does that seem plausible to you?"

"Not in the least."

"Exactly, sir." The genius, Cadover found himself absurdly reflecting, would make quite a promising detective-inspector of police. "No criminal would undertake the immense hazards of murder to effect so tenuous a piece of insurance. So where are we now?"

"We are looking for something sufficiently evident." Sir Bernard spoke a shade drily. "There must have been some more or less coincidental reason for Cox's being a particularly dangerous man. It certainly wasn't his brains that got him killed. And it wasn't even his V.C. It was something he *knew*. And that something it is desirable that we should know too."

For a man whose only son was indisputably in some unknown but large danger Sir Bernard Paxton was putting up an uncommonly good show. Cadover warmed to him. "We'll know," he said stoutly. "We'll know before the night's out."

"It is almost out now."

As he spoke, Sir Bernard rose a little stiffly from his chair and walked, a tall figure in a dressing-gown even more magnificent than that of his late butler, to a window heavily curtained in some ancient Eastern brocade. He pulled at a cord. And the dawn, bearing indefinably with it something ominous and urgent, slid into the too elegant, the obscurely vulnerable Chinese room.

CHAPTER XIX

I T WAS AN HOUR LATER, and a coffee-pot now stood between the two men. Cadover glanced at it and saw again the scared face of the parlourmaid who had brought it in. The gong, the disappearance of Jollard, this mysterious matutinal conference in Sir Bernard's study: all these must be occasioning a fine whispering in the servants' quarters. The conjecture was doubtless that Master Humphrey had been kidnapped. And the conjecture was doubtless right. Cadover, thus gloomily concluding, glanced up at Humphrey's father as the latter set down the telephone receiver.

"Yes, Inspector, you were right about that. There can have been no question of Humphrey's going to his dentist on Thursday. Partridge is down with influenza. And I fear that his wife didn't thank me for the early call. The first step in the affair was my unfortunate boy's practising a foolish deceit."

"You can put it like that if you like, sir." Cadover saw no profit in the introduction of this particular moral note. "He took the best means he had for securing a last meeting with his sweetheart"—here Cadover took some satisfaction at observing Sir Bernard wince at a word echoing, as it were, across a vast social gulf—"before he was hurried off to Ireland. I don't see much harm in it myself. And it is possible that in going out with the girl again he was showing that he wasn't going to be scared by the abominable Clodd."

Rather pathetically, Sir Bernard brightened. "Yes," he said, "there may be something in that."

"And there's another thing. It may be very important. If your son had not made this covert visit to the Metrodrome he wouldn't have sat beside himself—as he undoubtedly did. He must have been aware of it, you know. There is no other reasonable explanation of his leaving in the hurry that he did.

Now, just think of it. He knows that Captain Cox (whom he may have had a peep at when he was here) has sent that telegram crying off, and that another tutor is to take him away. And now here beside him are two people addressing each other, no doubt, as Captain Cox and Humphrey, and indicating, maybe, that they are off to Ireland that evening. And at that Humphrey grabs his girl and bolts from the cinema. A very healthy bolt, I should call it. But what happens then?"

Sir Bernard took a moment to answer this. His eye, so apt to converse with astronomical distances, looked as if it might be discovering some unexpected horizon nearer home. "What happened next? I don't think we know."

"I hope we do." And Cadover in his turn took up the telephone and made a call. Getting the number he wanted, he asked a brief question and then for the space of a minute intently listened. Then he put down the receiver. "We've taken only half an hour to get hold of *that*." He spoke with the satisfaction of a man whose organisation has served him well. "I've been a little anxious about that telegram from Thewless at Killyboffin. We've had one fake telegram already, after all. But I think it's all right. At least those two *set out* for Ireland. They picked up Humphrey's baggage at Euston, and there was some sort of little scene over the gun—the gun that Cox brought along with his bogus pupil, and that he had sent on to the station by messenger. It served to fix our two in the memory of a fellow in the Left Luggage. . . . So there you are." And Cadover paused, as with a decent sense of the magnitude of the moment. "Your boy, Sir Bernard, went to Ireland. *That's* what happened next."

Humphrey's father was at his most cautious. "You judge that to be surprising, Inspector?"

"Come, come, sir. I take it that Humphrey is not a densely stupid boy?"

"Certainly not."

"Nor abnormally phlegmatic?"

"He is abnormally sensitive and imaginative." Sir Bernard's voice had risen a pitch. "And of late he has actually been beset by obscure anxieties—by all sorts of baseless and fantastic fears."

"And you have been anxious about this?"

"Certainly I have."

"Would it be fair to say that you suffer from that sort of thing yourself?"

"I don't understand you."

"Would it be fair to say that what you have called your obstinately rational mind would not in itself have taken you a tenth of the way you have gone; and that you are at bottom abnormally sensitive and imaginative; and that you pay for this by being frequently beset by all sorts of baseless and fantastic fears?"

Sir Bernard had risen to his feet, and for a moment Cadover thought that he was going to flare into anger. The great man, however, looked merely surprised—as he well might do at this sudden transmogrification of the policeman before him into a modish psychological inquisitor. "What you say is of great interest. But I suggest that it is a little more speculative than is appropriate to the present occasion."

"I think not. For we shall get at this most quickly, you know, by having some idea of how the minds of the people concerned are working. Now, sir, you have been fussing and over-protecting this only boy of yours—and particularly so, I should guess, since his mother's death. That is no more than to say that you have been letting your own hidden fears loose on him; that you have been using him as a channel for the discharge of your own anxieties. It is a considerable burden to impose on a lad."

Sir Bernard Paxton had walked to the window and was staring out at a morning sky still darkly red in the east. "Well?" he asked.

"The boy is aware of this situation—or say, rather, that he is sensitive to it. You are worried, scared; you plainly need support. Being your son, he feels bound to stand by you; to take on his own shoulders as much of the burden as he can. That, Sir Bernard, is the Paxton family situation. There's nothing occult about it. It must be evident to your parlourmaid or your knifeboy, if they have an ounce of brains and observation. And it is decidedly one of the facts in the situation confronting us."

"You have a considerable power, Inspector, of succinct exposition." Sir Bernard paused as if to inspect this defensive irony, and found it unsatisfactory. "We get back to what Humphrey did on leaving the cinema."

"Yes, sir. Imaginative boys know a hawk from a handsaw, and he knew very well the difference between the insubstantial fears he obscurely shares with yourself and the tip of an actual, down-to-earth threat to your security."

"To *my* security, Inspector? It would strike him essentially in that way?"

"Of course it would! The picture that emerges of him is of an extremely intelligent boy. He knows very well that, although enormously interesting to Humphrey Paxton, he is nevertheless only an unknown small boy, of no interest whatever to the great outer world. If anyone looks at him twice it is because he is Paxton's son. More than commonly, the father-image towers above him. At the same time, as you and I know, he has the job of giving that image a hand"—Cadover paused—"of shoring it up, in fact, with whatever he can lay his hands on."

Sir Bernard Paxton walked back across the room, peered into the coffee-pot, and rang a bell. He was, in a way, taking all this with flying colours. And now he turned to Cadover. "So Humphrey came out of that cinema feeling the need of a stouter prop than usual?"

"He must certainly have had a more than usually urgent feeling that something must be done. But, chiefly, he felt the challenge in the thing?"

"Challenge?" Sir Bernard turned to the parlourmaid who had entered the room. "Coffee," he said briefly.

"Exactly—but excuse me for a moment." The telephone bell had rung, and now Cadover grabbed the instrument. He listened for a moment. "I see. . . . I see. Well, I think we ought to have been told. They should never play that sort of lone game. . . . Unofficial?—stuff and nonsense! And what name did you say? . . . Never heard of her. But it's better than nothing, I suppose. . . . Yes, not later, I hope, than ten o'clock. And look here!—the Dublin people simply *must* be kept right. Go and get the Commissioner himself out of bed and make him telephone through. . . . No; don't worry; he'll thank you in the end. The main point is that it must be quite clearly explained as something big, but quite without political colouring. Otherwise they may take fright, and hold us back while they hunt up their own big-wigs. . . . Yes—ten o'clock."

Cadover put down the receiver. "I think it may be said we're starting to move."

"I hope in the right direction." Sir Bernard had returned to the window and was staring sombrely out at distant chimney-pots. "What was that about a challenge?"

"Your son realised that, quite accidentally, he had been warned. What he had heard in the cinema said, 'Ireland means danger.' It must also have said, 'Get home as quick as you can and tell Daddy'—something like that. But the boy decided to meet Thewless, all the same, and set off. He is seeing the thing through himself. I think it may be said that he is seeing to it that danger and you have the Irish Sea stretched between you. But we won't exaggerate. We'll put it simply that Humphrey has seen the chance of an adventure and has taken it."

Sir Bernard Paxton made a noncommittal noise, and as he did so the parlourmaid returned with the replenished coffee pot. She set it down, retreated, hesitated by the door. "If you please, sir," she said, "is it Master Humphrey?"

Her employer stared at her in surprise—altogether, indeed, as if something out of nature had transacted itself. "You may go," he said. "And tell your fellows not to gossip."

Beneath this displeasure, the girl trembled visibly. But she held her ground. "It was only that, if it *is* Master Humphrey, there is something the policeman ought to know."

Cadover, who had hardly supposed himself to have been identified after this manner, promptly took the matter in hand. "In that case," he said, "you had better speak up."

"When Master Humphrey went away before lunchtime on Thursday he told us he wasn't coming back. He was going to Mr Partridge, he said, and after that straight to Euston. But he *did* come back. And he can't have been leaving himself very much time to catch his train."

"I see." The movements of the son of the house, Cadover realised, must be of considerable interest in the servants' hall. "But was there anything very remarkable in that?"

"It was the *way* he came home, sir. It was only Mary saw him."

"Mary?" Sir Bernard Paxton interrupted rather as if this was a particularly opprobrious name.

"Mary, if you please sir, is Evans, the second housemaid. She was in Master Humphrey's room, sir, taking down some curtains that were to go to the cleaners. And she saw a taxi stop at the end of the mews, and Master Humphrey get out and come up the mews and in at the back. And she says he was looking like a ghost, poor lamb."

"That he was looking like a ghost is conceivable. But that he is reasonably to be described as a poor lamb is a proposition that we seem hourly more able to contravert." And Sir Bernard, in whom paternal vanity, like almost everything else, seemed apt to take decidedly polysyllabic form, glanced swiftly at Cadover. "You may, however, proceed."

"Well, sir, there was Master Humphrey creeping into his own house no better than a thief. And for a while Mary waited, thinking that he might have been taken ill, and didn't want everybody to know it, and would be coming up to his room. So she went down, and through to the little door at the back, the one that isn't used even by the tradespeople any more, and there was Master Humphrey slipping out again. He gave a terrible start at seeing her. And then he gave her a——" The parlourmaid hesitated.

"Do you mean"—Sir Bernard was displeased—"that Master Humphrey gave Evans a sum of money?"

"No, sir. It was a hug and a kiss, sir. And then he made her swear by all sorts of things that shouldn't rightly be mentioned that she wouldn't say a word about it to anyone."

Master Humphrey, it seemed to Cadover, was not un-possessed of some knowledge of the world. "And after that?" he asked.

"That was all, sir—only Mary and me felt we ought to mention it. Master Humphrey went straight out after that, and Mary heard him drive away in his taxi."

"Thank you." Cadover waited until the girl had left the room. "Now, sir, what do you make of that?"

Sir Bernard considered. "Perhaps he did mean to come home and tell his story, after all. His covert manner of entering may have been a boy's natural reaction to the atmosphere of melodrama in which he found himself. And then he may have changed his mind and decided to go through with it after all."

Cadover shook his head. "That leaves the taxi unaccounted for. I mean his apparently having kept the taxi waiting at the end of the mews. He *meant* to go off again. In fact, he came home to fetch something. And that something wasn't in his own room, since the housemaid, it seems, was there until she went down and found him leaving." Cadover paused. "Well, let us take up another point. The Bolderwoods—what about them? I understand that they are cousins of yours. Are they reliable people?"

"I have gathered that Cyril Bolderwood—who, actually, is only a distant connection of mine—is a person of substantial means and considerable position. His interests have been mainly in South America. His son, Ivor, has called upon me. He appeared a very sensible young man."

Cadover scratched his jaw. "Does it occur to you——"

"Of course it does!" Sir Bernard, for the first time, was vehement. "I have been criminally careless. The boy is a problem during the holidays. He and I are, at present, obscurely out of sympathy. This chance of dealing with a difficult period came along, and I snatched at it. I considered that if I found a reliable man to go with him—Cox or Thewless—then nothing could go radically wrong. But I acted rashly. I ought to have considered that these people's manners and morals were virtually unknown to me. I ought even to have

237

taken into consideration the special risks—one may call them professional risks—to which my position might conceivably expose not only myself but my child."

"Perhaps you ought." And Cadover again scratched his jaw. "By the way, Sir Bernard, to whom are you responsible for the work you are doing at present?"

"I am directly responsible to a committee of the Cabinet —that is to say, to the Prime Minister and three of his colleagues."

"I see." Cadover's lips formed themselves into what might have been the position for a low whistle. "Do you think that, about that, they would mind if you told me a little more?"

Sir Bernard Paxton looked grim. "I should certainly need permission before speaking another word."

Cadover looked grim too. He pointed to the telephone. "I suspect," he said, "that they won't keep you waiting long at Number 10."

Sir Bernard made the call. Cadover faintly heard first an unfamiliar and then a familiar voice; he heard, too, the tiny ticking of the watch on his own wrist—it suddenly suggested to him the remorseless effluction of time in the heart of a delayed-action bomb. . . . Sir Bernard explained himself. The answering voice came incisive and faint, like a political broadcast almost tuned out. The watch ticked—but now there was a voice in it too. *Amorous-arrogant-armed, amorous-arrogant-armed*: the voice in the watch was an urgent and imbecile whisper. Vaguely apprehended masses formed themselves in Cadover's vision, took intelligible shape as a scantily-clothed female form, no more substantial than plywood but with the power to flex in a lascivious langour its grotesquely elongated limbs. . . . Cadover jerked himself awake. He had hours of vigilance ahead of him yet.

Sir Bernard had rung off and was talking to him; his brain cleared and he was listening with narrowed eyes. "I see," he said; ". . . yes, I see."

"And I collate the reports once a month, Inspector, and revise the plan in the light of them. The plan exists in a unique copy that stays with me. And when I have completed each revision I appear before the committee in person and report. It all requires, as you may imagine, a great deal of interpretation to the lay mind."

"No doubt." Cadover had turned slightly pale. "But that sort of thing will require singularly little interpretation when one day somebody drops it out of a plane on London or Moscow or New York. The understanding of the lay mind will be instantaneous and complete."

"May the world's cities be spared that understanding, Inspector." Sir Bernard looked for a second so like a lost child—so like, conceivably, the missing boy—that Cadover almost repented the grimness of his pleasantry.

There was a moment's silence. "Now—Cox," Cadover said abruptly. "We've got no nearer to why he was a threat against which such violent means had to be taken. He couldn't, in any way, belong to this world you have been telling me of?"

"Good heavens, no! The poor young man possessed, as I have said, only the most moderate share of brains. I had the impression, indeed, that he had been in on some queer affairs about the world—but definitely, I should think, as a reliable subordinate. Good physique, no nerves, and a straight eye."

"He probably had no precise notion of the sort of work you do?"

"His ideas on that would almost certainly be of the vaguest."

Cadover thought for a moment. "And there is nothing—absolutely nothing—further of any significance about him, or about your interview with him, that occurs to you?"

"I think not." Sir Bernard Paxton frowned. "And yet—at luncheon, I think—there was something——" He broke off. "There *was* something, and it just eludes me. And yet something, connected with yourself a few moments ago——"

"Something about me?" Cadover was surprised.

And suddenly Sir Bernard snapped his fingers. "You offered a pleasantry—something about atomic warfare and the world's cities. It was not—you will forgive me—quite to my liking. Now, *that* was what happened with Captain Cox at luncheon. He said something that I took to be intended as a jest, and it displeased me for the moment. I judged it to be somewhat familiar and a little fatuous." Sir Bernard paused, aware that in this there might be an implication not altogether polite. "I need hardly say that in *your* jest it was not similar qualities that disturbed me. Yours, far from being fatuous, held a little too much salt."

Cadover could still hear his watch ticking. But, even with his adored son's safety at unknown hazard, this august personage had his own tempo.

"I was proposing to give Captain Cox some sketch of the Irish household in which he would find himself, and I began— I recall the word precisely—by saying that the Bolderwood family was most respectable. Whereupon the young man said, 'Ah, they wouldn't be the Bolderwoods I know.' I supposed him to be making the facetious suggestion that he himself was without respectable connections and moved only in rag-tag and bobtail circles." Sir Bernard Paxton hesitated. "I even suspected mockery of what I am aware of in myself as a certain stiffness of manner to which, by persons uncharitably inclined, the name of pomposity might be given."

For perhaps the first time since he had seen Peter Cox's dead body, Cadover felt a momentary disposition to laughter. Genius apparently had its *naïf* side, and nothing could be more exquisitely pompous in itself than the complicated cadence in which Sir Bernard had framed this confession. He checked himself. "But actually, sir, you think——?"

"It now comes to me that he may have meant exactly what he said. He happened to know some disreputable Bolderwoods, and he was dismissing the supposition that I could have anything to do with them. Viewed in that light, the unfortunate young man's observation was a perfectly proper one."

"Perfectly proper. But I don't see——" Cadover broke off with a sudden exclamation. "Could that fellow Jollard have heard all this?"

"Assuredly he could. He was waiting table at the time."

"And after this happened Cox remained with you for a substantial interval? There would have been an opportunity, I mean, for Jollard to contact his associates on the telephone and arrange for the bogus Humphrey to waylay Cox when he left?"

Sir Bernard thought for a moment. "I am fairly sure there would. We had coffee together, and then we spent about an hour in going over Humphrey's school reports."

"That would certainly be time enough. And now I think we may be said to have got quite a long way." Cadover paused. "It would be nearly all the way, indeed, but for one thing. You remember, sir, my mentioning the blackmailer, Clodd? He hoped to make a victim of your son, and recently he seems to have had little that was more hopeful on his hands. As a result, he has had your household under pretty close observation. You might call it professional observation, so far as a knowledge of crooks and their ways goes. And Clodd—who is probably dead by now—came to the conclusion that it was not a matter of *one* gang or organisation being interested in your affairs. He was convinced that there are *two*. If that is true, and if we now go all out in one direction, we may simply be leaving Humphrey—and in some danger, let us admit— farther and farther behind. And there is something else that I am uneasy about as well. You have spoken of this vital plan which you revise monthly as existing in a single copy that stays with you. Does that mean here in your own house?"

Sir Bernard raised his eyebrows. "Good heavens, no! I mean simply that, so long as the present organisation of things holds, nobody ever sees it except myself. It stays in a place of security—of quite fantastic security, I may say—to the inner-most part of which I alone have access, and access that is very strictly controlled at that."

"That sounds good enough."

"But it is true that I do keep one file of highly confidential ancillary papers here in the house. It is an essential time-saving convenience when I am visited by any of the people with whom I am permitted to discuss—well, the project in general. That file tends to get known, quite inaccurately, as the plan. And it is important enough, goodness knows."

"It might have been known to, say, Jollard as the plan?"

"Quite possibly. And he has seen it in my hands half a dozen times."

Cadover considered. "I think I should like to see it myself."

"See the file, my dear Inspector? I hardly think——"

"I mean, see it in your hands—safe and sound. Where is it kept?"

"In a strong-room in the basement, which was put in for me by the Government during the war. It opens on a combination known only to myself, and I am given to understand that it represents about the last work in security available today."

"Well, sir, I think I'll just ask you to make sure. Would you mind? And I'll stop here and make one or two more telephone calls."

Without a word, Sir Bernard Paxton left the room. Cadover made two quick calls, and then walked to the window. Broad daylight had flooded this prosperous part of London long ago. The vista disclosed was unexciting, but it spoke of a security so massive as to be almost smug. Here and there one could perhaps spy signs that it was on the down grade; nevertheless, it was civilisation's (as *Plutonium Blonde* was art's) supreme achievement to date. Taking civilisation, that was to say, as meaning the commercial civilisation built up in the nineteenth century. It had all, Cadover reflected, come out of the spout of James Watt's kettle. And the probability was that it would all dissolve again in some more extensive manufacture of steam contrived by Sir Bernard Paxton and his kind.

Cadover turned round at the sound of a door thrown violently open behind him. Sir Bernard stood framed in it, pale and trembling.

"It's gone!" he said. "The strong-room was locked as I left it. But the file has gone."

CHAPTER XX

DAWN HAD FOUND MR. THEWLESS fast asleep. The regular pulse of light flowing over his ceiling had grown faint before the early approaches of the sun and then had ceased—the lighthouse-keeper having first turned off his machine and then betaken himself to slumber. The day promised to be calm and bright. From far below, the sea murmured its suggestion of just such another obstinate refusal to come awake as that of Humphrey Paxton's unconscious tutor; had one looked out at it, however, one would have judged it impossible that any sound at all could come from a sheet of silver so unflawed. No wind ruffled it, and in the little hamlet by its side the pale blue peat smoke was beginning to rise straight to the deep blue of heaven. No keel furrowed it, for the foreign trawlers were already gone from the harbour, and gone too was the motor-cruiser whose riding-light Mr Thewless had remarked in the darkness not many hours before. Only on the horizon the brown sails of outward-going fishing-smacks were already vanishing through the faint line between sea and sky.

This marine solitude at one distance was matched by a mountain solitude at another; indeed, the actual appearance of the sun had been delayed a full hour by the interposition, to the east, of a single peak, obtuse and massive, about the bare slopes and outcropping rocks of which clouds were still lazily disparting. Below this, where the white cottages in their invisible lanes glistened like sparsely-strung pearls flung down upon a mantle of brown and green, more tenuous vapours drifted, broke, fragmented themselves to a point at which, mere fleecy wisps, they matched the nibbling sheep now moving slowly up the hillsides to meet them. Nearer still, from little valleys yet lost in shadow, diminutive figures in bright homespun or sombre black climbed to the potato fields or set out, a donkey beside them, on the long trudge to the turf. Another day had begun.

And about Killyboffin itself there was some stir of life. The poultry, perhaps indignant at having been so unjustly cast under a cloud in the estimation of their owner, maintained a constantly augmented volume of angry cackle; the half-Ayrshire and several of her fellows, sequacious of the milkmaid, mooed impatiently outside a byre; dogs barked; Billy Bone clumped noisily about a cobbled yard; and through the house itself sundry servants, presumably released by their employer from their nocturnal segregation, bustled amid floods of lively conversation. And still Mr Thewless slept.

When he was finally aroused, indeed, it was by olfactory rather than by auditory sensation. His eyes, prompted by some titillation of the nostril, opened upon a large and steaming cup of China tea. It was a composing sight; nevertheless, Mr Thewless sat up with a celerity that spoke of a clearly returning consciousness of something untoward in his situation. A glance about the room told him that he had a visitor. Cyril Bolderwood, in an ancient and unassuming bath-robe made of turkish towelling, was sitting in his familiar position in the window embrasure. And now Cyril Bolderwood, observing that he was awake, gave him a cheerful smile. "Ah," he said. "Good morning, my dear fellow."

Mr Thewless remembered with something of an effort that he was this genial person's guest—his dear fellow, indeed—and that Ireland and the Atlantic Ocean lay around him. He stretched out his hand, secured the handsome cup, and sipped his tea. "Good morning," he replied. He was aware of something circumspect—provisional, almost—in his own tone.

"A really nice day. In fact, I should say that we are in for a spell of fine weather. And in August, on the west coast of Ireland, that is something, I am bound to admit."

Mr Thewless considered this—and also certain matters now returning somewhat confusedly to his mind. "Um," he ventured.

"And—what's more—I have some rather good news." Cyril Bolderwood got up and obligingly tested the temperature of a jug of hot water standing in Mr Thewless's washbasin. He shook his head disapprovingly, picked up the jug, and, not without some splashing and accompanying imprecation, ejected it from the room. "Gracie," he bawled down the corridor. "What good-for-nothing, idle, chattering chit brought this disgustingly tepid stuff to Mr Thewless? Don't they know what's due to a man of his great learning? Don't they know that in London there's but the turning of a shining tap and you can scald yourself like a milk-pail at will? Send up a great jug, now, that won't disgrace us all, you worthless woman." And the master of Killyboffin, flushed and irate, banged the door to and returned to his perch in the window. "Yes, indeed," he pursued with instantly recovered equanimity; "capital news. Last night, you know, I put my foot down. I made a real row."

Mr Thewless remembered a row—and although it had begun in dreams he was tolerably confident that it had indeed been a real row in the end. "Ah," he said cautiously.

"The result is that at breakfast, I'm glad to say, there will be a couple of eggs all round. I was afraid, you know, that there would be nothing but champ."

"Champ?" said Mr Thewless. The constitution of this dish was not one of the matters upon which he felt any urgent wish to be informed. But for the moment he was at a loss how to broach more relevant topics.

"Yes, champ. I won't say that I haven't had a very tolerable champ in the north—and particularly in County Down." Cyril Bolderwood was judicial. "But here in the south I don't recall anybody as being able to make it really palatable. They're too lazy, I should say, to pound it properly with the beetle. That means that it comes out sloppy. And nobody, you'll agree, could pretend to enjoy a sloppy champ."

"No," said Mr Thewless. "Nobody could do that."

"But I expect young Humphrey—a nice lad, I'm bound to say, although his father is said to be uncommonly stiff—I expect young Humphrey will enjoy his couple of eggs. If he turns up for them, that is to say."

"If he turns up for them!" Mr Thewless set down his cup in frank dismay.

"He was off and away hours ago. Exploring, I don't doubt.

245

There's a strong streak of wanderlust in Humphrey, if you ask me."

Mr Thewless was fleetingly conscious that this suggestion—in which he saw no special cogency—had been made to him before. "You think he will be all right?" he asked. "I am bound to say I feel a little anxious for his safety."

"As right as rain." Cyril Bolderwood's reassurance was so confident as to have no need of being emphatic. "Of course, this countryside is full of every sort of rascal, as I think I've told you. But they wouldn't harm a lad—and especially an English lad. It's astonishing how popular the English are in Eire. Just the same as in India, nowadays. Nothing too good for them. And all because they've climbed down and cleared out. Why, if it wasn't for the presence of yourself and Humphrey, it would probably be champ this morning after all—and that in spite of all the fuss I made yesterday."

Mr Thewless had by this time finished his tea, got out of bed, and wrapped himself in a dressing-down. It ought to have been pleasant to shave while enjoying the society of one so informally companionable as his host. But somehow he felt slightly intruded upon—he was growing old and secretive, he supposed—and in an endeavour to dissipate this churlish feeling he too moved over to the window. "Ah," he said; "I see that the motor-cruiser has gone."

"It has—and I don't think we'll see it again."

"I don't see any sign of Humphrey." Mr Thewless, dazzled by the morning light, was peering vaguely at the distant mountain, rather as if his charge might appear in infinitesimal silhouette on the summit of it. "And I *am* rather anxious, I must repeat."

"The boy will be quite all right, you may be sure." Once more Cyril Bolderwood was soothing. "As a matter of fact, I rather think that Ivor must have gone with him—or, at any rate, that Ivor has followed him out. They had some plan, you may remember, of going off early together."

"Yes, of course." Mr Thewless wished that he could be certain of just what he *did* remember. That the night had held wild doings he was well assured. But there might, he judged, be humiliating reasons for his preserving only a somewhat distorted recollection of them. "I am afraid," he pursued, "that —after last night, you know—I am in a decidedly nervous state of mind."

"Last night?" Cyril Bolderwood looked momentarily puzzled. Then he laughed heartily. "To be sure—and I am afraid you really had rather a bad time. It's not being used to nonsense of that sort."

"I see." But Mr Thewless was very certain that he did *not* see. "Nonsense?" he queried diffidently.

"Atrocious and rascally criminals," said Cyril Bolderwood. He spoke with the greatest good humour. "Abominable and thieving ruffians, breaking in in the middle of the night. And yet one can't be angry with them for long. Children, my dear fellow—mere children. And, of course, you must remember their religion."

"Ah," said Mr Thewless. He was beginning to feel slightly unnerved.

"I've had them break in before. It's why I shut up so carefully at nights. But the tiresome villains managed to get in somehow. They were after the whiskey, you know—nothing but the whiskey. How could they tell that you and I hadn't left much of it, eh?" And Cyril Bolderwood laughed more boisterously still.

Mr Thewless's discomfort increased. He took his host's last reference to be by way of tactful reminder that any distorted picture of the night's adventures which he might cherish had its origin in potations which could not with delicacy be more specifically referred to. It was true that he *had* drunk rather a lot of whiskey—and, moreover, to Irish whiskey he was quite unused. Conceivably it had some quite special hallucinatory power. Yet by all this he was not, in his heart, quite convinced. "My impression," he said boldly, "was decidedly different. I thought they were after not the whiskey, but Humphrey."

"Humphrey? Good lord!" And Cyril Bolderwood delightedly chuckled. "Why, that's just the sort of notion the dear, fanciful lad would think up himself."

This was disturbingly true; it cohered absolutely with Mr Thewless's own obstinate reading of much in his recent experience. Nevertheless, he tried again. "I have a recollection—really quite a distinct recollection—of these intruders dogging me through the house. I was convinced that they were trailing me to Humphrey's room."

"Odd," said Cyril Bolderwood easily. "A very odd trick for the mind to play. But, of course, we must remember that you had been thoroughly fatigued."

"And my recollection stretches further. I had, just before the general alarm, a direct encounter with one of the prowlers. He was wrapped in a sheet."

"A sheet!" Cyril Bolderwood looked blankly at his guest.

"And I threw something at him. I think it was a candlestick. The sheet fell and I had a moment in which I recognised him. He had travelled with me on the train from Euston to just before Heysham."

"Dear me." This time Cyril Bolderwood was not amused. He was mildly embarrassed, as a man must be to whom a guest obstinately propounds fantasies that have come to him *in vino*. "That is very curious, to be sure—very curious, indeed. But I must really leave you, my dear fellow, to finish dressing. Breakfast will be in a quarter of an hour. I think you may find that a cup or two of strong coffee may do you a world of good. And—don't forget!—champ is off and eggs are on. Now I'll go out for a stroll and try if I can see the others."

And thus, with a smile of more than customary joviality, the master of Killyboffin left the room. Mr Thewless, before turning to his shaving water, remained for some moments staring out of the window. He was browbeaten, bewildered, worried. He was also, had he known it, on the verge of being extremely angry.

The breakfast-table was generously appointed for four. But only the elder Mr Bolderwood and Mr Thewless faced each other across it. A massive silver contraption, which opened at a touch upon at least a dozen boiled eggs, emphasised the depleted condition of the company.

"Ivor," said Mr Bolderwood, "must still be hunting

Humphrey up. I took a turn in the grounds, but there was no sign of either of them. A bit odd, eh? One would expect two hungry young people—guns or no guns—to be waiting for the gong. I hope that egg isn't too hard for your liking."

"It is quite excellent; a great treat." Having made this eminently conventional response, Mr Thewless was silent for some moments. Then, rather abruptly, he spoke again. "I suppose, sir, you will inform the police?"

Cyril Bolderwood looked mildly startled. "You mean if Humphrey runs away? I hardly think so. It would be my inclination to get in touch with his father first."

"I certainly mean nothing of the sort." Mr Thewless was as emphatic as he was surprised. "What I refer to is last night's housebreaking."

"Oh, that!" Cyril Bolderwood's laughter—and with a quality now really irritating to his auditor—rang out anew. "Yes, I suppose I better had. Yes, I must ring up Sean Cushin, and he must go round and give the horrible scoundrels a talking to." He glanced at his watch. "I could do it in about ten minutes."

"Ten minutes?"

"When the girl opens the telephone exchange in the village for the day. At night, you know, we are quite cut off from the world. In all these ways, my dear chap, we are shockingly unprogressive here in the south. This ruffianly Government in Dublin dislikes anything it can't find an ancient Irish word for. Telephones must be included. For the purpose of getting news about the country those fellows would probably prefer beacons on the top of Slieve League and Ben Bulben." And Mr Thewless's host, as he offered this political information, chipped the top off his second egg.

There was silence for a minute. Mr Thewless was conscious that he was listening with some eagerness for the sound of approaching voices. The vehement tones of Humphrey Paxton, even if raised in some tiresome chronicle of fictitious perils, would at this juncture have been music to his ears.

But *were* the perils with which Humphrey tortured or entertained himself indeed merely——? Mr Thewless, before the

249

half-apprehended threat of something like a Copernican revolution in his thinking—or better, perhaps, of a return to the primitive, the monstrous, the Ptolemaic hypothesis, the Humphrey-centric theory, as it might be called, of his own first alarms on the Heysham train: Mr Thewless, confronted by this, wisely suspended speculation for a while and sought the material recruitment of another egg.

Cyril Bolderwood, too, ate silently. There was now a slight frown, as of the first dawn of anxiety, on his normally candid brow. He rose, walked to the window and stared out at the limited prospect commanded from the ground floor. Then he moved to the door, flung it open, and fell to his familiar shouting to invisible retainers. His instructions, it seemed, were for some sort of search to be made for the late-comers. Then he crossed to a sideboard, poured himself out a second cup of coffee, and returned to the table. But immediately he was back at the window. "Those foreign trawlers," he said abruptly. "Did you notice if they've sailed or not?"

Mr Thewless looked up in surprise. His host's tone forbade the supposition that this question was asked merely in a conversational way. "Why, yes," he answered. "I noticed that they had sailed."

"Um." Cyril Bolderwood reached gloomily for the marmalade. "And Ivor is usually so very discreet. If anything, he is a young man too much to the circumspect side. May I offer you the marmalade? I shouldn't have thought it of him."

To Mr Thewless this was, for the moment, altogether mysterious. He possessed, however, very considerable intelligence—was he not eminently capable with capable boys?—and this fact (which conceivably had not become apparent to his host) did now result in a dim apprehension of being "got at." But at least the marmalade was excellent, and he helped himself to a little more of it.

"All that talk," pursued Cyril Bolderwood presently, "about the North Cape and the Midnight Sun. Unwise, I fear, with so imaginative and restless a boy."

"My dear sir"—Mr Thewless was suddenly impatient—"I

must say, quite frankly, that I judge you to be indulging a bee in your bonnet. For you are apparently apprehensive of Humphrey's attempting to run away to sea, or something of the sort. And it seems to me entirely unlikely." Here Mr Thewless paused, abruptly visited by suspicion. "But your anxiety *is* really about that? You are not attempting to divert my mind from the consideration of risks of a different order? For a number of things that have happened do make me occasionally feel——"

"Other risks?" Cyril Bolderwood interrupted with brisk incredulity. "Of course not! Mere fancies, my dear fellow—like your odd notions about the whiskey-thieves last night. But about Humphrey's perhaps cutting and running I am a little anxious, I admit."

At this Mr Thewless felt so exasperated that he paused before framing a reply. And in the resulting silence the sound of a telephone bell was heard shrilling in the next room. Cyril Bolderwood jumped to his feet. "Ah," he said, "that worthless girl has opened her exchange at last. And here's somebody been waiting to get through, I'll be bound, this last half-hour. Excuse me, my dear Thewless, while I take the call myself."

Cyril Bolderwood hurried out. He was absent for a long time. Mr Thewless looked at his watch, looked out of the window, took another piece of toast. Could his host, conceivably, be right? His own acquaintance with Humphrey Paxton was brief—hardly sufficiently substantial, certainly, for the hazarding of any very confident opinion. But Cyril Bolderwood's acquaintance with the boy was briefer still; and there was no sign that of this distant connection he had previously known very much by hearsay. Yet Cyril Bolderwood had been talking as one might do from a settled familiarity with Humphrey's character. There was surely something artificial in this; there was, as it were, a perceptible forcing of the pace. . . .

Mr Thewless paused on this conception, and as he did so his host returned to the breakfast-room. He looked, Mr Thewless thought, oddly pale—and moreover it was visibly with a trembling hand that he now poured himself out a third cup of coffee. Could he have had some calamitous news, and was he now nerving himself to break this to his guest? Mr Thewless took another look, and was convinced, by indefinable but powerful signs, that he was in the presence of a man in a panic. And at this, inevitably enough, all his own repressed anxieties surged up in him. Could Humphrey really have run away to sea in a trawler? He nerved himself to speak. "Mr Bolderwood," he said, "I hope you have not had bad news?"

"No, no—nothing of the sort." And the owner of Killyboffin Hall sat down heavily. "The telephone call was about something entirely trifling. A mere matter of domestic economy, nothing more. I must really apologise for having left you so abruptly. But none of the servants is reliable with the telephone. The miserable rascals——" But here Cyril Bolderwood's voice tailed off, as if he had not the heart for entering upon one of his familiar imprecations. "The fact is, I have been thinking." He broke off again, and stared into his cup. It was, Mr. Thewless thought, demonstrably true that his host was thinking very hard indeed—much as if, on the issue, his whole life depended.

"I beg your pardon. You struck me as rather upset." Mr Thewless hesitated. "For a moment I had a horrid feeling that you might have been right, and that Humphrey had really bolted."

"Dear me, no." In Cyril Bolderwood's glance as he looked up there was a momentary gleam that told of swift decision. "To tell you the honest truth, my dear fellow, I have never really been afraid of *that*. In fact you were more or less in the target area a few minutes ago. I have anxieties about Humphrey that I was anxious to conceal from you. And being unable altogether to conceal my feelings, I rather played up the run-away notion."

At this Mr Thewless set down his cup and presented his entertainer with an expression that was altogether new. "Explain yourself," he said sternly.

"Well, my dear chap, we must admit, to begin with, that you had a deuced queer experience yesterday afternoon. The more I think of it, the odder does that affair in the railway tunnel appear to be. And then consider last night. Consider the fellows masquerading as whiskey-thieves. I didn't want to alarm you, you will understand, and I made light of it as far as I could. Still, it was a bit sinister, wasn't it? Trailing you like that in order to get at the lad. And one of the criminals having been on your train the day before. I don't like that— I don't like it at all. It is suspicious, my dear Thewless; positively suspicious."

"Suspicious?" Mr Thewless would probably have recognised within himself a rising tide of indignation had this not been overtopped for the moment by bewilderment and dismay. "You surely don't think——"

"Ivor and I noticed at once that your mind was quite at rest. The significance of your adventure had quite escaped you. And we were most anxious not to spoil your holiday. But we have ourselves been uneasy—very uneasy. It is why we shut up the house so carefully last night. But the criminals managed to break in. Had we not changed the boy's room—an excellent thought of Ivor's, since information of where he was first put no doubt leaked out through the servants—they would have got him, you know; they would infallibly have got him. Tell me—did anything else out-of-the-way happen on your journey?"

"Humphrey certainly told me a very odd story. The suggestion seemed to be that he had been kidnapped on the train, shut up in a dark, confined space, and then in some mysterious fashion rescued or released again. It seemed an extremely tall tale."

"Not at all. It would be the fellow you saw last night, you know, when you made such an excellent shot with the candlestick."

"I see." Mr Thewless was a good deal put to a stand by this incontinent promotion to a secure reality-status of what his host had so lately aspersed as mere vinous imaginings. And now a thought struck him. "Good heavens! I'll tell you rather a significant thing. The man who was with us in the carriage —a bearded man with glasses, whom I really *am* sure I saw

253

again last night—left the train at Morecambe—the stop, that is, just before Heysham Harbour. He appeared to be a fisherman, and he had a rod and so forth with him in the compartment. But when he did get off, and I saw him on the platform, he had a case containing some enormous musical instrument. It seemed quite unnaturally heavy. It could almost——"

"Have held Humphrey!" Cyril Bolderwood, triumphant for a moment, paused perplexed. "But it *didn't* hold Humphrey so how——?"

Mr Thewless answered this abrupted question as by sudden inspiration. "In the luggage-van, when I come to think of it, as well as this double-bass or whatever it was, there was a weighing machine with a set of pretty heavy looking weights. So somebody——"

"Exactly!" Once more Cyril Bolderwood interrupted. "Somebody could have released Humphrey—it would tally perfectly with the story he told you—and tricked your friend for a time by shoving in the weights instead. I don't like it—I don't like it at all. The whole situation that is revealing itself, that is to say. Here is a responsibility that we ought positively not to have undertaken. Our invitation was ill-advised. And Bernard ought certainly not to have accepted it." Cyril Bolderwood shook a severe and judicial head. "The son of a man in his position, not only immensely wealthy, but doing secret work of the utmost national importance, ought not to have been sent off into the blue—not even to quiet relations like ourselves; not even under the guardianship of so responsible a person as you, my dear fellow. And I'm surprised—indeed I'm positively astounded—that the English authorities don't provide a lad in such a position with a bodyguard. Now, in South America——"

Mr Thewless had risen and taken yet another prowl to the window. "Still nobody to be seen," he said. "Oh dear, oh dear!" He turned back again. "I fear I have been extremely remiss."

"And in this countryside, of all places in the world!" Cyril Bolderwood spoke from out of the deepest gloom. "Full of lawless wretches, ready to cut your throat as soon as look at you. Danger on every side."

"On *every* side?" Mr Thewless's alarm grew greater still. "You think there might be more than one—gang, organisation, or whatever it's to be called—plotting against Humphrey?"

"Oh, no—oh, dear me, no!" Cyril Bolderwood was more swiftly emphatic than he had yet been. "That would be a most extravagant suggestion. *One* gang, my dear fellow, led by this abandoned desperado with the glasses and the beard. And quite enough, too, in all conscience. He probably had that motor-cruiser we saw in the bay. Any amount of resources, you know, agents of that sort have."

"Agents?" Mr Thewless stared. "You mean emissaries of a foreign power?"

"No, no—nothing of the sort." And Cyril Bolderwood violently shook his head. "Quite the wrong word. Straightforward kidnappers, I should say, out for a big ransom." He looked at his watch. "This is bad—really bad, is it not? I wish these two would come back. I wish I could contact Ivor and have his advice!"

Mr Thewless, for whom the excellent Killyboffin marmalade had ceased to have any savour, pushed away his plate and looked in sudden, perplexed speculation at his host. It struck him that in this last cry of the elder of the Bolderwoods there had been more sincerity than had sounded in anything uttered to him for some time.

CHAPTER XXI

"I suppose you know," Ivor Bolderwood had said quietly as soon as he and Humphrey had gained the open air, "what those fellows in the night were after?"

"Oh, yes—I know. Look, Ivor—is that a kestrel?"

And Ivor Bolderwood had stared upwards at the small black shape poised above the dawn—but not before his glance had travelled curiously over the lad at his side. Humphrey, he thought, was in some uncertain stage of development, and ready to take a push either way. It would not, surely, take much to thrust him back into childhood and its helpless fears; correspondingly, it would not take so very much to make a man of him. "A sparrow-hawk," he said. "It's looking for something small and defenceless to pounce on, and carry off, and deal with at leisure. . . . I was talking about these men that are after you."

But Humphrey was still looking into the sky. "Did you ever," he asked, "see an eagle fighting with a snake—high up, like that?"

"No, never."

"Do you think Shelley did?"

"Shelley!" exclaimed Ivor. "And what has Shelley got to do with it?"

Humphrey turned to him in surprise. "Got to do with what, Ivor?"

"Why, this that you're up against. This situation."

"Oh, that!" Humphrey's gaze went seawards. "Are there any gannets?"

"Gannets? If we went along the cliffs we might see some now." And for some minutes Ivor obligingly talked about gannets—and only the more coherently because he was aware of the unexpected appearance of something imponderable in the situation. Was it possible that the boy's fantasy life had led him to a point at which he was a little astray in his wits? Or—a totally contrary hypothesis—had somebody already been on that job of making a man of him? Ivor paused to fill a pipe. It was a disordered thing to do long before breakfast, but the last few minutes had made him feel oddly in need of steadying. Much more so than the mere fact that, as things had turned out, it was necessary to keep a revolver next to his tobacco-pouch, and to scan every hedgerow as he neared it. That sort of thing was part of the day's work with him; he had made his life of it. But this. . . .

He let the subject of gannets, sufficiently explored, easily drop. "You are fond of Shelley?" he asked.

"Yes."

There was a silence. The subject seemed one upon which Humphrey was indisposed to be communicative. But for a moment Ivor kept it up. "I don't know much about him," he said. "But I seem to remember that he once lay down on the bottom of a pool just to see what it would be like to drown. And, if somebody hadn't interfered, drowned he would in fact have been. I suppose people do sometimes court danger even of quite a deadly kind just to know what it feels like."

"Oh, yes—I'm sure they do." Humphrey's reply was entirely ready. "In fact, Ivor, I'd say you were rather the type yourself."

"We go down this little path." Ivor glanced first warily about him, and then with an almost equal wariness at his companion. "But look here, Humphrey, would you like to go back? The truth is, you know, that we're courting danger ourselves, and I don't know that I ought to do it."

"Do you think this might be gold?" Humphrey had picked up a stone and was pointing with childish *naïveté* at a streak of copper pyrites. With an inconsequence that was equally childish, he threw the stone away, and it bounded down the cliff they were now approaching. "But you are armed, aren't you?"

"I certainly am. I have a revolver in my pocket."

"Then I think we may perfectly reasonably go on. How green the sea is between the rocks!"

"Good. That at least means that you trust me." Ivor paused for another of his wary reconnaissances. "You *do* trust me, don't you?"

And at this Humphrey stopped. His glance—as a glance should do upon such a question—met Ivor's direct. It was wholly candid. "Of course I do," he said. "I trust you as much as I trust any man."

The reply had an oddly mature ring, and for a moment it held Ivor up. But Humphrey, he realised, did mean what he said. "Good!" And he touched the boy lightly on the shoulder. "Then we can face it out quite comfortably. Be careful at this next corner; there's a pretty sheer drop."

257

"I don't mind heights. What I do hate is the dark. Sometimes it can make a kid of me at once."

"Is that so?" For an instant Ivor might have been detected bearing the appearance of one who makes a useful mental note. "Don't you like the headland straight in front? And there's a big cave beneath it. We might just have time to get to it now. You might as well see what you can *while* you can."

"While I can?" Humphrey was startled.

"Well, you see, this can't go on. There has been an attempt to kidnap you, and that is a very serious thing. My father and I couldn't possibly take the responsibility of not letting Sir Bernard know at once; and Mr Thewless is certain to feel just the same. It will certainly mean policemen investigating, and that sort of thing. And I am afraid it is likely to mean the end of your Irish holiday as well."

"I see. I'm glad I saw the gannets."

Ivor received this with a glance askance; it was too like a remote irony to be altogether comfortable to him. But presently he spoke again. For the right ideas had to be injected, and moreover he was increasingly curious about this out-of-the-way boy. "It all sounds more like America than England or Ireland, doesn't it? But there it is. You are the son of a very rich man. And somebody wants to kidnap you and extort, no doubt, a very large sum of money. You understand that that's it?"

"That's certainly it." Humphrey paused, apparently in hopeful inspection of another ore-bearing stone. "And *precisely* it, isn't it?"

A stone rattled on the cliff-path behind them, and Ivor swung round upon it. Nothing was visible, and its dislodgement must be a delayed effect of their own passage. But had something else startled him as well? "We should hate to think of your father having to pay up some enormous sum," he said.

"Yes—it would be too bad."

Was there, for a fraction of a second, something like a secret smile about Humphrey's mouth? Ivor was prompted to heartiness. "Well, we jolly well won't let them get away with it."

"No, they won't get away with it—whatever it is."

"That's the spirit!" But, to a greater extent than before, Ivor was sensibly troubled. The peculiar confidence with which the boy had spoken might be mere childishness—but could it be something else? "I'm glad you're quite sure of it, Humphrey."

"Oh, I'm sure, all right. It comes of not playing the game."

"Not playing the game! I don't think I understand you."

"I suppose they've told you that I am a problem-child?" And Humphrey turned upon his companion a glance of which the innocent seriousness was decidedly baffling. "It's been going on for some years—and, of course, one of the grand signs is that I don't play the game. If I get a hack at rugger I think they're being nasty to me, and I bite. If I'm bowled at cricket I say it isn't fair, and I throw the bat at them."

"How very odd." Ivor found himself quite unable to decide whether these shocking revelations were fact or fantasy. "But I don't see what they have to do with——"

"Just that I've cheated this time too. They think I'm playing the game according to the idiotic rules they've thought up for it—the sort of rules that mean that they're bound to win. But I'm jolly well not. You see, I've kept the ace up my sleeve. Or rather——"

"Yes?"

This prompting word had escaped Ivor in spite of himself. Almost certainly, Humphrey was now delivering himself of no more than the meaningless boasts of infancy. And yet——

"Yes, Humphrey?"

It dried the boy up at once. "Where's the cave?" he asked. "Does the sea go right inside? Do you need a torch for it?"

"You'll see in a few minutes. But you were telling me how you were going to cheat them. I'm awfully interested. Do go on."

Humphrey laughed. "You would pluck out the heart of my mystery, Ivor." He paused, suddenly frowning. "Hamlet said that, didn't he? Who did he say it to? Was it a friend? Can you remember?"

"I think it was to a thoroughly bad hat." Humphrey, Ivor realised, was momentarily suspicious of him after all; some drift of association from Shakespeare's play—the false professions, presumably, of Rosencrantz and Guildenstern—had disturbed him.

"I know! It was one of the men that Hamlet thought was on his side, but who took him away to England to be murdered." Humphrey had stopped on the perilous little track they were following down the cliff, and now he looked at Ivor with what really was swift distrust. "Shan't we be late for breakfast?"

"Good gracious, no! We got up ever so early. But of course, if you like, we can turn back. Look! There's the first of the trawlers going out."

"And the motor-cruiser's gone already. It's a terribly lonely sea. From up here it looks like a single toy steamer on an enormous pond." Humphrey moved to the very edge of the track and gazed down. "We're still tremendously high up. Like one that gathers samphire, dreadful trade." He repeated the line, and his spirits seemed to rise. "Come along, Ivor! Does the cave have an echo in it? Is it very cold?"

They climbed down steadily. The face of the cliff now screened them entirely on the land side. Below them, where first a line of tumbled rock and then a long, thin sickle of sand separated the base of the cliff from the sea, the prospect was utterly deserted at this early hour—and looked, indeed, as if it might commonly remain so all day. They walked in shadow; the rock face was cold as they pressed against it; with the smell of brine there was as yet only faintly mingled any of the awakening scents of heath and ling. But already the sea was a sheet of silver under the sun, its surface disturbed only by the long, lazy undulations in the wake of the vanishing trawler, or by the sudden plummet-fall of a gannet from the sky. Lesser gulls were wheeling above and below them as they walked, making the still air vertiginous to the eye, exploiting in shrill cries their power to evoke haunting suggestions of loneliness, desolation, pain. The path turned and for a few yards ran through the cliff like a cutting. Ivor, who was ahead, walked with one hand always in his jacket-pocket. His expression, as soon as his face was averted from Humphrey, had hardened into that of one whose senses are on the stretch for tiny physical things. And Humphrey too, when he ceased to converse, had a look not altogether ordinary. Sometimes his glance rested on the figure immediately before him, and in these moments a spectator would have found it readily interpretable, for it was the glance of one who sees, and would fain solve one way or the other, a known and finite problem. But at other times his eyes changed focus and glinted upon something very far away; his breath came faster through parted lips; his chin went up; he trod with a certain automatism the rough path beneath his feet. The swooping gulls, had they been anthropologically inclined, might have reflected that here was a stripling warrior advancing upon unpredictable rites. And thus this odd pair picked their way—having nothing the appearance, to an intimate regard, of persons proposing a before-breakfast stroll to a place of local curiosity. They were almost at sea-level now, and could hear the flap and murmur of small waves stealing in from an ocean still half asleep—an ocean wholly and vastly indifferent to what transacted itself upon its verge. Ivor turned his head for a moment. "It will be dark in the cave. Did you say darkness frightens you?"

"Sometimes I could follow it like a dream."

Ivor was silent for a moment. He found Humphrey's unabashed—his positively monarchal—raids upon English poetry very little to his taste. "And all this," he said presently, "doesn't that frighten you a bit?"

"This?"

"The fact of these desperate and unscrupulous people being on your trail."

"It frightened me most terribly."

They moved on again mutely, Humphrey with some obtrusiveness offering no elucidation of the tense into which he had cast this statement. Presently, however, he did speak: "And I'm very glad I'm not taking this walk alone."

There was a lurking appeal for reassurance in this. Ivor

laughed. "We certainly can't have you scouring the country by yourself just at present. That ambulance would roll up again, and away you'd go. They wouldn't bag the tutor instead of the pupil a second time."

"It was odd they did that, wasn't it?"

This brought Ivor up. "Yes," he said. "It *was* odd."

"And I had another escape on the Heysham train that was odd too."

"Did you, indeed?" And Ivor's eyes came swiftly upon his companion. "Tell me about it."

But again prompting proved to be a mistake. Something—it seemed three parts mischief and one part caution—held Humphrey back from pursuing the theme. Instead, he returned to a confidence of another sort. "I suppose," he said thoughtfully, "that some people are brave and some cowardly in a settled way. I mean the one thing or the other all the time. They're usually like that in books. But with me it's intermittent." He paused on this impressive word. "Last night, you know, when I heard old Thewless yell, and I grabbed my gun in the dark and ran out, I think I was more terribly scared than I've ever been before. There seemed to be no safety . . . anywhere. But then, when I saw that he'd had a rough time again, poor old chap, and I was afraid he might be badly hurt, and I got my arm round him and told him to cheer up, I just stopped being frightened without so much as noticing that I *had* stopped. Of course you and your father were about by then. That must have been it."

"That must have been it. Mr Thewless is an excellent man. But I don't think he'd cut much of a figure in a crisis."

"Oh, no—you're wrong there." Humphrey's eyes went off into distance, so that he looked for a moment very like Sir Bernard conversing with the æther. "You ought to be right, but I'm sure you're wrong. Perhaps he really——" Humphrey abruptly broke off. They had reached the bottom of the cliff, and beyond a strip of boulders, rock-pools and shingle the long beach stretched before them. "What wizard sands! I'll race you, Ivor." And the boy went off at a bound.

For a second Ivor was irresolute, his eye on the firm, shining surface, printless save for the criss-cross tracks of gulls; he might have been a man recognizing in a situation some factor of which account ought to have been taken long ago. "Stop!" he called. "Come back at once!" And he himself advanced a few paces, as if meditating pursuit.

Humphrey turned back in surprise. "What's wrong, Ivor? You—you haven't spotted the enemy?"

"No, not that. But those sands are dangerous. We must keep along the rocks. Rather a shame, isn't it? This way! Look, the cave is over there."

"Dangerous! You mean it's quicksand?" Humphrey's eye travelled swiftly over the long beach, and his intelligence was working swiftly behind it. "Why, it looks impossible! I've seen——"

"Not all over, of course. Just in patches. And that makes it thoroughly treacherous."

"Treacherous?"

The word, as Humphrey echoed it, hung upon the air rather longer than Ivor liked, making him wish that he had phrased his warning differently. "But it's rather fun going by these pools. There are crabs, and sea-anemones, and some astonishing seaweeds."

Perceptibly, Humphrey hung back. Perhaps it was merely that the proffer of these interesting marine exhibits struck too juvenile a note—as if the graduate in Biggles, the student of Captain Hugh Drummond, the explorer of the pastoral loves of Daphnis and Chloe had been questioned on a forgotten command of the creations of Miss Enid Blyton. Or perhaps it was something else. . . . "We'll be there in five minutes now," Ivor said. "You can see the opening. It's that dark patch just before the next headland."

"It's going to be a long way back to breakfast. And I'm hungry. I'm tired, too." The corners of Humphrey's mouth were dropping, and his mental age was clearly threatening to drop with them. For a moment he dragged one foot after another across the rock—a gesture very sufficiently childish. "I want to go——" He checked himself, and was evidently confronting the fact that Killyboffin Hall was not precisely his native ground. His shoulders squared themselves. "Then come on!" he said. "But straight to the cave. Never mind the beastly seaweeds and jellyfishes." And he scrambled his way forward, avoiding further talk—and also, perhaps, a little heartening himself—by whistling some altogether vulgar tune. But every now and then his glance went out across the empty sands, and his high forehead grew puckered under its crown of untidy black hair.

The gulls wheeled around them, crying out as if in some futile warning. The mouth of the cave, foreshortened to a jagged slit in the face of the cliff, lay in front—obscurely sinister, like an unsutured wound.

CHAPTER XXII

HUMPHREY PAXTON'S DOUBTS HAD grown as he walked. But when he entered the cave he knew at once that this was where the thing must act itself out. It was a cave such as adventure stories own—and must have owned, indeed, from the beginnings of story-telling, so familiar was it, so much part of the already existing furniture of the dreaming or day-dreaming mind. The low orifice; the vast twilight chamber, vaulted and silent, with further dark *penetralia*, forbidden thresholds, beyond; the deep waters flowing, mysteriously and excitingly, inwards: these were part of the archetypal cave, recognized at a glance. And orthodox too, if at a more superficial level, were the smooth ledges that ran, like narrow and sinuous quays, on either side of the darkly gleaming water. One of these, a resolute man might hold against a whole gang of smugglers, a whole nest of spies; from such a narrow footing, a well-directed blow might send some pirate captain, his cutlass helplessly flailing the air, sheer into his own element. Such fancies were the natural promptings of the place.

Such fancies, too, Ivor Bolderwood designed. Walking behind Humphrey, and glancing at his watch by the last clear light from the open sky, he saw that in just eight minutes' time the boy was to be kidnapped. His tutor—and the world, should it be disposed to enquire—might believe for a time that he had run away to sea. His father might guess the whole truth if he had a mind to. But the boy himself must guess no more than half of it—and, in a manner, events had conspired to just this end. Humphrey, returned crumpled and scared to the paternal roof in so many days' time—or weeks, if that were needed—must have no story other than that of his brutal snatching from kindly relatives in Ireland. The crux of the plan lay in that. And did not this unexpected complication of rivals at the game, although it introduced a fresh hazard formidable enough—marvellously second what was aimed at? Something had happened on the Heysham train; something more had happened on the light railway—yes, and something yet further at Killyboffin Hall in the small hours. And in none of these things was a Bolderwood implicated or implicatable. Decidedly it all went well. And Ivor smiled to himself in the growing darkness—unconscious of his father, at this very moment (the girl at the telephone-exchange having consented to begin her day's duties), listening to calamity on the line from London; unconscious of *Bolderwood Hump*, of *gun for boy 1.15*, of the fact that the late husband of the indigent Mrs Standage had once coxed an eight at Cambridge, of the outraged moral feelings of Soapy Clodd, of Detective-Inspector Cadover now grim and silent in a police car hurrying out to Croydon. There had been ticklish moments, as in a design so fantastically intricate there were bound to be. The strange chance of Sir Bernard Paxton's having chosen Cox for a tutor —Cox with whom he had had that uncomfortably revealing clash in Montevideo some years ago—that, as hurriedly revealed by Jollard, had required action swift, tricky and nasty. But it had gone off very nicely indeed. There was great advantage in being after something really big. The resources one could draw upon were enormous.

"Have you seen *Plutonium Blonde*?"

The boy's question came out of the near darkness like a pistol-shot, and was followed to Ivor's ear by his own sharply indrawn breath, his own voice raised a pitch in too swift answer. "What do you mean?"

"It just occurred to me to wonder. . . . I say, Ivor, old man, I suppose you've brought a torch? Does the sea go right in? Is the air all right? Ought we to have a candle-flame to test it with?"

He knew by now Humphrey's trick of rapidly fired questions. They covered hard thinking. But this time they covered too his own first alarmed sense that, after all, there might have been some flaw in the design. It was simply impossible that this inconsequent question could be coincidental. Humphrey had framed it, hoarded it, and at last fired it off with what had been, perhaps, triumphant success. The boy suspected something—and that was bad. The boy, reported as immature, unstable, and apt for his part in the plan, proved to have a clear head and an ability to go on using it—which was surely worse. And Ivor began to wonder—as his father, had he known it, was desperately wondering now—whether there were not some alternative way of going to work that would better meet the situation as it had come to stand. But yet he must not exaggerate his misgivings—nor, in the boy, what were still, perhaps, no more than drifts of suspicion, forming only to dissipate themselves moments later, like the pockets of mist still at play on the hillsides when they had begun to descend the cliff. Moreover, the little drama about to be enacted ought to be convincing enough even to the keenest-witted boy, the more especially as it had, all unexpectedly and thanks to the bearded and bespectacled rival desperado—the immense advantage of kindred incidents affording an ample "working up" of the sort of responses required.

Ivor became aware that he had permitted a silence, conceivably sinister in effect, to fall upon the tail of Humphrey's questions. "A candle?" he said. "No, we need nothing like that. I've been through here scores of time. It was my favourite hide-out when I was a boy. But here's a torch." He let the beam play past Humphey's bare legs. "Straight ahead."

266

"Am I to walk in front of you still?" There was a touch of resignation in the boy's voice.

"Yes—straight forward. It's a perfectly secure path. But, if you don't want a ducking, don't take too big a jump when anything startles you." Ivor was gay. "And one or two things *can* do that. Look"—and he flashed the torch upwards—"the roof is stalactitic, as you can see. That means an occasional drop of very cold water on your nose or down the back of your neck. And do you notice how we have started whispering?"

"I certainly do."

"It's because any noise multiplies itself quite astoundingly. For instance, fish swim right in, and sometimes they leap. The row is quite surprising. It might be the body of the murdered man going overboard in a sack."

"I see." Humphrey's tone acknowledged the perfect appropriateness of this image to the spirit of the place. He halted and peered down at the water a few feet below him. "What I don't understand," he said, "is why it *flows*. It's like a subterranean river."

"It's the flow that makes a little current of air all through, and keeps the amosphere pure. And it flows because the whole cave is in the form of a horseshoe, with a second, rather smaller, entrance at the other wide of the headland. That the sea goes slowly through is some trick of the currents here."

"Don't you feel that the whole place is a trick?"

"The whole place?" Ivor was again disconcerted.

"A *papier-mâché* cave in a fun-fair. You pay sixpense to drift slowly through in a boat, and there are all sorts of prepared surprises. Romantic views of Venice behind dirty gauze, and luminous skeletons that drop down from the roof. I don't think I'd feel it out of the way if we met one or two prepared effects here. It's in the air, as you might say."

"I doubt the romantic view of Venice." Ivor answered readily, but he was now more conscious still of the boy's power to set him guessing. He was relieved to think that in five minutes the present ticklish phase of the affair would be over.

"Well, I think I'd have more stomach for the skeleton not on an *empty* stomach. Do we turn back presently, or go right through?"

"I'm all for breakfast too. But it will be just as quick, now, to go right through, and up another track through the cliff. Only"—Ivor's voice was regretful—"we shan't have time to look into any of the little caves."

"Little ones?"

"They ramify out from this. We'll pass several entrances presently. Some are quite long; others are odd little places, rather like side chapels in a cathedral. You must never explore them by yourself, though." Ivor delivered this caution with benevolent emphasis. "Not all of them are safe, as the main cave is. Some have crevasses you can't easily see, with stalagmites like needles at the bottom. Others have deep pools, with smooth sides, like wells. And in some the roof is unsafe, and one might be walled up."

Humphrey laughed softly. "To be entombed in *papier-mâché*—what a horrid fate!" For the first time the boy glanced round. And Ivor, glimpsing his face, felt considerably relieved —for the boy's expression was not that of one taking matters so lightly as his mocking words suggested. He was—rather magnificently, Ivor acknowledged—keeping up a part: a part out of some favourite book, perhaps, in which the hero marched insouciant upon his fate. But he was as pale as a sheet in the torch's beam, and his lower lip faintly trembled. Better still, he was puzzled; he had found, in whatever conjecture he had formed, no absolute certainty. And, so long as his mind hung in the balance between one interpretation of his situation and another, the event now imminent could scarcely but take it down on the desired side in the end. Reassured as to this, Ivor could spare a little admiration for the boy's performance. And how superb the intuition of the *papier-mâché*, the factitious and contrived, essence of the scene!

But the cave itself—or rather the vast cavern that, in fact, it was—stretched sufficiently substantially around them. It had now taken in its course a turn entirely excluding the daylight, and the water flowing perceptibly through it, together with the unintermitted unfolding before their torch's beam of the gentle curve from which it took its essential form, gave it all the suggestion of some interminable subterranean river projected from the imagination of Humphrey's favourite poet. The rock face was damp and chill as they brushed it; and neither chill nor damp would wax or wane, whatever change befell external nature—for here the varying cycle of the year had no power to probe. Owning thus no pulse, no rhythm, the place was lifeless and ungenial, propagating only an unnatural and abundant brood of sounds. The waters that were now, as they climbed to a greater height, almost invisible beneath them, whispered ceaselessly like conspiring maniacs in some Tartarean bedlam. Single drops of water, falling from the fretted vault, exploded on polished stone with a strange resonance, like that of a distant harp string snapping in an empty house at night. And their very footsteps, as if each in alarm at the other's tread, fled before them and behind them in a constantly repeated diminuendo of frenzied escape. When they spoke their voices, like every other sound, were distorted strangely, so that it was as if they were beset by their own travestied images in some hall of misshapen mirrors. And above them, as perceptibly present as if some muscular effort of their own must hold it off, was the vast suspended burden of living rock, so that one could think up through it until at length, at what might be almost an aeroplane's elevation, one came upon sheep nibbling the turf directly overhead.

"Here's the first of the smaller caves." Ivor's voice called Humphrey back to what was no more than a narrow slit in the rock face. The torch, thrust through at the length of an extended arm, played upon a blank surface only some yard ahead—the meagre aperture making it impossible to see what lay on either side. Ivor laughed softly. "I haven't been in there since I was a kid—for obvious reasons! It's not exciting, though—just a small, almost square chamber, like a cell. I think you could just get in, although I certainly could not. If we thrust you in, Humphrey, and fattened you up on nourishing dishes, or just left you till you'd grown a bit——" He broke off, again laughing softly—laughter through which there for the first time incautiously sounded as it were the overtones of an unlicensed and sinister imagination.

"I think," said Humphrey, "that'd we better go on." They moved forward again. "How soon do we see daylight?"

"I should say it's just a little more than as far again. . . . Hold hard! Here's another one."

This time the aperature was larger, and gave upon an oval chamber, low-roofed, down the longer axis of which the light of Ivor's torch led the eye to two further openings, set close together, that led apparently to further cavities or passages. And of this place the form was at once unreasonably alarming and mysteriously compelling or attractive; it seemed to tug at the very roots of the mind. "And behind," said Ivor, "there's a sort of maze of interconnected tunnels. One could bring a picnic and play hide-and-seek."

"I still think we'd better go on." There was now a tremor in the boy's voice, and he pushed forward even before Ivor had swung his torch back to the ledge—it was perhaps three feet broad—which had now climbed to something more than a tall man's height above the water below. He walked for some moments in silence. Then his voice came back—and this time it was once more level, but very serious. "Ivor," it asked, "why have you brought me here?"

The direct challenge was curiously difficult to meet. There really seemed, for the moment, to be no colourable reason. And, because of this, Ivor, it may be, a little over-pitched his reply. "Why? Because it's such tremendous fun!"

"Of course I see that." Humphrey's reply was now not so much level in its tones as drowsy, and it was almost as if he spoke with some ambiguity he scarcely understood. "I can see you find it that; I can see . . . the fascination. But it's . . . well, so decidedly underground and isolated."

Ivor felt the torch twitch in his hand, felt indeed his whole body twitch as if a touch had been set to his mainspring. It was true that he had for long—and for no very pressing exterior necessity—found his fun in a world uncompromisingly subterranean. But now, blessedly, the definitive moment had come, and he could neatly enough introduce it by elaborating upon his reply. "Rather fun," he repeated. "And at the same time quite safe for us in our present odd situation. Not that this wouldn't be rather a neat place for an ambush." He let the torch play idly around them as he spoke. "But it's only the local people who really know about the caves. The kidnapping crowd would never find their way in here." He laughed lazily—injecting into the tone of it all the suggestion of unweariness, of relaxed vigilance, that he could. "By the way, there's another little side-cave just here." For a second his torch touched a dark concavity beside them. "And it's here that there's an echo. If we stand with our backs to the little cave"—and he swung Humphrey round—"we'll just catch it. . . . *Cooee!*"

There was certainly an echo—although no very remarkable one, perhaps, in this home of echoes. They listened to it die away. "Yes," said Humphrey doubtfully. His voice was almost that of one who catches from the air some hint of defeated expectation.

"*Coo-ee!*"

In its turn, too, Ivor's second call ebbed away. There was a second of something as near to silence as the place allowed. And Ivor received it rigidly, his every muscle quivering. He turned—his motion was at once swift and indecisive, blundering—and strode into the small cave behind them. Humphrey —driven by darkness, led by curiosity and the full store of courage he had brought into these recesses—followed.

The boy followed—and it was as if he had dived head foremost into a maelstrom of violence whose buffeting made all mental process impossible, made observation as discontinuous, as phantasmagoric, as it was terrifying. Immediately before him was a flailing octopus-shape, uncertainly resolvable into the locked bodies of struggling men. From amid them Ivor's torch, as if in a clenched hand forced upwards, circled wildly on the dripping, gleaming roof. From some farther corner another torch was at play upon the scene, and through its beam Humphrey dimly glimpsed two further figures that seemed to be of men bound, gagged and thrust out of the way, like supers whose moment was past in the advancing play. Then all his attention was swept to Ivor's face, sprung into fierce illumination, as by some searing light thrust hard against it. Desperation and rage glared from it, and with these emotions were mingled still the mere surprise of the wary man, betrayed against all expectation. His head went back, blinded; and from amid the confusion of. pants, and groans, and blows driven hard upon a human body—grievous sounds multiplied and distorted into indeterminable agonies by the configuration of the place—Humphrey heard his companion's voice straining for a command of articulate words. "They've got us! Run, Humphrey, r——" A fist came up hard against the working jaw. He saw blood spurt from Ivor's crushed mouth. The panting and groaning grew of heavier respiration more desperate.

For a moment Humphrey stood motionless—paralysed by his fear, paralysed by the vast injustice of the road his thoughts had lately been travelling. For here was revelation. Here was his cousin Ivor—whom he had monstrously suspected, whom he had even believed himself by cunning questions to have lured into self-betrayal—here was Ivor straitly beset by his, Humphrey's, true enemies; here was Ivor literally defending him to the death. . . . And Humphrey's legs, which for some seconds had been no legs at all, but clammy columns rooting him to the rock—Humphrey's legs became compact of nerve and muscle. Even his lungs obeyed him, so that it was with a shout of passionate anger, admirably calculated to wake the remotest echoes of the caves, that he charged into the fight, raining blows where he could.

And the struggling mass of heaving limbs and straining torsos gave for a moment. under this fresh impetus, gave sufficiently for Ivor to heave himself partly free and snatch out his revolver. But they were upon him again in an instant, and it was without aim or any effective control that the weapon, twisted into air, now again and again spat fire—spat fire and vomited thunder, cataclysm, chaos as of the ruining down of the very pillars of the world. For this rapid succession of reports, which would have been sufficiently ear-splitting in itself, the caves in their farthest extension, their remotest and most intricate honeycombing, rose to nobly, as to a challenge. Second after second the uproar only grew, as if straining to some hideous consummation, some final shattering of the ear, the begetting of some last, all-embracing Noise by which, as by the angel's terminal trumpet, all noises should be ended. . . . It ebbed; hearing, exhausted, slept even in the midst of continued turmoil; another, and sluggish sense took over; the universe was all gunpowder and sweat.

Humphrey's arms were pinioned. There were shins before him and he kicked; there was some fleshly part, straining through stretched cloth, and he bit it—deep. He felt himself lifted bodily and pitched through space; he might have been in mid-air still when his reawakening ear heard what was surely Ivor's last shuddering cry; he fell shatteringly on rock and for a moment lay still, knowing only that the pain he would presently feel would be deep and sickening in belly and groin. But the fight, he realised, continued after all; gasps and grunts attested it to his ear even while nothing but a swimming blackness hung before him. He staggered up on one knee, and as his eyes cleared saw standing before him, looking dispassionately down, the bearded man of the Heysham train. The man smiled at him—a sweet, evil smile, far more terrifying than any expression of ferocity could have been. The man smiled and then—expertly, with cold brutality—kicked the boy's raised knee, so that he tumbled again, as through a wave of agony, to the ground. His consciousness mercifully flickered; he was fadingly aware of the fight rolling out of the little cave to the narrow ledge beyond, and then of a reverberating splash, as of some inert body being pitched into the dark waters below. Instantly, as if it were his own fate, some cold element closed over him.

Ice-cold water deluged him. But it was not that they had thrown him in too; it was simply that they had found means to give him a good soaking by way of restoring him to consciousness. And at least it worked. His mind suddenly was very clear; he lay on his back and stared up into dazzling torchlight; beyond this hung the faces of his bearded enemy and two other men. They looked down on him in grim proprietorship, like people who had run some troublesome pest to earth. The bearded man spoke. "He's cost us a good deal," he said. "But there he is. Bring him along."

Humphrey was in great pain. In the attempt to smother it, he rolled over on his stomach. One of the men bent down and took him hard by the hair, dragging him up upon his hands and knees. Weakly, he began to crawl. The second man kicked him hard behind.

Had it not been for this last savagery it would all have been over with Humphrey, for he had believed himself—and with substantial reason—to be beaten. But in this there was sheer indignity as well as pain; it confronted him with obscure memories he had resolved never again to entertain; a flame of anger rose in him and brought him supernaturally to his feet; he saw the dark cave and the men around him through a milky mist. And he found that he had a weapon in his hand. It was no more than a short length of heavy rope, brought by his antagonists for their own sinister ends. But involuntarily he had grasped it—and now, straight before him, was the bearded man's face. He put all his strength into the lash; he heard a scream that went through his veins like wine. He swung round and one of the other men confronted him— surprised, straddled, vulnerable. Humphrey praised God for his stout shoes and kicked. The man went down howling. Humphrey jumped his body as it fell and ran out of the little cave.

He was in darkness and on the narrow shelf that led—but over interminable distances, as it seemed to his memory—to daylight and the possibility of freedom. A dozen feet below him, and flowing between walls of sheer rock, was the sea; and somewhere down there the dead body of Ivor drifted. Behind him were two ruffians recovering from unexpected overthrow, and a third, uninjured, who must be coming hard after him now. They would have torches. He had only eyes which— from sheer necessity and the love of dear life—had at least some apparent power of distinguishing between the greater and the lesser darkness of rock and air. But this served him

274

only as he stood and with concentration peered. Whereas his only chance—his only ghost of a chance—lay in the rapid flight that might gain him a flying start. He must race along this winding ledge in blind precipitance, with nothing to guide him but his finger-tips stretched out and brushing the rock face beside him as he ran. Yes, that was decidedly his single hope: to wring from his sheer desperation a speed more hazardously headlong than any his enemies, equipped with torches though they were, would willingly venture on.

It is not easy to run full-tilt through any pitch darkness; it outrages an instinct against which the will can scarcely urge the muscles on. Much less is it easy in the knowledge that ice-cold waters, through which a corpse is drifting, await one at the length of an extended arm. But Humphrey, having come at the intellectual necessity of running, ran. He remembered that the path, worn smooth whether by generations of smugglers or by the operation of the sea, had presented a reasonably level surface underfoot, so that there was comparatively little danger of a stumble. But in places, and even when he had been moving with care the other way, it had been too slippery for comfort; and in this there lay one of the dangers that he could afford now only to ignore.

For now they were after him. The cave was alive with their footfalls—footfalls that appeared to recede from him with miraculous speed, others that with an equal speed overtook him, but died away as they came. He was skilled to interpret this echoing confusion now; he knew that all three men were in the pursuit; and he knew that they were failing to gain on him as they ran. Hope in him grew suddenly strong. They could of course, pinning him down in the beam of their torches, shoot. But there was no reason to suppose that a dead boy would be of any use to them, and he knew enough of firearms to realise that only an exceptional marksman could, under such conditions, with any confidence fire only to maim. Certainly it was not unlikely that, if their pursuit failed them they would shoot to kill rather than let him carry his story out of the cave. But this was simply another of the dangers about which nothing could be done.

His path was sloping downwards now, and an occasional glint from the water came up to him as he ran. His breath was coming very short and his heart was pounding; he had the swift, horrible knowledge that, unexpectedly soon, his strength was going to fail. He had been pretty roughly handled in the little cave; his knee as he ran hurt in a fashion quite outside his experience, and it was this that took it out of him most. Hitherto, moreover, he had thought of his danger and this hideous subterraneous place as being coterminous. But now he realised that there was only childish instinct behind this coupling of daylight and safety. He remembered the long beach, the long climb across the face of the cliff. Barring the unlikely chance of some sufficiently numerous assemblage of persons in that solitary spot, he had really no hope at all. He was simply giving the creatures behind him a run for their money.

Meanwhile, he was still heading them. But his start, after all, had been of the slenderest, and they were so close that, on rounding a bend, the torch-light they cast before their own feet afforded him, too, some illumination as he ran. And now one of them, realising this, advanced his beam, for an instant let it rest on him, and then made it dance in rapid zigzags immediately before him. It was a cunning move, so bewildering as almost to take him into the water at once, and for the time he could only reduce speed so that he knew that they were gaining on him—so that he expected to feel, indeed, at any moment the hot breath of a pursuer on his neck. But still he ran, for the good reason that there was nothing else to do. They were not even the sort of urbane kidnappers who had frequently entertained him in fiction; if he was not to be booted and wrenched and tugged—treated worse than one might be treated at the most horrid of schools—he must keep out of their heavy hands. Particularly, he grimly thought, after having so gloriously landed that wallop with the rope's end, that extremely ungentlemanlike kick. . . . One of them had begun to shout. The sound, although in itself alarming, raised his spirits once more, since it seemed the distinctly futile expedient of an angry and baffled man. But this luxury

he enjoyed only for a second; there was an answering shout
from straight ahead, and the darkness was cut by a dazzling
ray that leapt up and took him full in the eyes like a blow.
It brought him up dead. And as the torches behind him
advanced, and as the first blinding effect subsided, he saw
enough to know that any faint hope of its being succour that
lay ahead of him was vain. For here was simply another
ruffian of the deepest dye.

The man advanced. The footsteps behind were now only a
score of yards off. Only one resource was left to him: to take
a header into the black waters below. But, even so, he could
not swim *away*; he could swim only up or down, and most
certainly not so fast as his enemies could run. They would
only have to wait, and presently haul him out like a half-
drowned rat. . . . And now from in front and from behind
they were upon him; their hands were stretching out to
clutch, to wrench. Terror pouring over him, he cowered,
shrank back against the face of the rock as if in very pity it
might open and receive him. His shoulders were crushed as in
a vice; he twisted, thrust, squirmed—and the rock *had* received
him. He was *through*. In a fraction of a second's complete
clarity he realised what had happened. This was the little
cave into which Ivor had not been since he was a kid. This
was the little cave through the narrow cleft to which no
grown man could hope to penetrate. He fell on his hands and
knees, and a strange new clamour was all around him. He
listened to it with curiosity, but without alarm. It was, he
discovered, his own wildly pealing laughter.

There was clamour from outside too, and for the moment
it was merely bewildered. The speed of what had so unexpectedly happened had given to his disappearance all the
effect of something out of Nature, and his adversaries were
utterly at a stand. But his laughter had betrayed him; there
was a shout of comprehension; once more torch-light was
playing full upon him as he crouched. And like a minnow in
a tank Humphrey started into movement and scurried to the
most inviolate corner of his fastness. There he huddled, his
heart pounding with the force of hammer strokes in his chest.

Had Ivor's calculation been correct? Or could one of these men, if not too bulky, actually, fatally, squeeze through? There was a sickening sound from the aperture of successful heave and shove; then an exclamation of discomfort, of pain; there was a grunt as somebody freed himself from the constricting rock; there was imprecation, hurried and murmured talk. Humphrey waited, and this process repeated itself—again with no ill result. And at this Humphrey stretched himself out in utter luxury on the ground, his every limb relaxed. And as he did so the possibility of an ease yet more exquisite dawned on him. He could allow himself the extravagance of speech. "Hullo," he said. "Hullo, you silly asses—won't you come in?"

At his words, the murmur outside stopped. He heard heavy and exhausted breathing, and realised that the condition of these great brutes was altogether inferior to his own; it was out of *them* that the headlong chase had really taken it. The knowledge went wildly to his head; his sprawled body curled itself like a spring; he was once more doubled up, dissolved, in helpless laughter. Through this he struggled again for speech, and presently it gloriously came—a torrent of childish mockery, rude epithets, snatches of verse, lavatory humour, farmyard imitations, puns. And when he had done himself this ease he was suddenly serious, practical, assured. There was a stick of chocolate in his pocket; he took it out and ate a piece with slow deliberation. Then again he spoke. "Hullo, chaps—you still there?"

"We are here, Humphrey." It was the voice of the bearded man; Humphrey remembered it as it had sounded on the Heysham train.

"Don't you think you'd better be cutting along, you great ugly, stupid, incompetent, clumsy brute? You've lost, you know—and that's that. If you hang about in this very unintelligent way you only increase your chances of an early appointment with the gallows." Humphrey paused, pleasurably savouring this superior flight of rhetoric. "The others realise that, you know. Just have a look at them; they're dead scared at what they've done—the dirty, murdering swine." Exultation had suddenly left the boy; he was shaken from head to foot by what he realised was hatred and rage. "You killed my cousin, you low maggots! You killed him when he was fighting to get me out of this. And if you *do* cut off now, if you bolt to the furthest corners of the earth, I'll never rest until I know that the law has brought you back and snapped your filthy necks."

This speech was evidently not without effect. The murmuring outside was renewed, and this time it held a note of altercation. Presently, however, there was silence, and then the bearded man spoke. "We are going to wait for you, Humphrey. We are going to wait until you come out."

"And whatever is going to bring me out?"

"Thirst might, for one thing."

"Never believe it. The moisture coming down these walls isn't even brackish. Besides, the idea's absurd. Ivor and I have been missed by now. And it's very likely that the racket those pistol-shots made has been heard over half the countryside. Look at your low friends again. *They* feel that. They'll be off without you, if you don't quit. And I'm not absolutely convinced that they won't put a bullet in you first—just for luck, you big stinker."

"We can smoke you out."

"Absolutely useless." Humphrey was in command of the situation, and he knew it. "I only got in with a tremendous effort and all my wits about me. Do you think I'd ever manage to get out again when half-stupefied? Besides, you sadistic moron, I'd rather die than fall into your hands. You know that—don't you? And it goes for shooting, too. Fire often enough into this little cave and, sooner or later, a ricochet would get me. But it wouldn't do you much good, would it? . . . Do I hear people coming?"

This last stroke was admirably calculated; it produced a moment's near-panic in the enemy. On the strength of it Humphrey had another piece of chocolate.

"Your only real chance is to clear out now and try again to-morrow. Or why not *pretend* to clear out now, and lurk somewhere for the innocent lad as he breaks cover and makes for home?" And Humphrey laughed comfortably. "I expect you can answer that one. I'm not *going* to break cover; not until they've come down from the house to hunt for me. And not then either; not until they've sent for half a dozen armed policemen. I'm through with this as private fun, you great big ugly maggot. You've done something too jolly beastly. I'll have detectives and all the rest of it now. So be off, and crawl back into the woodwork. After the rotten show you put up last night, creeping all round Killyboffin and getting nothing but a clip on the ear from Thewless, I wonder you have the face to stay in business. And besides, you know, that feeble performance hasn't gone for nothing. It means that the police and the madhouse folk are out by now, scouring the country for a pack of half-wit, yellow, incompetent crooks."

If there was much in all this of Humphrey's that was deplorably lacking in elevation of thought and dignity of tone, it was a speech nevertheless persuasively grounded in solid sense. The assistant ruffians were now audibly for immediate retreat; only the bearded man was obstinate—was, indeed, whipped up to fury. There was a moment's silence and then Humphrey was startled to hear the old heaving and straining begin again. The most formidable of his adversaries was having another try. But the boy was confident now. He crept up close to the aperture and substituted for his late loud tone a bloodcurdling whisper! "Come on, old mole—work away! Do you know what I've got here? A really nice lump of jagged rock. And when your rotten head comes six inches nearer I'll pound and pash it into a pulp."

There was a moment's stillness, followed by a sound of rapid extrication. The bearded man had given up. And Humphrey—who was undoubtedly behaving very childishly— had just begun to cast about in his mind for some further contumelious strain when the silence was cut, to positively electrical effect, by the shrill blast of a powerful whistle. The sound came apparently from that larger of the entrances to the long cavern by which Humphrey and Ivor had entered, but in a fraction of time its echoes were everywhere, so that it was impossible to tell by how many actual pairs of lungs the

wild alarm was being sounded. By the ruffians without—
whose morale, indeed, must have been considerably under-
mined by the implacable eloquence of their young antagonist
—it was taken as a plain signal of whole cohorts advancing to
the vindication of law and order. Humphrey glimpsed the
torch-light through that blessedly narrow cleft waver and fade.
Then he heard, first, a single, deep, panic-striken curse; and,
second, the sheer music of four heavy men taking to their
heels. Again, and this time nearer, the whistle shrilly blew;
and again echo wrought the same rich confusion of effect.
With surprising speed the pounding footsteps—themselves
augmented and distorted to render effects as of a whole herd
of buffalo in stampede—faded and ceased. There was a
second's silence and then, from the direction in which they
had departed, the roar of a powerful marine engine starting
into life. Perhaps, Humphrey thought, it was the motor-
cruiser. They would have had it lurking at that farther opening
of the cavern by which Ivor had proposed that they should
themselves leave it.

Anyway, they were gone. And—quite suddenly—Humphrey
felt queer; far queerer than he had ever felt in his life before.
There was now only darkness round him, but it was a darkness
that danced and sickeningly swam. He had believed himself
to be standing firmly on his feet. But to his surprise—the dim
surprise of an already fading consciousness—he found that he
was really crumpled up in a deflated, a quite desperately
small and weary, heap. He had an uncertain impression of
light footsteps near at hand; of his own name being called,
and called again, in a familiar voice. But his bruised and exhausted body had already curled in upon itself. He lay in a
posture of infancy, a thumb stolen to his mouth. Perhaps he
had fainted. Perhaps he was simply asleep.

CHAPTER XXIII

IT WAS TEN O'CLOCK. Mr Thewless had retired to his bedroom and was finishing his unpacking. The operation was not exacting, and it need hardly be said that he performed it in almost complete absence of mind. His chief concern—apart from the almost intolerable one of simply *waiting*—was to decide whether the situation demanded any immediate initiative on his own part. By this he meant, say, action within the next half-hour. For it was quite clear to him (and he marvelled, indeed, that it was not quite clear to his host) that the sensational situation now admitted and to be faced decidedly forbade the whole morning's passing without the taking of some quite obvious steps. He himself, he saw, had been extraordinarily obtuse; but he was by no means now—as the elder Mr Bolderwood appeared to be—markedly confused and dilatory. His initiation into the guardianship of Humphrey had been, thanks to the boy's seemingly bizarre behaviour at Euston, a matter of wild and blundering suspicions; from this he had passed into a phase of stubborn scepticism; and that phase his host, until not much more than a few minutes ago, had sustained him in with what might appear, to a scrutiny more leisured than that which Mr Thewless now commanded, a positively mysterious answering obtuseness. But the events of the night had constituted a fence stiffer than any reassuring interpretation could readily take. And Mr Bolderwood, after what appeared in the retrospect a merely muddled endeavour to do so, had come round—dramatically and, to Mr. Thewless' recollection, upon no fresh presentation of argument or evidence—to the view that Humphrey was, and had been, very startlingly in danger. This being so, certain necessities were clear. The police must be told, and their protection claimed—a proceeding that doubtless involved calling upon forces considerably more substantial than the hamlet of

Killyboffin could provide. If there was likely to be delay here, the making of some immediate appeal was only the more desirable. And, again, Sir Bernard Paxton must be communicated with at once. And this in particular, Mr Thewless thought, was his own responsibility. Only it raised one issue the undetermined nature of which would sound awkwardly on a trunk-line to London. Was the threat against Humphrey merely impending still? Or had it accomplished itself?

The boy had gone out early, perhaps accompanied, perhaps only followed, by Ivor Bolderwood. And neither the boy nor the young man had returned for breakfast. This, looked at squarely, was occasion for the blankest dismay; and the mounting irritation that Mr Thewless felt at something obscurely equivocal in the attitude of his host was for the moment swamped by an even larger tide of self-reproach. The very moment of his waking up from the heavy sleep that had unfortunately followed upon his night's adventures should have seen him hurrying to his charge's side, should have seen him raising a hue and cry when the boy was discovered to have made off. Instead of which, he had allowed himself to be half cajoled and half bullied into some hours of passive spectatorship. What ought he now to do?

He was at the immense disadvantage, had he known it, of having never had other than the most respectable persons within, so to speak, view-halloo; and it was thus his instinct, when a rat was scented, to peer rather remotely at the horizon. He did this in sober fact now, crossing to his window for perhaps the twentieth time and gazing out as if in the expectation of discerning a band of cut-throats on the farthest hill-top. Suspicions altogether more domestic were, indeed, dimly awake in him, but they had as yet taken no effective grip on his mind. He knew simply that he was perturbed by more than he could bring to the surface. He knew, for instance, that he had distinctly failed—had, unaccountably, over the last few minutes so failed—in taking some effective measure which it had been open to him to take. His inability at all sharply to focus this perception agitated him physically, and this agitation now had a small but fateful consequence. He let slip from his hands a small note-book which he had taken from his suitcase a moment before. And as it fell to the floor he was vividly reminded of an incident of the previous evening. Just so had Humphrey, while still occupying the room next door, dropped a note-book upon his tutor's entering. But Humphrey had done something further. He had then kicked the note-book deftly beneath the carpet.

It might well be there still. And Mr Thewless—the tiny episode showing vaguely portentous in the light of subsequent events—resolved at once to retrieve it. He slipped into the next room, pulled back the carpet, and found that the note-book indeed lay to his hand. He carried it back with him, glancing at it the while. Why should Humphrey have been embarrassed when discovered having dealings with it? It was a plain exercise book such as one might buy for sixpence, with the name "H. E. H. Paxton" written in a bold if inelegant hand in one corner. Presumably, Mr Thewless thought, it served as a private diary. He opened it gingerly at the first page and found this surmise amply confirmed:

DAIRY
(*cont.*)
Seecret!
Confidential!
Stranger, do not read!
H. E. H. P.

Mr Thewless frowned—partly at Humphrey's orthography, which was deplorable in so capable a boy; partly at the moral problem which he was himself confronting. But his perplexity lasted only for a moment and was resolved with great good sense. He opened the diary and scanned it rapidly.

While Mr Thewless was unpacking—slowly and in some absence of mind—his host, oddly enough, was engaged in the inverse operation—and if with an equal absence of mind certainly with much greater speed. This, he was reflecting, was it. To this his cherished and inimitable son, venturing at length too high a flight, had brought them both at last. In all probability there was nothing for it but a quick get-away and a going underground for good. One can, of course, engage in espionage and sundry related activities without cutting oneself off from the possibility of retiring, upon any discomfiture, to a number of pleasant asylums in one or another part of the civilised, or approximately civilised, world. But when one has been masterfully concerned in a murder in a London cinema one is almost certainly at the troublesome necessity of changing one's identity for good. The dubious South American magnate, the eccentric Irish squire, were both *personæ* from which the last grains of sand were falling. Or so, at least, to the elder Mr Bolderwood it appeared. Ivor, when he returned, might yet contrive a more hopeful view of the matter.

But Ivor—such was the necessity of their plot—was not to return for a good many hours yet. Bloody but unbowed, he was to stagger in with the news of his own near-murder and the snatching away of Humphrey. And in the interim—such still had been the plan—the dimly perceptive Thewless was to have been put off with vague speculations of the boy's mere truancy—a truancy from which Ivor was to be represented as no doubt busily recovering him. . . .

Thus did Cyril Bolderwood, nervously stuffing bank-notes and negotiable securities in a convenient grip, doubtfully recapitulate to himself the plot that had seemed so admirable so short a time ago. Abundantly wishing for his son's return, he yet felt with some misgiving that it might not be easy to justify his own deplorably abrupt and implausible change of front to the wretched Thewless hard upon the shattering telephone call from Jollard. Up to that moment he had played heavily (and in the light of the night's events even absurdly) on the "run-away" theme which was to keep the tutor quiet for a vital twelve hours, and which was to be exploded only by the reappearance of a grievously battered Ivor. But when it had become apparent that the police of two countries must know enough to be moving against them now, and at the best they would find themselves faced with the closest questioning, it had appeared to him essential to drop at once an attutide

285

that cool enquiry must inevitably brand as grossly irresponsible. Moreover, he had at last fully seen the advantage, the blessed hope of safety, resident in the fact that others besides themselves were "after" Humphrey. *That* was the card that they should have played for all it was worth as soon as ever the truth of it was apparent to them. For its astonishing interlocking with their own design, its vast scope as both corroboration and obfuscation, surely by far outweighed the few hours' grace that the pretended belief in a mere truance was designed to secure them.

But where were they now? Just how far did the news from London carry them? Was he perhaps precipitate in his feeling that all, or nearly all, was lost? And Cyril Bolderwood looked at the preparations for panic flight which lay around him with something like embarrassment. Conceivably this was just the sort of mistake that, in Ivor's absence, he was prone to make. . . . He sat down to think it out.

Murder is always undesirable. And the fatal mischance that had befallen them was the necessity Ivor had discovered for arranging the liquidation of Peter Cox. The police had moved on that rapidly. They had identified the dead man. And they had traced his connection with Humphrey Paxton.

And now Humphrey Paxton had been kidnapped while staying with his cousins, the Bolderwoods. That was by this time an accomplished fact. There was no going back on it. Even if they were to cry off now, and present the appearance of the boy's having been freed by his misdoubting captors, stringent enquiry would inevitably follow. That, of course, they had always envisaged; the whole elaboration of their plot was designed to withstand it. So—after all—were things so very much altered?

Cyril Bolderwood paused on this flicker of hope, and in a moment saw that it was delusive. Cox had been killed on the eve of his setting out with Humphrey for Ireland. The police knew this. And the police would ask *why*.

Perhaps it was to secure the boy's going with some other tutor, a tool of the kidnappers? Very little investigation of the blameless Thewless, Cyril Bolderwood grimly saw, would eliminate any such hypothesis as *that*. And only one other explanation was reasonable. Cox was killed because Cox must not go. *Why?* Because he would discover something. *What?* The crux lay here.

If the kidnappers were indeed persons working, as it were, from the dark, mere anonymous conspirators without identity, they would have no reason to fear anything that a particular man might *know*. And what Cox had known must be something at the very heart of the design; not something that some minor variation of it could get round. For—once more—murder is undesirable; one does not perpetrate it as a matter of minor convenience. What should it be, then, that Cox so fatally knew; what should it be but something compromising about persons who *had* identity; who, somewhere, stood, and were bound to stand, openly in the picture? And so (the police would say) we must cast about. What, to begin with, of those distant cousins in a remote and wild country, with whom the boy, so conveniently, had gone to stay? Is their respectability, their integrity, as unchallengeable as it seems? And is there conceivably some point at which their history, traced back, would be found to cross with the history, similarly traced back, of Peter Cox?

And Cyril Bolderwood, who in this analysis knew himself to have captured something of the cool intelligence of his son, once more reached for the bank-notes. For it *was* all up. This precisely, was the degree of investigation that they could by no means stand up against. So now——

At this point he broke off, hastily thrusting the so convenient and bulging grip out of sight. For his study door had opened and Mr Thewless had entered—very pale, very quiet, with a small note-book in his hand.

"It's much worse than we thought—or, at any rate, much more complicated."

Mr Thewless, as he spoke, sat down and looked gravely at his host—looked at him, Cyril Bolderwood swiftly noted, entirely without distrust.

"They *are* after the boy, without a shadow of doubt. He is in

287

deadly danger. But I judge that your son—if he is endeavouring to guard the boy—is in graver danger still. You see, Humphrey they must have alive. But about others—the rest of us—their ruthlessness would be absolute. Already there has been murder. And the thing is so—so *big*."

"Murder, Thewless? Good God—what do you mean?"

"In a cinema. I can't quite make it out. But it certainly connects up. Humphrey, you see, has been keeping a diary. This is it." And Mr Thewless held the little note-book up in the air.

"Good heavens! Let me look at it."

But Humphrey's tutor, though apparently in no distrust, put it quietly in his pocket. It was still a private diary, after all. "I think I can sufficiently explain. He went to a cinema. He went to see a film called *Plutonium Blonde*. There's a kind of irony in that."

"An irony?" Cyril Bolderwood looked blank.

"You'll understand in a moment. The film is about atomic warfare—that sort of thing."

"Well?" said Cyril Bolderwood. "*Well?*"

"And what these villains are really after—— But I'll come to that. He went to this cinema just before joining me at Euston. And something disturbed him. Actually, he talked to me about it on the Heysham steamer, and I took it to be all moonshine. It must have been this mysterious shooting—probably you noticed it—that was reported in yesterday morning's papers. I bought one in Belfast."

"But I don't see——"

"The point is this. What he saw, or heard, in the cinema gave him an inkling—it's not made clear how—that there *was* some plot against him; that in coming to Ireland he was walking straight into danger. And, all the same, he came."

"What!" Cyril Bolderwood had paled. "You mean that he came as a sort of decoy; that the police——"

"Not that at all." Mr Thewless too was very pale. "He came because he read it all as a sort of challenge, as a test of his power to control himself, to grow up. It's all in the last pages of this queer little book. But there was something else as

288

well. He seems to have had some idea—not a very rational one, surely—that he was drawing the danger away from his father; that he was protecting *him*."

"What extraordinary nonsense!"

"I don't know. Humphrey appears to have formed one idea in which there is a good deal of sense. Sir Bernard is extremely wealthy, as you know; and it would be natural to suppose that the kidnappers would be after money. But, of course, Sir Bernard is something else as well—one of the key men, at present, in the—well, in the country's power to wage war. And he has in his possession some sort of plan of an extremely vital sort. Humphrey has concluded that what the kidnappers would be after—privately, as it were, and beneath any more overt demand for money—would be *that*."

Cyril Bolderwood, who had been standing rigidly before his guest, sank into a chair much as if his legs had been knocked from under him. "The *boy* worked that out?"

"Why, yes—so it would appear." Mr Thewless looked momentarily puzzled at the form this question had taken. "And then there's a most remarkable thing. Humphrey—who must have been scribbling all this under my very nose, on that interminable light railway—Humphrey really has the queerest insight into character. He writes that his father, in his opinion, pays for his towering intellect in not having much guts."

"Guts?"

"He appears to mean will-power, moral fibre—things like that. And he thinks that that was part of the calculation."

"You mean that Humphrey worked it out that the—the criminals would rely——"

"Precisely. Humphrey himself is the one point at which Sir Bernard has an emotional life worth a tinker's curse. That, I may say, is the boy's very turn of phrase. He has, you know, streaks of extraordinary intellectual maturity."

Cyril Bolderwood gave a sort of groan. "If only we'd remembered," he said, "that he was Bernard's son and Ivor's cousin!"

"I beg your pardon?"

"Nothing—nothing, my dear Thewless. I am becoming utterly confused. But, for Heaven's sake, go on."

"Humphrey judged that his father, secretly receiving unnerving threats as to what would happen to his kidnapped son, would simply crack up and part with anything he had—not with anything he had of his own, you understand, but with what he had, so to speak, of his country's. It was a thought unbearable to the boy. And he felt that he had to protect his father; that it was his job to protect him. He has the notion, you see, that *he* is the strong member of the family, and that he must always give his father a hand."

"I wish to heaven Ivor were here!" Cyril Bolderwood, by an association of ideas not altogether obscure, came out with this with considerable vehemence. "But I don't see—I can't for the life of me see—how it was going to help his father to—to——"

"To come to Ireland and put his head into the lion's jaws?" And suddenly Mr Thewless brought out a handkerchief and mopped his brow. "Well, it's here we come to the bit that's really grim; to a point"—for a moment Mr. Thewless was vaguely magniloquent—"where all these personal issues, Humphrey's fate and ours—are transcended. At this point the boy's faculties—terribly at a stretch, after all—seem to have broken down. He makes an obscure, rather childish note to the effect that he has cheated, broken the rules, taken some underhand way of baffling his enemies. What he means by that isn't quite clear, but I'm afraid it's something pretty appalling. He had access to the plan."

"*What!*" Cyril Bolderwood was suddenly trembling all over.

"With some sort of child's cunning, and in the pursuance, one may suppose, of an innocent fantasy of secret service work and that sort of thing, he had possessed himself of the combination of a safe in which the thing is kept."

"I can't believe it! It's incredible! You mean—simply in Paxton's own house?"

"So it would appear. And the boy resolved that, before coming to Ireland and running the risks of which he'd had so odd a warning, he would put it out of his father's power to comply with the demand that might be made on him. So he went straight home from the cinema, possessed himself of this vital document, and brought it along with him."

Cyril Bolderwood made a choking noise in his throat, so that his companion positively thought for a moment that he had suffered an apoplexy. "Do you mean that—that it's in this house now?"

"It may be, if he has hidden it cunningly. I have come straight from ransacking his room—I took that responsibility at once—and I could find no sign of it. He may simply be carrying it on his person. The diary, you understand, breaks off without being specific on the point. It is only apparent that as he sat opposite me yesterday in the little train, scribbling this astounding matter in his note-book, the document may have been somewhere within a yard of us. Or that is how I read the matter. And you see how catastrophic is the situation that confronts us."

"Quite—oh, quite so, quite." Cyril Bolderwood was staring with an almost glassy eye into space. The sudden, enormous hope in the thing had actually dazed him. What would the disappearances of the South American magnate, the Irish squire, matter if he and Ivor, in disappearing, took the thing with them after all—the whole speculative business of the pressure upon Sir Bernard short-circuited, obviated, by his son's crazy act? "Quite—it's too terrible for words. But I still can't see why the child did it. It's quite mad."

"I judge that he is not capable of thinking in terms of a nation's safety; that he has no realisation of the vast public issues involved. His vision stops short with his father's honour. And he *had* saved that. If caught—and he was going to do his best *not* to be caught—he had the document to hand over and cry quits with. The thing then could not be charged against his father's weakness, but only against his own childish folly."

"I see. I see." Cyril Bolderwood was almost impressed.

"And *I* see too."

The voice was a weak whisper. Both men turned in surprise. The study door was open. And just inside it lay Ivor Bolderwood in a pool of blood.

291

CHAPTER XXIV

WITH HUMPHREY THE FIRST flush of returning consciousness had been sheerly pleasurable, like waking up on his birthday. He had behaved in a heroical manner; he had been extremely clever; he had eluded, confounded, mocked his enemies. It was matter to compose a song about, full of thrasonical brag. Not Toad himself, when he had outwitted the barge-woman and sold her horse, was more outrageously pleased with himself than was Humphrey in these seconds during which his faculties were coming back to him.

But he was extremely cold, extremely bruised, extremely stiff. And there was something like a tiger gnawing at his right knee. Opening his eyes with some idea of investigating this phenomenon, Humphrey realised that it was dark.

Naturally it was dark. Lying quite still, he summoned hasty argument on the matter. This was the little cave—the one into which the entrace was a mere slit—and beyond that was the big cave; and of the big cave there was perhaps as much as a hundred yards before its gentle curve admitted a first gleam of daylight. . . . So *naturally* it was dark.

But this, although it located him, orientated him, really helped very little. A box of matches, or the nursery nightlight for which he had never entirely shed a lingering regard, would have helped a great deal more. He shut his eyes once more—it was absolutely his only means of *dealing* with the darkness—and thought again. His pursuers, if they had been outwitted and adequately insulted by himself, had yet been finally routed by some exterior agency. There had been a police whistle which had sent them, already rattled as they were, pell-mell to their motor-boat waiting at the other end of the cave. But what had happened after that? Not—his recollection, although it was dim, told him—any massive irruption of the blue-clad (or here, rather, green-clad) forces of the law. And certainly no comfortable tramp of constabulary feet echoed in the cavern now. There were noises—and noises reverberating so that he by no means had to strain his ears to hear them. But they were only the murmurs and lappings, the dull explosions, the odd and muted musical notes, that the place contrived, as it were, on its own steam.

He must wait. Quite simply, he must do that. He had suggested to his enemies that their best chance was to retire a little and lurk—and might they not be doing so now? Whatever had disturbed them was apparently departed, and the possibility that they were themselves still a force actively in the field was at least something too substantial to take chances with. He had practically told them so, given his assurance that he would in no circumstances emerge until substantial and authentic succour had appeared. And it *would* appear; there could be no doubt of that. Let a man and a boy disappear in this district, and such a cavern as this would suggest itself as one of the first places to be hunted through. Even were he to fall unconscious again where he lay—or, worse, in that corner of the little cave inaccessible to inspection from without—competent searchers would not neglect the possibility. Ultimately, he was entirely safe. . . . And thus Humphrey comforted himself, as he was so frequently able to do, by the slightly complacent exercise of his own good brain. Only, of course, he was neglecting the factor of the dark.

And it *was* dark. Here in the little cave the very most attenuated quiver of the sense of sight was absent. This was something he did not at all like. And in a flash he realised that there was still danger. Or rather there was a choice of dangers. Another five minutes here and he would have lost his nerve, would be battering himself wildly against the rock in a panic so catastrophic as to deprive him of all chance of finding and negotiating the narrow cleft leading to ultimate sunlight. That was one, and a very horrid, danger. The other danger, of course, was simply that they *were* waiting. He had said that he would die rather than fall into their hands, and he had abundantly meant it. But to die was one thing; to buffet himself into madness against invisible rock was quite another.

. . . He got to his feet—it was an action surprisingly difficult of accomplishment—and felt his way cautiously round the little cave. It occurred to him that there might be bats. He resolved to keep on remembering this, because a bat when one was *thinking* of bats would be rather less upsetting than, as it were, a bat from the blue. And, now, here was the narrow slit.

It was the worst thing yet. When he had come through it from without it had been in blind escape from imminent seizure; and, although bruised and breathless, his fund of nervous energy had been sufficient to honour the draft. Now he was stiff all over; danger lay on either side of the cleft; and danger lay, too, *in* it. Surely, surely, it was now narrower by far! He squeezed and strained himself to a dead stop, crushed in a brutal vice of stone, with nothing but his sense of touch to help him, with even that sense hopelessly crippled as his arms, his wrists, his very fingers seemed no longer to have an inch's play. Terror rose and lipped the threshold of his strained possession of himself. Panic *here* and he was done for. All that rescuers would find *here*—pinned in the rock—would be the wreck of a small boy, irretrievably insane. Or so it seemed to Humphrey, who was prone, as we know, to dramatic views. He gave a last shove—it would certainly mean one thing or the other—and found himself outside. He found himself, too, *seeing* something: the ghost of a glint of water. And this meant that he must be reeling crazily on the narrow ledge's verge, the sea flowing between its fatally smooth walls below. He took a step backwards and sat down.

At least the bearded man and his associates had not simply been lurking there, ready to pounce. And, if they were still lurking at all, would it not be here rather than in the open air beyond the cavern—a place which, however lonely, was yet within possible observation from the cliff, and from the sea, and by possible wanderers on the shore? Humphrey, taking fresh heart from this, got to his feet again and groped his way painfully forward.

It was incredible that along this ledge, that through this utter darkness, he had actually run headlong less, as it must be, than a couple of hours ago. Now, he could achieve nothing that could be called a walk, a crawl; he edged his way forward, fumbling and shuffling, as his very grandmother, similarly placed, might have done. And his heart was in his mouth throughout every instant of his progress. It was almost as if he were enjoying the luxury of manageable, of assessable fear.

And then he saw the light. Incredibly, alarmingly almost, like the first appearing sliver of the sun's orb after the long arctic night, it filtered in from distance and reached him; another moment only, and it distinguishably lit the remaining path before him. At this he paused, irresolution taking him like a strong hand. Would it not be best to wait at this spot—here, with the nursery night-light comfortably glimmering in its corner? Then, should his enemies appear, he could retreat to the fastness from which he had just issued. But he had no sooner made this proposition to himself than he knew it to be nonsense; knew, that was to say, that he would never enter that little cave again. It had been the scene of his greatest triumph, of his most vulgar exultation. And it had been the scene of his life's most staggering scare. That, decidedly, was enough. Humphrey walked rapidly forward and out of the cavern.

The sea had been silver and now it was blue, a deep, deep blue; it had stirred into life, moreover, and there were little ridges of dazzling foam, whiter than any white thing had ever been before. The sky, too, was blue and brilliant; it was dressed with incredible clouds; gulls in enormous freedom cut it with their passionate geometry. Humphrey ran forward, let himself be received again into the abundant world, tumbled himself out upon its bosom with the tears streaming down his cheeks. Straight before him was the gleaming, empty beach. Across it—the only sign of change he could discern—a double row of footprints led to and from the cavern, traversing the lovely sand that poor Ivor had deemed so treacherous. And where they had gone Humphrey could go. He took them as a line and ran—a limping run with a stab of pain in every stride. He would have shouted—why ever should he not?—had he not preferred to keep all his breath for joyous speed. The footprints—they were as small, almost, as a child's—

ended in a little eddy or sortie of others in a familiar spot. It was the place where he had himself made that brief dash across the sand before Ivor had called out to him to halt. And now before him there was only the path that slanted up the cliff. When he had climbed that the strange, the blessed populousness of rural Ireland would lie before him: tiny fields dotted with the bright homespuns of the labouring folk; dykes and hedgerows along which were strewn the same bright colours of the drying wool; white cottages with their open eyes and pricked ears; donkeys, sheep, goats; the absurd and suspect poultry of Killyboffin Hall.

He climbed, and that really hurt his knee badly. He braced himself against the pain by thinking, not very laudibly, of the deep weal that must now lie across the bearded man's face. Perhaps that would help the police to nobble him. And perhaps the man whom he had kicked—Humphrey, wallowing in atrocious satisfactions, reached the top of the cliff. Everything was as he had imagined it, with one additon. At the end of the commanding headland to which the cliff here rose there stood the solitary figure of his friend, Miss Margaret Liberty. He took to his heels and ran to her as if she offered all the security of the Brigade of Guards. Then, becoming aware that this was a childish performance, he slowed down to an exaggerated saunter. "Hullo," he said—and his tone was extravagantly casual. "It's a lovely morning, isn't it?" He paused, reading in her faint amusement an indication that this had been a little overdone. He gave a sudden incongruous sob. "They've killed my cousin."

But behind her moment's relaxation Miss Liberty had been grave. And at this, indeed, her gravity scarcely increased; it merely became shot with surprise, with the rapid recasting of some picture with which she was preoccupied. "In the cave?" she asked.

Humphrey looked at her with answering surprise. "You know about the cave?"

"I have been watching you come across the sands from it. Why didn't you answer me, Humphrey? Where were you hiding?"

The boy was now open-mouthed. "*You?*"

Miss Liberty smiled. But at the same time her eye was attentively studying the boy's battered condition. "I took a walk quite early and noticed your cousin and yourself. Later I noticed your footprints where you had stepped for a moment on the sands. I followed the shore and came to the cave. And when I had gone a little way in I heard something that persuaded me it might be wise to do a little clearing of the air."

"Clearing of the air?"

By way of answer, Miss Liberty took a small object from her bag and raised it to her mouth. And faintly, as for their private edification only, Humphrey heard the note of a police-whistle. "It is," Miss Liberty said modestly, "one of the pre-scriptive devices. We have often come across it, my dear Humphrey, in our common reading. And it certainly had an effect. But when the air *had* cleared, and I went further in to look for you, I got no reply. What had happened?"

"I'm afraid I had—well, gone to sleep. In a little cave in which they were besieging me." Humphrey paused. "Please, may I ask a question now?"

"Certainly, my dear boy. This is scarcely a cosy spot for a little chat. But it has advantages. We are in full view of a good many of the people working in those nearer fields. And if I stand *so*, and you face me—yes, just *so*—then you will be keeping an eye open *this* way, and I *that*. I think you scarcely need be told by now that keeping an eye open in this part of the country is an *excellent* thing."

"Indeed I don't!" Humphrey's tone was grim. "But listen, please. I think it must have been you who rescued me on the Heysham train. And it was you who talked—well, so as to put guts in me. And it was certainly you—I see it now—who fixed it so that poor Mr Thewless found himself in the place meant for me in that ambulance. And then you turn up in a most frightful crisis, blowing a police-whistle like mad. And a police-whistle, after all, isn't a thing that old"—Humphrey blushed and stammered—"that ladies commonly carry about with them. So—well, what I mean is, you're *not*, are you, just an accident?"

"No, Humphrey; I must admit to being distinctly intentional. You see, my brother, Sir Charles, has the duty of keeping an eye on certain most *important* matters; and he had grown a little uneasy. So when he found difficulty in the way of taking *official* action, he just asked me to come along—to keep half an eye, you know, on your little holiday."

"Gosh!" Humphrey, round-eyed and awed, stared at his friend. "It must be pretty hot when you get *both* eyes on the job."

"Well, that precisely describes the position now." Miss Liberty glanced at her watch. "There doesn't seem to be much chance of your tutor's turning up."

Humphrey could only stare again. "Mr Thewless was to turn up here?"

"I endeavoured to convey to him a hint that he should do so—at ten o'clock. It seemed time that he and I had a *quiet* little talk. But he must have failed to take my implication. And now I think you had better tell me just what has happened this morning."

Humphrey did his best. Miss Liberty listened with the steady and unstrained attention of a judge. "And so," she said when she had heard him out, "for a time you almost suspected your cousin himself?"

"I'm afraid I did."

"But there can be no doubt of the fact? He *was* attacked—genuinely attacked, and overpowered, and thrown—dead, you think—into the sea?"

"There's no doubt of it. And the same chaps—at least the bearded man again and somebody else—raided us last night in Killyboffin Hall itself." And Humphrey recounted the history of this too.

Miss Liberty listened and nodded, frowning slightly. "The basis of success in this trade," she said, "is to keep on suspecting everybody all the time. But, of course, there has to be a limit to it."

"This trade? Is what you tell me about your brother Sir Charles not quite all the story?" Humphrey's wonder still grew. "Have you been at it—often?"

"Ah, my dear Humphrey—we all have secrets in our past. I expect you have some that are quite dark to me still. Had you better tell me some of them—in so far, that is, as they may relate to this *exciting* affair?"

And Humphrey told—or told much. Miss Liberty, as she listened to these further disclosures, had moments of undisguised perplexity. "And another requisite of success," she said when he had finished, "is that one should recognise when the waters become too deep for one. But I think our next step is clear."

"The police?"

"Decidedly the police. As a romantic adventure designed to exercise the faculties of Humphrey Paxton the affair definitely ended when your cousin went into the waters of that cave. And my brother's apprehensiveness has certainly been amply vindicated. We shall walk together as far as the Hall, still with our eyes *extremely* wide open. You must go straight inside. But you need not tell your uncle about his son's probable death if you feel unequal to it, my dear boy. For as soon as I have walked on to the village and made one or two telephone calls I shall come straight back, bringing the local police with me. And then we can have it all out while waiting for more substantial help to arrive."

Humphrey nodded. "Yes," he said. "That seems all right. And I don't think I shall too much mind telling. It has to be faced, after all." He spoke with the sober confidence of one who had himself faced a good deal. They walked on for a time in silence, their senses alert to what was happening round about them. It was only when they had taken a cut through the ragged park, and were within hail of the front door of the house, that he spoke again. "I suppose I *had* better go in?"

And for an instant Miss Liberty hesitated, caught by something in the boy's tone of which he was himself, perhaps, unconscious. Then she nodded. "Yes; I think you had better go. The sooner the facts are spread beyond just our two selves the better. I shall follow you in less than a quarter of an hour."

Humphrey watched her go—a slight, quick, upright figure

glancing alertly from side to side as she walked. He noticed how she kept her right hand in one roomy pocket, much as Ivor had done on their walk to the cave. But at the thought of Ivor Humphrey's eyes misted with tears.

He turned and once more entered Killyboffin Hall.

CHAPTER XXV

CYRIL BOLDERWOOD HAD at first viewed his prostrate son with considerably more surprise than alarm. He was immensely struck, that is to say, with the abundant quality of the verisimilar in Ivor's presentation of one who has, in the handy American phrase, been "beaten up." Ivor, indeed, looked, to the point of extravagance, a man who had been beaten *down*; he was now crawling across the room to prop himself, with a low groan, against the back of a chair. "The boy!" he gasped. "He's been kidnapped."

The scene was taking place hours before it was due; and, thanks to the efficiency of the London police, it was taking place in a context the wider reaches of which were vastly other than had been planned. Apart from this, Cyril Bolderwood had no fault to find with it. "Kidnapped?" he exclaimed. "Good heavens—it is just what we feared!"

The tone of this—much that of Lady Macbeth's "What, in our house?"—produced in Ivor a sort of weak gasp of strangled fury. "By the people," he said hoarsely, "who broke in last night. They got us in the cave before—before we had finished looking at it."

And light dawned on Cyril Bolderwood. "You mean," he shouted—a shade strangely to Mr Thewless's ear—"that Humphrey has been . . . *kidnapped?*"

"Of course I do. And snatched from us, it now seems, with the plan—the vital plan—actually in his pocket. . . . Get a bandage out of the cupboard there, will you? It's only a hack on the scalp, but it makes me bleed like a pig."

Ivor's father did as he was bidden, but with the air of a man not at all knowing how to proceed. "Thewless," he said suddenly, "would you, like a good fellow, go up to the bathroom beside your room, and fetch some lint and sticking-plaster from the cupboard? We must do what we can until the doctor comes."

Mr Thewless, although his concern was much more for the vanished Humphrey than for the injured Ivor, hurried away. When he returned it was to find Ivor sitting up in a chair. The young man, however, looked by no means better; he had turned yet paler and was breathing fast; it was clear that such intelligence as father and son had exchanged in the interval was far from having any composing effect. And one might, moreover, have formed the impression that something like a brief altercation had been in the air.

"Well," Ivor was saying, "these people have taken the boy, haven't they—after more shots at it than one? And the police must go after them for all they're worth?"

"Certainly—certainly." Cyril Bolderwood, glancing rapidly at Mr Thewless now ministrant with the sticking-plaster, appeared to find difficulty in the easy expression of his feelings. "The police *must* go after them, of course. And I'll telephone the moment we've fixed you up. The police, my dear boy, must investigate the *whole* affair from the start, you know; they must follow up whatever seems remotely connected with it. And they *will* do that. We can trust them, absolutely."

Ivor received this for a moment in silence, and Mr Thewless took the opportunity to speak. "I must get in touch with Sir Bernard at once. I feel about this quite terribly, since I was given his confidence in the matter. I wish to Heaven the other man had been able to come. He would probably have been far more competent than I in such a disaster."

Cyril Bolderwood pounced upon this. "Another man?"

"Another tutor, who was Sir Bernard's choice on the first place. But he was prevented at short notice from taking up the post——"

"Now, that's just the sort of thing I mean." Cyril Bolderwood, who had finished bandaging his son's head, drew back, fixed him with an urgent gaze, and proceeded in a sort of rapid gabble. "Just before these plots begin—as a prelude to them, you may say—this other tutor suddenly drops out. Well, the police must go after that even, for what it's worth. Find him, you know, alive or dead—and find out all *about* him. They *must* do it. Exploring every avenue. Leaving no stone——"

"Yes, of course." Ivor held up an impatient hand, and at the same time uttered what, since it could scarcely have been an imprecation, Mr Thewless took to be a muted exclamation of pain. "The police are bound to go right through the whole thing. And—well, you'd better get on to them now."

"Exactly." And Cyril Bolderwood—obscurely, it seemed to Mr Thewless, as if he had carried some urgent point—turned to the telephone. Then he stopped. "But, Thewless—I wonder if you'd make the call? I don't like Ivor's look; I don't like it a bit. I think I had better get out the car and drive him straight to the doctor's. Ivor, wouldn't that be best?"

And at this Ivor did unequivocally produce a murmur of weakness and agony. "Yes, I think it would. I have lost a shocking amount of blood."

"Good. I'll get it out straight away." Cyril Bolderwood made for the door, checked himself, seized from beneath his desk a bulging leather bag. "Brandy," he said. "And that sort of thing. Kept for an emergency. Get the police, Thewless, and insist on being put straight through to the county office. I'll have the car round for Ivor in a couple of minutes."

Again he made for the door. But it opened before he reached it.

"Ivor!"

Humphrey Paxton, his face alive with amazement and joy, ran across the room and threw himself into his cousin's arms.

To Mr Thewless the sheer relief of this apparition was so great that it was a moment before he could identify in himself the further pleasurable sensation arising from the affecting nature of the scene; arising, basically, from all that was generous in his pupil's character. Twenty-four hours before Humphrey would not have known Ivor Bolderwood from

Adam; but in the interim his cousin had fought for him against superior odds; and now Humphrey felt for the bandaged figure before him as Hamlet might have felt for a wounded Horatio. And at the sight Mr Thewless turned to Cyril Bolderwood, as if from an impulse to share with him something so decidedly worth sharing. What this movement brought into his field of vision was a state of affairs so entirely unexpected that an appreciable interval elapsed before it made, so to speak, any intelligible statement. His host was still standing by the door through which he had proposed to depart to fetch out the car. He had, however, laid down his bag—and what first dawned on Mr Thewless, oddly enough, was the extremely unlikely appearance that this receptacle presented as the repository of a bottle of brandy. And in place of the bag Cyril Bolderwood was now handling something else. It was some small contrivance of gleaming metal. Mr Thewless placed it provisionally as being—what seemed in itself unlikely enough—a species of surgical instrument. But now Cyril Bolderwood was advancing it, pointing it, in the oddest way—in what was surely the most *threatening* way. . . . Thus laboriously did Mr Thewless analyse out the wholly unfamiliar experience of finding himself covered with a revolver.

The boy understood first. His disillusionment, if even sharper, was almost instantaneous. He let his hand fall from Ivor's arm very gently and reluctantly, like a child who perforce abandons what he cannot, after all, "take away." And then he sat down on the edge of a chair. "Yes," he said. "Yes . . . I see."

And Ivor Bolderwood squared his shoulders—a man who had been roughly handled, indeed, but who by no means urgently required medical aid. His cheeks were faintly flushed. "My dear father," he said, "I think you make it all rather unnecessarily dramatic. But, no doubt, we had better proceed to business."

"We certainly better had." Cyril Bolderwood kicked the door shut behind him. "The police may be here in half an hour."

"That is distinctly unlikely. But half an hour will be time enough, I don't doubt." And Ivor turned to Mr Thewless. "It's a great shame," he said with a faint grin, "but I'm afraid we shan't be able to show you that defensive earthwork at Ballybags, after all."

"I think it very unlikely that either of you will be in a position to show anybody anything for a great many years to come."

Ivor's grin widened, as if in amiable acknowledgment of the very proper spiritedness of this reply. "That's as maybe—and I won't deny we take a risk. But you ought to be grateful to us, Thewless. We took much our biggest risk simply in order to ensure that you should come on this nice trip—or that somebody else *shouldn't* come. And things certainly haven't gone quite right. My father and I are obliged to quit these ancestral halls for good to-day. We certainly didn't envisage *that*. Nor did we envisage that the game of kidnapping this delightful Humphrey would become so deplorably popular with the underworld of which we are ourselves, so to speak, honorary members. I wonder who that bearded fellow is? And so you think that all *he* has been after is cash? That isn't *our* object, I need hardly say."

"Not"—Cyril Bolderwood interrupted—"that with things going well we mightn't have taken it out a bit in cash as well. Poor Bernard would have been in no position to refuse."

Mr Thewless looked from father to son. "You strike me as two singularly foolish, as well as two singularly wicked and contemptible, men. The bearded ruffian of whom you speak is, after all, a ruffian merely. He could not, in fairness, be described as basely treacherous. Nor has he concocted a futile and elaborate plot such as yours. He has simply tried to grab—and he has come uncommonly near being successful. The same cannot be said for you. And you don't cover the complete failure of your design by whipping out and brandishing a revolver. Your servants, who are as numerous as they are clearly innocent, must many of them be within hail. You haven't a card in your hand. My blindness has been great. But I can see *that*."

"I don't think you have the situation quite clear." Ivor spoke in a reasonable voice. "Our boats are burnt, you know. And our strength lies precisely in that. By noon Cyril and Ivor Bolderwood will simply have ceased to exist. And the question is just this: Will anyone else have ceased to exist as well? For instance, there are Billy Bone and Denis. It seems most unlikely that they would regard anything you started shouting at them as other than the outcries of madmen. But if they did come in on your side, so to speak, it would cost us nothing to shoot our way out. It would cost us nothing, for that matter, to shoot our way out through the whole of Killyboffin." Ivor paused. "But I think it is with Humphrey that we had better do the talking at present. He strikes me, my dear Thewless, as having a much clearer head than his tutor can boast of. Come, Humphrey, are you ready to talk?"

Humphrey was still perched on the edge of his chair, like a very small boy uneasily present upon the fringes of a grown-up party. But he answered with a strange tranquillity. "Yes, Mr Bolderwood, I'll talk."

"Very well." Ivor had faintly flushed again at this address. "I think you and I can still be very good friends."

"And I think you are almost as reliable a friend now as any I shall ever again be able to feel that I have." Humphrey was tranquil still as he enunciated this rather complicated belief. And he turned to his tutor. "Do you know, this must be what I came for, really? Not to discover if I could keep the stiff upper lip of a great big boy while being chased by thugs through horrible caves. But to see what I could salvage out of —well, of being utterly betrayed. And I do salvage something —although it's a very little something, I suppose. The power, you know, to take it quietly." The boy paused, and for a moment he might have been thought to be anxiously listening. "Well, Mr Bolderwood, talk away. You do it very well. Better, really, than you arrange bogus kidnappings in caverns. They had you caught out nicely, hadn't they? And—by the way— what happened to the chaps you must have had lurking and ready to go through their act? I seem to remember them now, uncomfortably trussed up in a corner. Did the rival gang pitch them into the sea as well; and did they have poorer luck than you?"

"The point is this." Ivor had stood up rather unsteadily and now planted himself before the boy. "We were going to have you held as by persons quite independent of us—were they not to have knocked me out in that cave?—and while there was the appearance of their demanding money from your father we were quite quickly and quietly going to get from him— well, something else. That has all broken down. And, as a result, we should have completely failed but for one fact. You yourself, with incredible folly, my poor child, brought that something else away with you from London. And so my father and I are in a position very nicely to retrieve our fortunes. You understand?"

It was evident that Humphrey understood. And in the little silence that followed Mr Thewless had his worst moment in the affair. "Humphrey," he said, "it is my fault. I found your diary, and I felt, since you had disappeared, that it was proper to read it for the sake of any light it might give."

"You were quite right." Humphrey had flushed, but his eyes went straight to his tutor's. "You did just what you ought."

"Unfortunately, mistrusting nothing, I confided what I discovered there to the elder of these base men. And now they both know."

"And now we *all* know." Ivor's grin had returned. "We all know precisely where we are. Humphrey has really been very fortunate. He does not need to suffer the inconvenience of being kidnapped, after all."

"I should have thought"—Humphrey's voice, interrupting, was still curiously mild—"that I am kidnapped *now*."

"Not at all. It is simply the second day of your Irish trip, and we are having a friendly family talk. Before my father and I are unexpectedly called away. Kidnapping is definitely off. The circumstances of our retreat, I can frankly tell you, are such that a reluctant small companion would be definitely embarrassing. But there will be no objection to our taking a small sheaf of papers. And the only question is this. Have you, my dear Humphrey, actually got them on you now, or have you hidden them somewhere about the house?"

Humphrey was silent, again like one who listens for a distant sound.

"Come, boy, you must see how the thing stands. We win—at least your father falls into no disgrace. He cannot be held accountable for a disastrous domestic theft by an imaginative small boy. Everything, you see, really falls out quite nicely."

"You are awfully considerate. But I think, you know, that these papers may be rather too important to be used as a sort of challenge cup in the Killyboffin annual sports." Humphrey paused, evidently rather taken by this image. "You win, and we all shake hands, and then it will go to the shop to be engraved 'Cyril and Ivor Bolderwood.' These papers—let's call them simply the plan—are quite unsuitable for that. And I've thought so, Mr Bolderwood, for some time. You just can't have the plan."

Ivor shrugged his shoulders. "You foolish child! Will you force us to give this talk a really unpleasant turn—to think of the really nasty things that might presently happen to you?"

It was at this point that Mr Thewless saw what seemed likely to become his necessary course of duty. That the Bolderwoods were utterly desperate and utterly ruthless he could see. And it might well be that their household would not be rapidly or readily convinced of their criminality. Nevertheless, some definitely criminal deed, if accompanied by sufficient uproar, would probably finish them; in such circumstances they would simply have to go while the going was good. It was his business to see that the uproar occurred; to sell his life if not dearly at least noisily. And no sooner had this thought come to him than he saw that he might have to hurry if he was to have the chance. For Ivor had walked over to his father, taking from his hand the revolver which he had been holding during these exchanges, and was now aiming it directly at his, Mr Thewless's heart. "Listen, Humphrey." Ivor's voice was now very quiet. "We have got to have that plan. It means the difference for us between penury and a fortune. So we are not likely to boggle at a little bloodshed."

"You can't have it." Humphrey spoke stoutly, but with fear creeping into his eyes. "It might mean far too big a difference for far too many other people as well."

"We have got to have it, all the same—and within a few minutes now. Well, we'll make a very fair bargain. We'll swop it for poor old Thewless here."

"What do you mean?"

"I don't, myself, think he's worth much. But it is possible that you think he is worth a good deal. I fancy he's been quite decent to you, and that you have grown rather fond of him. Well, unless you tell us at once where to find the plan——"

Ivor left his sentence expressively in air. And Humphrey looked piteously at his tutor. "Do you think he means it?" he asked.

"Never mind whether he means it or not, Humphrey. This plan is much more important than my life. And it is my duty to tell you that it is much more important than your life too. You ought not to have taken it, and your notion that by doing so you might be protecting your father's integrity was a mistake. You made a bad mistake, even if an honourable one. And I have made equally bad mistakes at every turn. If we are to be killed, my dear, dear lad, we must put up with it. These villains must on no account be told where the plan now is."

"As a matter of fact, I couldn't tell them, even if I wanted to."

"What's that?" It was Cyril Bolderwood who spoke, and as he did so he advanced threateningly upon Humphrey. "What's that, you horrible little rascal?"

"So that if you do any killing—of one or other of us, or both—it will be mere spite." Humphrey paused; and it might have been evident that if he was facing death he was also, in a manner, enjoying his moment. "Of course, I can tell you approximately where it is." And he glanced at the clock on Cyril Bolderwood's mantelpiece. "It must be somewhere between Preston and Crewe."

Ivor Bolderwood cursed, and a dark flush overspread his pale face. "You little brute! Do you mean you posted it back to London?"

308

"But of course! I only meant to hold on to it till I could *think*. And after what happened on the Heysham train I knew I hadn't much time. So I posted it back to London yesterday afternoon when we were changing trains at Dundrane. Only my diary hasn't got so far as to say so."

"By heaven, we're back where we were!" Cyril Bolderwood was pacing agitatedly about the room. "Bernard has the plan, and we have his boy. We must hang on to him. We must take him with us by hook or——"

"Oh, my *father* won't have the plan. I didn't post it back to *him*. Then we certainly *would* be back where we were." Humphrey was looking from one to the other of his captors as if almost amused by the simplicity of their minds.

"You mean that you posted it to somebody else?"

"Of course I do. I wrote a little note—what they call a covering note, I think—and posted the thing off to the Prime Minister."

"To the *Prime Minister*?" Cyril Bolderwood's voice held a strangled note.

"Why not?" And Humphrey looked mildly surprised at the sensation he had achieved. "He is—don't you know?—a terribly nice man. He'll *quite* understand."

At this Cyril Bolderwood, always inclined to display less finesse than his son, appeared about to hurl himself on the boy with a howl of fury. But in the same instant Humphrey himself gave a sudden shout. "Danger, Miss Liberty! Danger! Run!"

But this call, if heard, was without effect. The door opened and Miss Margaret Liberty walked into the room. Her eye travelled briskly round it, and evidently told her much. "Ah," she said. "Keep on distrusting everybody; I was remarking to Humphrey that it is the only safe rule. Mr Ivor, I see, has a revolver. Well, so have I. And that does just give us a chance."

CHAPTER XXVI

To Cyril Bolderwood nothing seemed to occur in this exigency but recourse to vituperation. "Why," he exclaimed, "you horrible old hag, what——?"

"Don't you dare to call Miss Liberty rude names!" Humphrey jumped from his chair, bounded across the room, and kicked his distant relative expertly on the shins. Cyril Bolderwood let out a howl of pain and grabbed at him; Humphrey dodged; the situation had all the appearance of being about to degenerate from melodrama into rough-and-tumble farce.

But Ivor was otherwise-minded. He put a hand on his father's shoulder and shoved him into a chair; he strode to the door, closed it and, weapon in hand, faced Miss Liberty. "If you have a revolver, madam, you will give it up to me at once."

"Don't madam me, young man." Miss Liberty walked composedly across the room and looked out at the window. "And, Humphrey, stop knocking people about."

Humphrey blushed. "They're quite horrid people; they've been wanting to kidnap me too, all the time; and they were going to shoot Mr Thewless in cold blood."

"I have no doubt that some of their ideas have been *most* foolish. But now that they are in so tight a corner we had better leave their shins alone. Particularly as *we* are in the tight corner too."

Mr Thewless, who had for some seconds found himself quite unattended to, had slipped over to the fireplace and possessed himself of the poker. "Miss Liberty," he said courteously, "I suspect that these are matters in which you have some experience; and I should wish to defer to your judgment. But it appears to me that, if I were to make a resolute attempt to dash out this elder ruffian's brains, the younger would be constrained to fire at me with his pistol, and this might give you the necessary opportunity of bringing out your own. Shall we proceed after that fashion?"

"Dear me! You are even more bloodthirsty than Humphrey. But the position is not quite so simple as that. Our friends here appear to have forgotten that they are not the only pebbles on the beach. It has really been very rash of them to suppose that their rivals were routed beyond recovery when Humphrey made one of his alarming attacks upon them in the cavern. That is not so. They are altogether more resolute than that. And they are, in fact, coming back at us now."

"I don't believe it!" Ivor Bolderwood spoke, but not with much conviction. "A gang of common kidnappers like that would never dream of actually assaulting——"

"But that is precisely where you have gone wrong. You suppose that you and your father alone breathe the high air of international intrigue; and that all that these other people fly at is a few thousand pounds extorted by menaces. Nothing could be farther from the truth. Their employers, I suspect, are, at a remote level, your employers too. But theirs has been an altogether more sensible plot."

Humphrey jumped up, round-eyed, from the chair on which he had once more perched himself. "*They* want the plan too?"

"Certainly not. They know that the plan as you call it—the real plan—is utterly inaccessible to them. The papers with which you walked off, my dear boy, are, of course, important. But the notion that they are in any sense the vital thing is a stupid misconception into which the Bolderwoods must have been led by some confederate in your father's house. You may be quite sure that the real thing is not, and never has been, in your father's uncontrolled possession. And, equally certainly, as soon as Sir Bernard Paxton's son was known to have been kidnapped, Sir Bernard himself would be very closely watched indeed. Your fear that he might be forced to part with something extremely confidential was quite groundless. And correspondingly"—Miss Liberty turned to the Bolderwoods—"*your* scheme was fantastic. But our bearded friend is after something altogether sounder. He knows just what he is going to have for sale as soon as Humphrey is in his hands and smuggled out of the country." She paused. "For I am afraid, Humphrey, that if *he* gets you, you are due for quite a long trip."

"What will he have for sale?" Cyril Bolderwood, who had been staring in distrust and dismay at his son, now peered uneasily out of the window.

"Simply Sir Bernard Paxton's inactivity—his immobilisation. With his son in those hands, he could neither be trusted nor could he trust himself. On the sort of work for which he is needed he would crack up almost at once. It has been 'the position, as you must know, with scores of scientists on the Continent whose families are in alien hands. *That* is what our friends are after. I have been watching them through binoculars"—Miss Liberty patted her bag—"holding a sort of battle conference. Their zero hour will be in about ten minutes. And we have an hour or so in which survival is all our own affair."

"An hour or so!" Mr Thewless was aghast. "But surely the police——"

"The first thing I did in the village just now was to get through on the telephone to my brother, Sir Charles. He told me quite a lot. The London police have got entirely on the track of the affair, and one has been given permission to fly here direct. He is in the air now. Two senior officers of the Irish police are coming, also by air, from Dublin. And a local force, available about forty miles away, will be setting out any time by car. I had learnt just so much when I was cut off. The girl at the exchange investigated, and she says that the line must have come down outside Killyboffin. Well, we know what that means."

"God bless my soul!" Mr Thewless tightened his grip on the poker. "It means that we are completely cut off in this singularly isolated spot."

"Exactly so. I went round to find the local *guarda*, for what his help might be worth, and discovered that he has been called away—no doubt on some fool's errand. The two cars one can hire have gone too. Your own car—it must have happened last night—has its tyres slashed to ribbons." Miss Liberty had turned to Cyril Bolderwood. "And, if you wonder how I managed to walk straight in, it was because your servants seem to have made themselves scarce as well."

"The good-for-nothing rascals! The dishonest——" Cyril Bolderwood, about to launch upon his old star turn as the irascible squire, thought better of it. "Ivor," he demanded, "whatever are we to do?"

Ivor said nothing, his brows knitted in thought. And Miss Liberty answered for him. "It is *quite* fantastic, is it not? Here is your son pointing a revolver at me—and knowing that, through this convenient tweed pocket, I am pointing one at *him*. Here is Mr Thewless standing over *you* with a poker. And here is Humphrey, who has had a very rough time, with the light of battle beginning to show again in his eye. One possible way of proceeding is, of course, clear."

"Clear?" said Mr Thewless.

"To our friends here, that is to say. They can try to do a deal with their rivals. Mr Ivor is thinking that out now. But you can see from his expression that he regards it as not altogether promising. Earlier this morning they attacked him in the cave and pitched him into the sea as dead. It was not a good prelude to any relationship of confidence. He knows these people to be as treacherous and dishonourable as himself. . . . I think, Mr Ivor, that that expresses the situation?"

"Certainly." Ivor remained calm. "It expresses it tactlessly, Miss Liberty, but accurately enough."

"Whereas you know equally well that Mr Thewless and Humphrey and myself are fowl of another feather. We subscribe to the old-fashioned idea of keeping promises, and that sort of thing."

"That is true enough." Ivor was positively handsome. "And the conclusion is that my father and I had better make our bargain with *you*."

"Then I will make a proposal to you. Our interests are different, are they not? We, on our part, are simply concerned to hold on until help arrives. You, on the other hand, are anxious to go while the going is good. I suspect that your normal course would be to get away in your car to somewhere along this coast where you keep a sea-going boat. But your car is out of action, and you must take what other means you can. Well, my suggestion simply is that you set about it." Miss Liberty was brisk, colloquial. "In fact, that you clear out."

"And you?"

"We shall endeavour to hold Killyboffin, or some part of it, until help does arrive. And we definitely don't want you as part of the garrison."

Ivor considered. "Just how are those people disposed?"

"They are assembling in surprising numbers in the village, where they have two large cars. And, of course, somewhere or other there is their motor-cruiser."

Ivor Bolderwood's eyes for a moment sought his father's—but less for counsel, it appeared, than in command. "Very well—we'll go. But we must have another revolver from the drawer of that desk, and also the grip that my father is pleased to describe as holding brandy."

"Agreed."

Mr Thewless, who was still grasping the poker, had listened to these exchanges with some reluctance. "I am bound," he said, "to express my heartfelt hope that you will both be in gaol before sunset. And it must be understood clearly that our engagement to let you go terminates two minutes after you leave this house. Thereafter we shall hold ourselves at liberty to assist in your apprehension and subsequent condign punishment by any means in our power."

"Dear old Thewless, full of choice eloquence to the last!" And from beneath his bandages Ivor Bolderwood gave his last malicious grin. "Well, you have about five minutes left to polish a period or two for our bearded friend. Goodbye."

The door closed and they were gone. There was a moment's silence. "I say," said Humphrey, "do you think they'll really beat it?"

Miss Liberty nodded. "I think they will—as long as the son stays in charge."

Mr Thewless demurred. "It struck me as being the father who is in a panic."

"Precisely. And it is he who might lose his head and senselessly turn and fight. Ivor is prepared to cut his losses and start life again elsewhere."

"Life? It strikes me as a grave responsibility to let him loose again on what he calls that."

"Our responsibility at the moment is towards Humphrey." Miss Liberty was grim.

Humphrey produced a rather battered smile. "I'm afraid," he said, "that I have a grave responsibility towards *you*. I did start all this."

"You must not be too hard on yourself." Miss Liberty too smiled. "After all, you were very young then, weren't you?"

"So I was." Humphrey, offering this reply with perfect seriousness, crossed to the window. "They *are* going. I think they're making for the shore. They're doubled up behind a dyke. Now they've vanished."

"Capital." Miss Liberty paused to consider. "One revolver, Humphrey's shot-gun—and, no doubt, other sporting weapons if we have time to hunt them up. A large and rambling house to defend against at least half a dozen armed men. A hamlet not far off, but with a population chiefly disposed to keep out of trouble. Rescue on its way, but uncomfortably far off still. Those seem to be the terms of the problem."

"Just so." Mr Thewless too had moved to the window, and was scanning a prospect that already seemed wholly familiar. "It might be called a problem that requires a little imagination in the solving. And that, of course, ought to be Humphrey's province. But do you know"—and Mr. Thewless looked at his companions in mild surprise—"do you know that, although my own mind is so desperately prosaic, I positively believe myself to have got there before him?"

CHAPTER XXVII

IRELAND, A BRILLIANT DISK of many greens, circled, tilted, side-slipped beneath Cadover's eyes. The pilot had slightly altered course and was now pointing straight ahead. There, beyond the shoulder of a mountain and an arm of ocean, a tiny speck of white showed dazzling in the sun. It was the lighthouse. Cadover took a deep breath and a little relaxed the pressure of his toes on the metal bar beneath them. Like a lover in an overdue train, he had been absurdly employing his muscles to urge the aeroplane on. He peered downwards and, leaning forward, pointed in his turn. On a long white ribbon of road his eye had caught the dark shape of three large cars. A trail of dust behind them told of their headlong speed. That would be the Irish police.

The mountain melted on their flank and in their place he saw cliffs, sea, a village like a scatter of white pebbles on grass, a single isolated house. These all dipped and swung away; the mountain had taken their place and was charging at him; again the mountain vanished and his ears were singing. He glimpsed the house again, close beneath him, in a violent foreshortening capped by expanses of ribbed lead. Then his horizon contracted to a rushing river of green and he bounced gently in his seat. They taxied on grass, their wing-tip almost brushing a hedge. On the other side a flow of darker green slowed and took form. Fleetingly Cadover's mind essayed comparisons with the back garden in Pinner. They knew about potatoes; there could be no doubt about that. He clambered out. His pilot came behind him, tugging off gloves, pulling out a revolver. They had polished off queer jobs between them before now. But this time their wireless had told them of astonishing things. They ran. A blackthorn hedge was before them and they burst through it. The lane led straight to the village. Everything was very still. Far away they could hear the cry of gulls and a wash of waves. The sunshine was warm on the fields, hard and brilliant on the white cottages ahead.

The peacefulness of it sharply taxed belief as to what could lie in front. As to what *did* lie in front—for suddenly the air was torn by a rapid fusillade. Cadover gave a gasp of relief as he ran. They were holding out.

The village stretched out two lines of straggling cottages and received them. But it might have been a village of the dead. Its doors were closed; many of its windows were shuttered; it was as if the Troubles had come again and pacific folk kept indoors when the gunmen were abroad. And the nearer fields were deserted. Only on the farther hillsides, a mile or more away, scattered figures in their bright home-spuns were going about their rural tasks. This gave, as it were, the scale of the affair. And it was a scale formidable enough. And now—as if to enforce this—Cadover's companion grabbed him by the arm and drew him sharply into the hedge.

They had been told of astonishing things; they saw them now. At a turn of the lane before them two large grey cars were parked, and on guard beside them was a man armed with a revolver. But it was to something else that Cadover's pilot pointed. Close beside them, on rising ground, was a tall white barn. Straddled on its thatched gable a hazardously perched figure slowly swept the countryside through field-glasses. Below him, two more men crouched on stationary motor-cycles, like competitors at the start of a road-race.

Cadover felt himself tugged through a hedge, and heard his companion's voice in his ear. "Can they have missed us coming down?"

"I doubt it. They saw the size of our plane, and feel they can still stick it out a bit."

"And when the Irish chaps come?"

"It will be a score of men with tommy-guns and a wireless transmitter. They'll know they're done for then, all right. Listen! They're still fighting back from the house."

Another fusillade had reached them. Stooping low, they pressed forward. The firing grew more rapid. But behind it now was another sound—explosive too, but accompanied by a low, deep roar, a dry crackling. . . .

"It's on fire!"

They had pressed on regardless and scrambled through another hedge, so that Killyboffin Hall was full in front of them. From now one and now another upper window came an intermittent flash from some species of small arms; this was drawing an answering fire from various points about the grounds; and inside the house, too, there appeared to be shooting. But more startling was the fact that a large part of the structure was indeed blazing—whether as the consequence of accident or design it was impossible to say. One wing, indeed, was almost consumed, and showed as a mere glowing shell against which was oddly silhouetted a line of broken statuary which lined a terrace in front. The effect of outrage and mutilation was sufficiently bizarre to hold Cadover for a moment at a pause. And upon this new sounds broke: the roar of an aeroplane engine overhead, and an answering roar, scarcely less loud, of powerful motor-cars rapidly approaching the village behind.

"That's them! The police and the Dublin men too!" And Cadover leapt forward with an impetuosity quite beyond his years. His companion followed. Bullets sang about their heads; from somewhere a whistle blew shrilly; they ran up a flight of shallow stone steps and dashed into the house through a broken window. The place was full of smoke through which they could see several forms in rapid retreat. It was clear that all effective siege was already over. From somewhere quite close at hand came the crash of a falling beam. Cadover, his eyes smarting, blundered out into a long corridor. "A staircase!" he shouted. "If we can't get them down in five minutes it will be all up with them."

They pushed along the corridor and found the smoke clearing; they passed through a baize door and found themselves in a part of the house not immediately threatened by fire. Presently they came to a narrow service staircase and climbed. They paused on a small landing, their eyes drawn to a window in which every pane had been shattered. Glass and splintered

318

wood lay everywhere, and a white-painted chest of drawers, apparently tumbled down from some further floor above, lay sprawled before them, its drawers fantastically spilling a profusion of housemaids' aprons and caps. Cadover glanced out, and glimpsed a number of men disappearing round a group of outbuildings, shooting as they went; glimpsed too, advancing across the park, a grim sickle of green-coated figures—police or soldiers—with formidable automatic rifles in their hands. Eire, he reflected, had done the situation proud. . . . And then he heard once more the crackle of flames and the roar of a ceiling coming down. Humphrey Paxton's kidnappers were a menace no more. The remnant of that astonishing organisation was in flight. But another enemy, quite as lethal, was advancing fast.

He turned to mount higher—and suddenly paused, aware that he himself was in new danger. For the top of this further staircase was roughly barricaded with wardrobes, cupboards, upholstered chairs; and the place reeked of powder. Here the real battle had been fought out. And it seemed only too likely that the defenders would still shoot at sight. "Hold your fire!" he shouted. "We are the police."

There was no reply. He heard instead only the crackle of the advancing fire, and the diminishing tumult outside, and his own voice strangely echoing in distant corridors.

"Answer!" he shouted. "Answer—whatever you think. The place is on fire. You must get out."

Again there was only silence—silence that bred a sudden and horrible suspicion. He thrust his revolver away and ran up the remaining stairs, his companion behind him. Together they heaved at the barricade, tore at it, broke the banisters, heaved cupboard and wardrobe pell-mell down the stairs behind them. Cadover, straining to dislodge a chair, slipped and put down a hand to save himself. He looked at it and found it smeared with blood. Blood was trickling over the topmost tread and forming a little pool below.

But now they were through. Beyond a narrow landing two doors were open upon two small rooms. Their several windows showed beyond—and of these also every pane was shattered.

A shot-gun lay on the floor of each. It was not to this, however, that Cadover's eye first went. Supine beside the barricade lay an elderly man, a revolver in his outflung right hand, his face blackened by smoke, blood welling in an ominous pulse from a long gash on his wrist. Cadover dropped on this like a plummet. "Look after the others," he called. "I'll fix this."

He busied himself with his task of first aid, for it was more urgent even than getting the wounded man out of the burning building. Intent on it, he heard sounds of rapid search around him. Then his companion's voice came for the first time since they had entered the house. "The others?" it said. "There aren't any others here."

Mr Thewless opened his eyes, aware of the fresh air, of a cool breeze from the sea on his temples, of brandy sharp on his lips. He saw, first swimmingly and then coming into clearer focus, the face of a man of his own age, sombre in cast, crowned by close cropped white hair. With considerable effort, Mr Thewless spoke. "You look," he said, "like an honest man."

"And you have behaved like one."

Mr Thewless made nothing of this. He felt very dizzy, very weak. "The house," he asked, "is it burning?"

"It is burning to ashes. Nothing can save it." The white-haired man paused to speak briefly to somebody behind him, and Mr Thewless was uncertainly aware of a background still of revolver shots, of shouted orders, of running men. "But what about the others?" The white-haired man had turned to him again and his voice was urgent. "What about Humphrey Paxton? What about Sir Charles Liberty's sister? Did they get the boy, after all?"

"I was extremely obtuse." Words still came painfully to Mr Thewless, but he felt that this was an important point to make. "I was a sadly inadequate person for coping with such a situation . . . although I did, to be sure, have this odd flash of imagination at the end. But even that was—well, literary and derivative. Poe . . . a very well-known story by Poe." He paused, reading in the expression of the face before him that this was judged to be mere delirium. "I think it is called *The Purloined Letter*—— What's that?"

"That?" The white-haired man paused while the rattle of firing died away. "There were a lot of them, you know— quite an amazing gang. And they're still rounding them up."

"All of them?"

"Only the small fry so far. Apparently the leader——"

"The bearded man?"

"Yes, the bearded man. He turns out to be somebody pretty big. And he's got down to the shore—somewhere under the cliffs—so that they haven't got him yet. But I want you to tell me——"

"He has a motor-cruiser!" Mr Thewless struggled into a sitting posture. "In a cave down there. If he is allowed to reach that he will get away."

"The devil he has!" And once more the white-haired man turned and talked rapidly to someone behind him. "We may get him, all the same. And I think we'll get the others."

"The Bolderwoods? I most unfeignedly hope so." And this time Mr Thewless did get firmly upright. "For I must confess to grave misgiving, Mr——"

"Cadover. Detective-Inspector Cadover."

"Ah. Now, what was I saying? But yes, of course! I was a good deal troubled by the morality of the bargain that Miss Liberty found it necessary to make with them. I should like to think that they had been laid by the heels."

"They have a boat too—somewhere on the other side of the headland. But they have been headed off from it and driven back here. It is thought that they must be in hiding not far away. Perhaps they——"

Here the police officer called Cadover checked himself—and with an exclamation so startled that it brought Mr Thewless swaying to his feet. They had brought him, he found, a considerable way from the burning building, and he stared unbelievingly for a moment at the flames still licking through those upper windows from which he had fought his strangely epic fight. But this scarcely detained him. For all eyes, he saw, were elsewhere.

It was like a little battle station pitched near the edge of the cliff. Green-uniformed men were around him—one with binoculars, one crouched over what he conjectured to be a field telephone. Below them he could see a line of cliff, a segment of beach on which more uniformed men were running, a great splash of sea. And it was the sea at which all were looking. There, from behind the headland where lay the farther entrance to Humphrey's cave, a gleaming craft had appeared hurtling through the water, the roar of its engines reverberating still among the rocks. And it was impossible to mistake that curbed and leaping prow, that low-cut stern. . . .

"It's him!" Mr Thewless cried. "He's got away!"

There were bursts of firing from the beach below, and little lines of cascading water marked the path of the bullets. But the motor-boat held on its course, heading at a tremendous pace for the open sea. In a matter of seconds it would be out of range. And Mr Thewless felt his shoulder gripped by the man beside him, heard an altogether new anxiety in that level London voice.

"The boy, man! Where is he? Don't tell me he can have got him out there?"

"The boy? I hope——"

Mr Thewless heard his own voice drowned in a new clamour, in the roar of an engine yet more powerful directly above him. A shadow skimmed the grass beside him; a wind tugged at his sparse hair; he looked up and promptly ducked —ducked in fear of sheer decapitation by the aircraft passing overhead. From a field behind them there came shots and the sound of men shouting, running. And from close beside him came an answering shout.

"Great heavens, it's my plane!"

And the London policeman grimly nodded. "We ought to have thought to set a guard on it. The Bolderwoods take the last trick."

Mr Thewless gasped. "The Bolderwoods . . . they're in *that*?"

"They've stolen it." Suddenly the grip that was still on Mr Thewless's shoulder tightened. "Look! I believe he can't——"

322

Cadover's voice died away. Steeply climbing, the little aircraft was now out beyond the cliffs; climbing more steeply still, it slipped, staggered, spun. . . . There was a moment's complete silence, broken by a soft Irish voice from the man with the field-glasses. "And no more he can, by all the saints! It's a mortal certainty he never held the controls of a plane before this fearful day."

The plane rose again, for a second hung sluggishly in air, turned over, fell. It fell, Mr Thewless thought, much as a gannet dives. . . . And directly beneath it was the hurtling motor cruiser. There was a single blinding flash, a single deafening detonation. Mr Thewless shut his eyes. When he opened them the man with the field-glasses was crossing himself, was muttering a prayer. And the sea was utterly empty. Where the bearded man, where Cyril and Ivor Bolderwood, had been urging their flight a moment before, there was only a sullen and spreading pool of oil, circled by a single screaming gull. It was an end at once horrifying and grotesquely theatrical—as if some trap-door had opened and incontinently swept half the *dramatis personæ* from the stage.

"Somewhere up *there*?" The officer with the field-glasses swept the hillsides before turning a puzzled face to Mr Thewless. "We don't quite see how——"

"How *The Purloined Letter* comes in." Cadover too had binoculars, and he spoke without taking them from his eyes. "I think you *did* say *The Purloined Letter*?"

"Certainly." Mr Thewless—rather to his own surprise—was biting hungrily into a sandwich which he held in his uninjured left hand. "You see, the ruffians were advancing to attack us in force; and the only thing seemed to be to get the boy away—and, of course, Miss Liberty as well. But there seemed no chance that they could slip away *unseen*, since the gang would almost certainly have the countryside under observation just as you have it now. So it occurred to me that they must be positively obtrusive—positively *staring*, so to speak—and find a sort of invisibility in that. And that was just how the letter in Poe's story——"

The man with the field-glasses exclaimed softly, his

instrument focused upon one of the highest fields beyond the village. "And when you were after thinking all this, Mr Thewless—what then?"

"We had noticed how brilliantly many of the peasantry show up against the green grass because of the rich colours in which they dye their homespun cloth. You can see them there" —and Mr Thewless pointed—"tiny splashes of red and blue right out on the mountain-side. So we hunted quickly through the servants' quarters and found a sufficiency of such things— for Miss Liberty a deep blue skirt, and for Humphrey some really brave claret-coloured trousers. Then Miss Liberty took a basket to balance on her head, and the boy a bundle for his back. Once they were a little beyond the house, and simply plodding openly across the fields, there was a good chance that they would be all right; that they would pass through whatever cordon the enemy had out. The danger was that the enemy might already have got into a position from which they were bound to spot them actually leaving. But it was necessary to risk that. And when they had gone—and I was never so glad of anything in my life—I prepared to give the effect of several people standing siege at the top of the servants' staircase. It proved to be excellently adapted for the purpose." And Mr Thewless nodded with an assurance that almost touched complacency. "I really believe I could scarcely have chosen better."

Cadover and the green-uniformed man now both had their glasses fixed on the same distant spot. It was again the latter who spoke. "Yes—to be sure! You'll be remarking, Mr Thewless, how they put out the long skeins of dyed wool to dry in the fields and along the hedges? Well, there's two folk at that up there now—and I'd say that one of them had claret-coloured trousers that are brave enough." He laughed softly. "Now, I wonder who he'd have persuaded to give him all that wool?"

Cadover too laughed—a short, deep laugh that spoke of a long strain broken. "And he is entering into the deception with a will. He's laying the stuff out on the grass like any-thing." He paused. "Hullo! I'm blessed if he hasn't formed letters with it. *He*. Now, why should the lad want to write *He*?"

Mr Thewless smiled. "Not *He*, Inspector. H. E."

"You're quite right. And he's going on. H. E. H. . . ."

"H. E. H. P. . . . Humphrey has a string of names, of which he is inclined to be rather proud. It's his way of letting us know, you see, that all is well with them up there. I wonder if we can send some signal back? I believe he would be quite glad to think that things have gone not too badly with me down here."

The green-uniformed man called out an order; there was a sharp report; a green Very light burst in the air. Mr Thewless watched it and judged it entirely beautiful.

"A capable boy," he said. "Really, a thoroughly capable boy."

THE PERENNIAL LIBRARY MYSTERY SERIES

Delano Ames

FOR OLD CRIME'S SAKE	P 629, $2.84
MURDER, MAESTRO, PLEASE	P 630, $2.84

E. C. Bentley

TRENT'S LAST CASE	P 440, $2.50
TRENT'S OWN CASE	P 516, $2.25

Gavin Black

A DRAGON FOR CHRISTMAS	P 473, $1.95
THE EYES AROUND ME	P 485, $1.95
YOU WANT TO DIE, JOHNNY?	P 472, $1.95

Nicholas Blake

THE CORPSE IN THE SNOWMAN	P 427, $1.95
THE DREADFUL HOLLOW	P 493, $1.95
END OF CHAPTER	P 397, $1.95
HEAD OF A TRAVELER	P 398, $2.25
MINUTE FOR MURDER	P 419, $1.95
THE MORNING AFTER DEATH	P 520, $1.95
A PENKNIFE IN MY HEART	P 521, $2.25
THE PRIVATE WOUND	P 531, $2.25
A QUESTION OF PROOF	P 494, $1.95
THE SAD VARIETY	P 495, $2.25
THERE'S TROUBLE BREWING	P 569, $3.37
THOU SHELL OF DEATH	P 428, $1.95
THE WIDOW'S CRUISE	P 399, $2.25
THE WORM OF DEATH	P 400, $2.25

Andrew Garve

THE ASHES OF LODA	P 430, $1.50
THE CUCKOO LINE AFFAIR	P 451, $1.95
A HERO FOR LEANDA	P 429, $1.50
MURDER THROUGH THE LOOKING GLASS	P 449, $1.95
NO TEARS FOR HILDA	P 441, $1.95
THE RIDDLE OF SAMSON	P 450, $1.95

Michael Gilbert

BLOOD AND JUDGMENT	P 446, $1.95
THE BODY OF A GIRL	P 459, $1.95
THE DANGER WITHIN	P 448, $1.95
FEAR TO TREAD	P 458, $1.95

Joe Gores

HAMMETT	P 631, $2.84

C. W. Grafton

BEYOND A REASONABLE DOUBT	P 519, $1.95

Edward Grierson

THE SECOND MAN	P 528, $2.25

Cyril Hare

DEATH IS NO SPORTSMAN	P 555, $2.40
DEATH WALKS THE WOODS	P 556, $2.40
AN ENGLISH MURDER	P 455, $2.50
TENANT FOR DEATH	P 570, $2.84
TRAGEDY AT LAW	P 522, $2.25
UNTIMELY DEATH	P 514, $2.25
THE WIND BLOWS DEATH	P 589, $2.84
WITH A BARE BODKIN	P 523, $2.25

If you enjoyed this book you'll want to know about
THE PERENNIAL LIBRARY MYSTERY SERIES
Buy them at your local bookstore or use this coupon for ordering:

Qty	P number	Price

	postage and handling charge	$1.00
	_____ book(s) @ $0.25	
	TOTAL	

Prices contained in this coupon are Harper & Row invoice prices only.
They are subject to change without notice, and in no way reflect the prices at
which these books may be sold by other suppliers.

**ᴴARPER & ROW, Mail Order Dept. #PMS, 10 East 53rd St., New
York, N.Y. 10022.**

Please send me the books I have checked above. I am enclosing $_____
which includes a postage and handling charge of $1.00 for the first book and
25¢ for each additional book. Send check or money order. No cash or
C.O.D.s please

Name_____

Address_____

City_____ State_____ Zip_____

Please allow 4 weeks for delivery. USA only. This offer expires 12/31/83.
Please add applicable sales tax.